A PRACTICAL GUIDE TO PSYCHOTHERAPY

A PRACTICAL GUIDE TO
PSYCHOTHERAPY

BY *Daniel N. Wiener,* PH.D.

CLINICAL PSYCHOLOGIST, VETERANS' ADMINISTRATION

ASSOCIATE PROFESSOR, UNIVERSITY OF MINNESOTA

1817

HARPER & ROW, PUBLISHERS

NEW YORK, EVANSTON, AND LONDON

FIRST EDITION

LIBRARY OF CONGRESS CATALOG CARD NUMBER: 67-22512

K-S

To Lois and Howard

Contents

Part V. Samples of Therapy Sessions

Acknowledgments

To FRIENDS and colleagues I owe much for listening to and helping to temper my views with fires of enthusiasm and dissent. The closest among them have been Dr. E. Lakin Phillips, an almost lifelong collaborator, with whom this book was originally planned; Dr. Philip Feinberg, a psychoanalytic therapist, whose good sense was dependable; Dr. Eugene Rinkey, an internist, who critically reviewed the drug and medical chapters. My editors at Harper & Row, Jeannette Hopkins and Norbert Slepyan, have sensitively encouraged and helped to improve the writing.

Foreword

OUR SYSTEM of political democracy and controlled private enterprise particularly challenge the consumer of psychotherapy to be knowledgeable and alert. The warning "Let the buyer beware" applies to services as well as to goods, for public bodies do not yet fully protect the consumer. Professional organizations and boards never exist primarily to educate and protect the public. At best they include as one of their functions adjudication between the public and the profession involved. At worst they seek to project a "good image" of that profession. In such a situation, the public's right to protection is probably best served through government. It seems axiomatic that the public will always need protection through the work of public offices as well as through the dictates of the law. Unfortunately, such full protection does not yet exist.

Even more important to the individual consumer in a democracy is his need for information by which to make his own judgments about the quality of goods and services. This is the most advanced and reliable kind of protection a citizen can have. When involved with decisions about psychotherapy, the consumer needs special protection. During his interviews with the psychotherapist, the consumer will find that the "power" lies overwhelmingly on the side of the practitioner. This stems in part from a grossly deficient scientific approach and in part from the mystical, even magical, nature of the situation. In the therapeutic relationship, the client tends to lean on the therapist as a strong, good man, a god-like or all-wise man, a compassionate, healing man. That most therapists are modest, simple, and humanly selfish men who have learned more than have most other people about the nature of human behavior and how to change it, is seldom realized by naïve consumers of psychotherapy. Yet, if the therapeutic relationship is to be democratic, that is, if the patient is not to be at the mercy of the therapist's particular theories and his personality, the patient must know enough to be able to choose his therapist wisely, and then to decide for himself if the relationship should continue. Therapy is often tumultuous and stressful, and the therapist should be able to help in making the decisions. Yet the consumer should no more depend entirely upon him than he should make his choices impulsively. Instead, the patient should be capable of making informed judgments independent of—and even contrary to—those of the therapist.

Man's distortions in seeing himself can be quite impressive. Thus, persons in trouble irrationally, stubbornly resist correction and help, and instead go on hating or loving their therapists, or flee from therapy at the first criticism or hint of rejection. In response, the therapist comfortably labels such behavior as "resistant" or "regressive" or "neurotic." Yet there must also be a way for the patient to handle a therapist who is himself resistant, regressive, neurotic, or, more simply put, mistaken. Therapists do exist who desperately want all their patients to like them, who become angry when patients do not agree with them, who are annoyed or indifferent when asked about other theories and therapists, and who insist upon large and current payments.

Somehow, within the context of democracy and private practice, the imbalance must be redressed so that the patient has resources to cope with the task of introducing more equality of give-and-take into the psychotherapeutic situation.

To provide the consumer with means of information and judgment by which he may do this is the essential purpose of this book. Such a book, it seems to me, is badly needed.

After an early period of enthusiasm about psychotherapy generally, and then after short bursts of excitement over its psychoanalytic and nondirective forms, I came to accept Hans Eysenck's famous conclusion (reached after he had reviewed all available research on psychotherapy) that no form of therapy was better than any other—or, for that matter, than no therapy at all. Although I developed a decade-long cynical attitude about psychotherapy, I continued—in my institutional and private practice—to work hard in the belief that I was actually helping my patients. This paradox was exemplified for me when a reader of a cruder, early version of this book (written ten years ago) asked me how one could practice a profession he viewed so dimly. In response, I could only feel vaguely uncomfortable, and hope that the results I was achieving did not square with the results of others.

In the course of collaborating on two other books about research and theory in psychotherapy,[1] my viewpoint became clearer, and I arrived at a view of psychotherapy that permitted me to practice it with zest, comfort, and optimism, yet without giving up the critical, scientific view that protects the therapist against arrogance, perversity, and a sense of omniscience.

Finally, it seemed, I could help clients to solve a wide variety of problems, and I was able to write down my views in detail for them and for my colleagues to inspect and criticize.

In the plethora of theorists, propagandists, and faddists, however, who is to be believed, who has carried the tablets down from the mountain, how can the client decide among the welter of strident therapist voices? More difficult still, how can he judge those who display nothing at all of their work outside of their very private offices and conversations?

The public display of results marks the work of practically all other professions. Lawyers talk in court and publish briefs; the handiwork of architects, engineers, and craftsmen is on open exhibit; physicians work their skills before colleagues, write hospital and laboratory records to be scrutinized, and record mortality rates; tax accountants succeed or fail in reviews by tax-department audits.

Of course, many practices in most professions are shielded from public view, and some of the same problems in finding the best practitioners exist in them as in psychotherapy. From within any profession one knows more about its practitioners, good and bad, than the public ever does. The problem is distinctively aggravated in psychotherapy, however, by the especially secret nature of the procedures—secret from colleagues as well as from the public. Information about the practices and competence of its practitioners is mostly based upon their own writing and talking—or vague

[1] *Dimensions of Psychotherapy*, with Donald R. Stieper (Chicago: Aldine Press, 1965) and *Short-term Psychotherapy and Structured Behavior Change*, with E. Lakin Phillips (New York: McGraw-Hill, 1966).

allusions to how they achieve successful clinical results—rather than upon public or scientific observation of their practices. The number of psychotherapists who are willing to expose their work to direct observation, movies, or tape recordings, verbatim reports of interviews, or objective follow-up of cases by impartial observers is minute.

The noted psychologist O. Hobart Mowrer has attacked the concept of secrecy in psychotherapy at its very roots—the patient's desire or need for privacy about his problem. He encourages patients to share their most private problems with others, thus earning the kind of feedback that can correct and help them. The secrecy of interviews which the therapist encourages, presumably to protect the patient from harm and to facilitate conversation about embarrassing material, also serves to preserve the therapist's secrecy of operations. Potential as well as actual consumers are in this way deprived of knowledge that would permit them to make decisions about psychotherapy and psychotherapists, and the primitive science of psychotherapy is denied the data it needs to study and improve the field.

While scientific needs are not our direct concern here, informed public pressure for a better science can surely improve the resources and methods of psychotherapy. So far, most research has been done in the laboratory or under the very limited and unusual conditions of special research agencies, projects, or institutions. Largely ignored for scientific purposes is the great bulk of psychotherapy practiced in private offices and public clinics. The profession as generally practiced thus remains scientifically crude, protected from the prying eyes of curious consumers and probing scientists alike, and both must depend upon bits and pieces of reflected information and subjective opinions.

In writing a guide to contemporary psychotherapy, the line between cynicism and realism—and also between realistic hope and banal enthusiasm—is thin. But cynicism about the multitude of fads and false prophets need not smear over tentative, modest, careful efforts, following the methods of science, to help troubled men as best one can. Nor need one damn all methods but one, nor fervently praise one and make devotions to a single road to personal salvation.

Practically any dedicated humanitarian effort will utilize some useful methods and be of some help. The four major forms of therapy have seemed to stand some tests of time or science to prove useful, though how much better they are than nature is uncertain. But in the large array of methods which has been used, there are almost sure to be elements of anything which will be used in the future.

There is a pre-eminently intelligent method of measuring any way of helping man, and that is the scientific one evaluating how effectively the means move him toward his chosen ends. This method calls for accumulating as much pertinent information as possible, applying it so it can be clearly judged, then evaluating results objectively. So far, unfortunately, professional researchers and practitioners cannot definitely tell you which therapist or way of therapy will yield the best results with your problems.

So you must do the best job you can for yourself. You must try to make sense of what facts there are, of the welter of conflicting claims and testimonials, and of speculations about what happens to produce results. You need the resources and courage to control wisely your purchase and use of psychotherapeutic services.

Can one observer be fair in commenting about the various methods and practitioners? Can the reader reasonably evaluate the writer and his biases to apply the material of this book differently from the way the writer does? Completely independent judgment is the goal. This is the most gratifying end the writer could hope for. Over and over again, we will plead for an informed, critical consumer who will learn to judge wisely for himself—if necessary in the face of strident, arguing voices in the professional market place. This writer is no more than another such voice. He will try hard to report on the other voices fairly and specifically and from an inside vantage point. His bias will clearly be for those methods and practitioners setting concrete goals with their patients which can be continuously evaluated, accomplished, and related to the patient's daily life; for working as efficiently as possible toward the goals; for modifying according to what does or does not happen when this or that course is followed; for sharing completely and equally with the patient the therapist's views, goals, and judgment of results.

These, then, are some of the purposes of this book, which is dedicated to making of psychotherapy a problem-solving process

—which needs to be as rational and intellectually resourceful as possible;

—which profits from an intelligent, wise, and well-informed consumer as much as from an intelligent, wise, and well-informed practitioner;

—which depends upon educating the consumer as well as the practitioner in the bases and processes of problem-solving and behavior change;

—which converts the psychotherapeutic situation from one in which magic and mystery prevail for the client to one in which they prevail for neither the client nor the therapist;

—which enhances in every way control and decision-making in psychotherapy by a well-informed consumer, in the democratic ways the constituent uses to direct his elected political representative.

Part I

BACKGROUND FOR
DECISION

CHAPTER I

Psychotherapy Today

EIGHTEEN MILLION Americans, nearly 10 per cent of our population, need some kind of professional help for what is called "mental illness," according to reliable estimates. Of this number, only about 10 per cent are identified and treated yearly. About half of all medical and surgical cases probably have emotional complications. Symptoms of mental or emotional disturbance afflict many other people. While some surveys place the number around 10 per cent of the population, some estimate as high as 75 per cent.[1] In the most carefully designed and controlled study available,[2] 11 per cent of the people sampled said they were "not too happy." If unhappiness is a consequence of emotional trouble, millions more persons have serious problems than ever seek or get help to solve them.

Each of these persons is an individual, facing conditions peculiar to himself and required to make what are for him unique decisions. The focus of this book, therefore, will not be on these millions, but rather on you, the reader, and your efforts to determine whether you need professional help for your own problems, how to choose help wisely, and how to gain the most from the help you get.

Choosing one's help can be a difficult and frustrating job. The claims made by various practitioners, "schools," and institutions are somewhat like those made for any other consumer product or service. Ultimately the consumer must choose for himself on the basis of as much information as he can obtain—or be at the mercy of the most persuasive propagandist, the most readily avail-

[1] G. Gurin, J. Veroff, and S. Feld, *Americans View Their Mental Health* (New York: Basic Books, 1960).
[2] *Ibid.*, p. 15.

able service, the most effective indirect advertising, or the most compelling advice of friends and strangers.

One father, who had sought help for his twenty-two-year-old son from a dozen prominent therapists and institutions over a seven-year period, asked me plaintively, "But how can I know whether you're any better than the rest I've consulted?" Each therapist had pursued his own course, each had differed at least somewhat from the others, and each had seemed confident about his answers. To improve your knowledge and confidence, as you confront the choices before you, is the aim of this book.

DIFFERENT VIEWS OF HUMAN PROBLEMS

Views, techniques, and practitioners of psychotherapy will be discussed at length in later chapters. To set the background for those discussions, we need to describe different views of the problems themselves.

The roots of human troubles can be viewed in many ways, but therapists tend to emphasize one of four views primarily: mental illness, or disease; internally disturbing feelings; frustrated efforts to reconcile personal needs with the social structure; unresolved problems in handling one's concrete life situations. Such causal categories have important implications for treatment.

The mental illness, or disease, concept is analogous to physical disease. It suggests specific diagnosis and, presumably, specific treatment according to that diagnosis. While it is the most agreed-upon category, the methods of treatment differ widely among its adherents. The main diagnostic groups are psychoses and neuroses. The major psychosis is schizophrenia, and the major neurosis is plain psychoneurosis, or anxiety reaction.

Certain kinds of treatment are popular at various times; some are "fads" for a period. Schizophrenia, for example, was commonly treated with insulin shock in the 1930's and by electric shock in the 1940's; today, heavy doses of tranquilizers are preferred. Middle-age depression is commonly treated with shock today, but even limited areas of agreement are rare and changeable, and are by no means universal.

The view that human troubles are best regarded as confused feelings about one's self in the world has a somewhat clearer implication for treatment. It leads to a more or less unitary psychotherapy based upon expressing and clarifying one's feelings, and trying to find one's place in the world. Its therapeutic conversation proceeds toward this end. Generally, this kind of treatment is called nondirective, or existential, psychotherapy.

The physician may also use drugs or sedatives as the major or sole treatment for tension or hypersensitivity, as if calming you down were all that you needed. A further cause for these feelings is not sought. It is assumed, sometimes correctly, that if you are calmed, you can better handle your problems; if the treatment doesn't work, other drugs, combinations, or dosages are often tried.

Human problems can also be viewed as arising from the painful effort to reconcile basic personal needs with social demands. Psychoanalysis emphasizes this theory, but not exclusively. As have all other theoretical opinions about human troubles and their solutions, this one has been adopted, in part, by many professionals who do not consider themselves bound to any particular theory. That a person must fight his environment to satisfy his fundamental needs, that society tends to be his enemy, and that the most serious personal problems are those that arise from this battle are widespread ideas that are held even among anti-analysts such as Ayn Rand. Such an approach to life, by whomever held, entails important consequences for psychotherapy. These will be discussed later.

Emotional difficulties can also be viewed as a function of the way you handle external problems. From such a perspective, your therapy should be grounded in a statement of what your specific problems are, and should be conducted to solve these problems as directly as possible. This view does not "take sides." It focuses on specifying what your goals are, how *you* (not society or the environment) defeat yourself or work ineffectively toward your goals, and how you can proceed reasonably to reach them. The problems you encounter (and feel), are, in this view, simply natural stumbling stones which must be accepted and then surmounted; all other considerations are secondary.

None of these views needs be exclusive of the others, but your therapist will usually show indirectly in his actions and words, if not in his direct presentation of a theory, that he really does hold one of these viewpoints—or at least he will talk and act *as if* he did. It is our view that you are entitled to know this ahead of time —and that the therapist should feel obligated to analyze his own attitudes and practices sufficiently to be able to let you know this about himself.

WHAT IS PSYCHOTHERAPY?

Simply stated, psychotherapy is help for your personal problems gained from persons professionally trained in socially approved ways to render such help.

Almost any other service to human beings can be related to or called psychotherapy. Morticians are sometimes called "grief therapists," librarians and psychologists utilize "reading therapy," dance instructors do "recreational therapy," and camp social directors practice "group psychotherapy." Perhaps insurance salesmen will soon label their work as "security psychotherapy." Any form of service to suffering human beings (whether they suffer from a lack of insurance or from anxiety about dancing with a partner) has been called therapy, and in the sense that it may help you solve a personal problem, it can surely be as effective as more technical professional help. But just as a friend who gives you an aspirin to cure a headache is not a physician and is not practicing medicine (even though the headache goes away), so a person who gives you psychological help may not be a psychotherapist or be practicing psychotherapy.

The distinction in terms of practices is often hard to determine. Often informal methods of helping people in medicine, law, education—or psychotherapy—are simple and successful. When your problems, of whatever sort, prove intractable and unresponsive to such aid, then you are wise to seek the most expert kind of help society can provide from social workers, psychologists, and psychiatrists. They are trained in various ways, but to be officially approved (through licensing or certification by a government agency or a professional organization), they must take graduate-level training at universities which have themselves usually been accredited by national organizations to offer such training. Social approval of the professional training of persons and institutions has many deficiencies, for untrained persons often do better work than trained ones. Nevertheless, some guidelines can be drawn to improve your chances of getting competent help.

TRENDS IN PSYCHOTHERAPY

The social history of man is replete with examples of psychotherapeutic techniques, which seem to have changed very little over the centuries. Ancient Egyptians practiced a form of shock therapy consisting of dunking the afflicted person in icy water, which may *seem* less humane, but actually has no worse theoretical implications than inducing convulsions and coma through shock therapy today. Wise men of all ages have counseled people to steady their lives with soul-searching, pursuing humanitarian goals, doing good deeds, selecting good companions, trying periods of rest, and taking prescriptions of wine, roots, and herbs.

Still, progress has occurred, in that man has moved toward more sophisticated, complex, and naturalistic views of the causes and possible solutions to problems. This progress, however, is *only* in terms of describing conditions and causes. Therapists as competent as any practicing today have probably existed in past centuries, just as counterparts of the witch doctor exist and practice in our time. Nor are success rates in therapy demonstrably greater today than in past years.

We are to some extent always victims of the fads of our times. Most approved psychotherapists fifty years from now will be practicing quite differently from the way the accredited ones work today. Though somewhat useful, social approval is the crudest screening device; one must still work hard to find the most skillful of the approved professionals.

The best practitioners of any era bear less similarity to their inferior contemporary colleagues than to their more talented counterparts of any era, future or past. About past ages some general distinctions may be drawn. Physical magic flourished as a therapeutic method. The results it produced, even its basic approach, might have been the same as those produced with placebo drugs today; but its use was probably far more widespread, its practitioners had more blind faith, and alternative treatment was less available. The laying on of hands and the use of potions, fire, and torture were thought to produce direct curative effects by physically purifying action.

Hypnosis, whose methods have remained practically unchanged for the past century and a half, was originally a kind of physical magic where "the magnetizer generally keeps the patient's knees enclosed within his own, and consequently the knees and all the lower parts of the body are in close contact. The hand is applied to the hypochondriac region, and sometimes to the ovarium . . ."[3]

With many exceptions in all ages, physical magic was succeeded by a psychological magic which did not assume a transmission or production of physical effects. The therapist was considered to possess psychological powers that could have curative effects on patients through unseen and unseeable forces which moved between them. This view probably represented a simple adaptation to the criticism that magical physical powers could not be seen. If they could not be seen, at least except rarely and unreliably, then why describe them as if they were physical? As mental or psychological effects, they did not have to be seen.

Modern psychotherapy began with Freud. His methods progressed from hypnosis, to suggestion, to analysis of developmental causes. His personal professional development thus paralleled the history of the field. He ended with a method that almost eliminated the magical powers of the therapist and substituted exposure and development of the patient's own powers.

We say "almost" because the power to move patients, to produce curative effects, which psychoanalysts ascribe to "transference," smacks of magic. The difference is that today's patients are considered to endow the therapist with what is really a remnant of imagined powers that children ascribe to their parents, whereas magic in the past was usually considered to be a power that the therapist possessed directly.

Other current psychological methods strongly resemble each other in that they depend upon the therapist's attempts to affect his patient primarily by means of the patient's own resources. The therapist's powers are presumably only those of developing or influencing the patient.

In all eras, these magical and psychological views have conflicted with the conviction that serious human disruptions are based upon body malfunctions and, more specifically, result from disturbances in the brain or nervous system. Much progress is being made in studying the electronic and chemical structure and function of the nervous system. Chemical and electrical changes

[3] From a report by French physicians to their King, written in 1784.

in the body in the presence of emotional upset can be observed, areas of the brain that produce specific sensations have been defined, physiological and chemical changes from drugs are being elaborately measured, and hereditary relationships in psychosis are being extensively studied.

Withal, there is absolutely no firm evidence that any organic means can successfully treat any large or important group of emotional disorders without serious disadvantages. Perhaps the closest thing to a major organic treatment of a psychological state is the use of heavy doses of tranquilizers for schizophrenics. It is, however, perhaps the biggest change in treatment of the emotionally disturbed of our own time. This method has the advantage of getting patients out of hospitals. They behave well enough to go home, for a while at least, but they frequently return to the hospitals and their adjustment in terms of supporting themselves or enjoying life may remain poor. That use of drugs represents permanent progress toward successful therapy seems doubtful, but the removal of persons from institutions to more favorable environments almost always represents better results than were previously anticipated —whether such persons are mental patients, criminals, delinquents, or the elderly.

The other major contemporary change, which will probably prove to be of much greater importance than drug use, is an increasing emphasis upon community care as an alternative to hospitalization. The community approach is tentative and fumbling so far, an amalgam mainly of individual psychotherapy and referral to conventional community agencies. But it could become far more: a way of planning the community to provide useful and productive ways to organize and direct the enormous groups of outcasts—the psychotics and psychopaths—and the disturbed parents and others who produce the outcasts. It could be a broad, nonindividualized attack upon a major social problem based on changing the social structure itself.

PSYCHOTHERAPY: ART, SCIENCE, OR SKILL?

Psychotherapy is usually described as an art, less often as a science, and sometimes as a combination of both. We propose to call it a skill that the therapist applies to help change the behavior of his clients so as to solve their problems.

As a healing *science,* psychotherapy is a failure. It can produce no proof that specifiable techniques produce specifiable cures. Its considerable research is almost all of poor scientific design: one cannot even say that a certain approach produces a certain result. Almost all its research lacks the basic elements of good experimentation. As a result, every therapist must depend upon belief in himself and his theories, rather than upon firm data, to sustain him in his efforts.

On the other hand, the elements for making psychotherapy a science are present. Dedicated researchers are seeking to discover what practices produce which results. Rigorous experimental methods are being developed and applied that will permit concrete measurement of results. These methods include the use of a "control" group which receives no treatment, so that "spontaneous" cures are accounted for; precision and reliability in making diagnoses; and statistical analyses of results to assure that outcomes are not attributable to chance.

Meanwhile, is psychotherapy merely an art? Art implies a practice not necessarily bound by rules; it suggest an intuitive posture, a creative enterprise. One admires the products of art, and may buy them if he likes what he sees, but would one buy the products of art unseen? One's preferences and tastes as a consumer are also important in purchasing psychotherapy. As an art, psychotherapy must be accepted without such a review. If it were merely art, it might make sense if one did not pay for it until sampling and judging its product.

So we hold that psychotherapy is best viewed as a skill, since it is not a science, that holds some promise of applying methods whose results with your problems can sometimes be predicted. Your therapist should be able to apply certain skills to the solution of the problems you present, skills he can describe generally to you in your first interview with him. Other problems will almost certainly appear later, and he will adapt his skills to means of attacking them, but these too can be made clear as they occur.

MUST HELP BE PROFESSIONAL?

Most human problems are solved without professional help or are at least controlled so that they do not become massively disrupting. By themselves, however, people do not think very usefully or objectively about themselves for very long. Fortunately most human beings constantly interact with others, so that the crucial help most people need to solve their problems most likely comes from nonprofessionals. A kind of wisdom which serves most people well seems to be transmitted in this way.

When you have a serious unsolved problem, you should seek out friends or acquaintances and even social groups which may have something to say to you about your problem. You must, of course, retain control of what you choose to do, picking as wisely as possible among the suggestions made; and you must further show discretion about the persons you consult. You should not, for example, burden children with problems they cannot understand, or employees, or supervisors you hardly know with problems they may use against you because they are unkind or self-seeking. But within very broad limits it would seem wise to expose yourself to nonprofessional reactions before seeking professional ones. It can seldom do harm and can often do good. It is the means by which most people settle personal problems. There is even good evidence that select "lay" persons can help disturbed persons as much as can professionals.[4] Freud wanted to train influential lay groups, including teachers,[5] to apply his methods.

There may come a time, however, when you wish to call upon the most skillful technical help obtainable. We will try to establish guidelines to help you determine when that time has come.

Meanwhile, since we are all continuously in the process of solving problems, and since, in mass terms, professional psychotherapy can never be an effective method for this process, the best nonprofessional methods the social structure can develop must be used.

HOW AVAILABLE HELP DETERMINES PROBLEMS

There is no reliable evidence that the incidence of emotional problems has increased or decreased from past times to the present. What has obviously increased, however, is the number and size of the helping professions. To the plea that we need thousands more professionals to help in treating such problems, the challenge can

---

[4] M. J. Rioch, *et al.*, "N.I.M.H. Pilot Study in Training Mental Health Counselors," *American Journal of Orthopsychiatry*, XXXIII (1963), 678–689.

[5] S. Freud, *The Question of Lay Analysis* (New York: W. W. Norton, 1950).

be made that what is actually most acutely needed is more efficient methods of treatment.

Patients and their therapists differ between themselves in their judgments of problems and therapeutic results.[6] Some writers claim that mental illness seems to be on the increase, while other observers point out that the same has been said in every era, that fads in diagnosis change, that people are becoming far more aware of emotional causes as the root of anxieties, and that as community resources become available more people recognize the presence of psychological problems. For all such reasons, trends in the incidence of mental illness cannot yet be securely interpreted.

Every new community mental-health center quickly becomes loaded with patients, yet private practitioners do not suffer from the competition. The number of community mental-health centers in this country has multiplied many times in the last ten years, yet no end to the apparent need for such resources is in sight. How is it that people survived before there were such agencies? One reason is that general medical practitioners and internists carried a heavy load of emotionally troubled people, ranging up to an estimated three-fourths or more of their total clientele. Many patients have no diagnosable physical disease, and most of them are treated through the reassurances of checkups and simple undifferentiated medicines such as tranquilizers, aspirin, and vitamins. Ministers, teachers, politicians, and many others have carried a large share of such cases. Persons with problems sought out lay helpers—politicians to provide jobs, elderly relatives to help to patch up marriages, or teachers to advise on school problems. Today mental illness or emotional disturbance tends to be regarded as a problem that only the mental-health professions have the competence to treat.

There is no reliable test for an outsider to determine whether your problem requires professional help. Some experts are wiser, better informed, more experienced, or more trustworthy than others; but in the long run you and you alone must determine whether you need help. Experts themselves weigh such a need on such different scales that, except in extreme cases, different judgments about you will occur within the group of experts. Where

[6] D. R. Stieper and D. N. Wiener, *Dimensions of Psychotherapy* (Chicago: Aldine Press, 1965), pp. 55–58.

services are readily available, professionals would probably tend to gauge need as most pressing; where services are thin, less need would be recognized. In localities where many psychotherapists are in private practice, a much higher proportion of the population seeks help. In countries such as the U.S.S.R. or Great Britain, where almost all psychotherapy is publicly sponsored, you must have a fairly obvious problem in handling your life before help becomes available. In the United States, among groups where money is ample, help is more eagerly sought and provided for philosophical as well as psychological problems.

Furthermore, in every society critical choices about solving such problems must be made. Which human problems should be attacked and with what priority? Shall treatment be in the form of additional mental-health services or through more jobs, housing, recreational activities, or education, all of which have impact upon some of the same problems of living? Society often makes haphazard choices about its own priorities.

HOPE FOR THE FUTURE

Major progress in psychotherapy as well as in maintaining good physical health must come with mass social methods of improving the ways people work on their problems. In such a scheme, the psychotherapist becomes more of a consultant to social planners than a technician available to individuals who seek help. This is the preventive approach.

Meanwhile, the individual must take advantage of what help is available among the various possible alternatives—seeking methods of mastering his environment and employing his own intelligence. In the meantime, as scientific progress is slowly made in psychotherapy, he can remain alert to developments and new choices through reading and listening to as wide a range of professional views and research findings as possible.

The most exciting current research in psychotherapy lies in what is often called "behavior modification" methods—direct, concrete, and relatively simple ways of changing behavior. This approach specifies its goals and means in objective, measurable ways, and for purposes of scientific progress represents an enormous gain over approaches which lack specific definitions of objective methods and progress.

Consumer education and protection also offer hope. Many years ago, Lee Steiner conducted a study of psychological services. Persons who pretended to be patients visited the offices of psychotherapists and recorded what happened to them. Yet Mrs. Steiner alienated her fellow professionals far more than she stirred the public. The time was then not ripe, but it may soon be, because exposés of poor consumer protection from quacks and incompetents are needed. Today it is nearly impossible for the consumer to determine when he is poorly treated and to obtain any redress. Professional psychological services should soon be in for their share of investigation and consumer protection. Professional organizations invariably are timid in policing themselves on behalf of their clients, nor is that their primary role. They will profit greatly, however, from the examination when it comes, for it inevitably will force them into intensive self-examination leading to better training and improved efforts at public education. Above all, it will encourage more sensitivity to the criticisms that they hold forth more hope than they can deliver, that they must make humbler claims to the public and to individual patients, and that they should vastly increase their efforts to develop a science of maximum usefulness.

CHAPTER 2

Realistic Expectations

REALISTIC EXPECTATIONS about psychotherapists and psychotherapy will permit you both to choose your service more wisely at the onset and to avoid much disappointment at the end. Disappointment usually results from false expectations—high hopes based upon ignorance, misinterpretation, or misleading information. The status of psychotherapy today enhances the development of all three.

Ignorance comes both from a true dearth of scientific information about the process and from the privacy with which the professions themselves cloak what is known and done. Practically none of the many therapists who criticize their profession and colleagues severely in private or even in professional journals and at professional meetings express themselves similarly to the public. Those rare professionals who do speak out publicly are often viewed by colleagues as publicity seekers or as unprofessional.

So a looser kind of criticism flourishes. Journalists occasionally expose shoddy professional practices without full understanding or information, and then professional organizations offer their sometimes true defenses. But usually neither the exposures nor the corrections come from the professions. It took a Nuremberg trial and a secret cancer experiment in New York to take physicians to task and to spell out or apply an ethical code in medicine. It took congressional denunciation to spur psychologists to further safeguards for the test-taker's rights. It will probably take a book by a clever reporter to trigger public concern about and control of psychotherapeutic shoddiness.

Misinterpretation and misleading information follow closely after ignorance, filling the vacuum with wrong answers to your questions about psychotherapy. Such bad information usually emphasizes optimism about the results. Ex-patients are far more likely to talk about their successes in therapy, however incomplete, brief, or distorted, than about their failures. A prominent ex-alcoholic may dramatically describe her rehabilitation through psychotherapy in a best seller, and soon inconspicuously slip back into alcoholism. A prominent therapist may publicly describe his wonderfully successful results in helping patients achieve "sexual fulfillment" with no reference to his failures, including the homosexuality of his own son. Newspaper articles may quote a movie star as saying he has begun a whole new beautiful life as a result of psychoanalysis; the next year they may report the star's attempted suicide.

You are almost certain to be disappointed if you enter into psychotherapy thinking that you will end up "unleashed" to enjoy life zestfully and without pain; or that you will change your job or your wife and find a much higher level of happiness; or that you will no longer have to work hard, feel guilty, or be depressed.

The fact is simply that very few patients who complete psychotherapy, however long, intense, or skillfully done it may be, feel radically changed or make basic alterations in their lives. Most say that they got *some* help toward solving their problems and achieving more satisfaction in their lives. Such a modest outcome, though often well worth the cost, is modest nonetheless. It bears in most cases no resemblance to the testimonials that many autobiographies contain, nor to the glowing accounts that frequently appear in professional books and journals.

Unrealistic expectations may thus becloud the real gains you make. They may also prompt you to go on for months and even years beyond the time for a reasonable return on your time, effort, and money, in the false hope that you are about to achieve nirvana. Actually, your greatest gains from direct forms of therapy are likely to come in the first few months. In indirect forms, such as psychoanalysis, results may show somewhat later. Still, dramatic turns are extremely rare, and gains usually occur on a decreasing scale as time passes.

Furthermore, false hopes may well lead you to change therapists. Most patients in psychotherapy at any time have had previous treatment. Sometimes treatment has failed because of a therapist's incompetence. But such changing about also reflects the patient's misconceived disappointment that grand results have not occurred.

Much of this book is devoted to trying to help you to set reasonable goals for your therapy, and then to raising the probability of your reaching them by selecting help well and guiding it wisely. Next to your home and car, your purchase of psychotherapy is likely to cost you more than any other single purchase you make in your lifetime. To avoid severe disappointment, you should know as much as possible about what to expect.

FALSE HOPES AND FOLKLORE

There are some specific fictions concerning psychotherapy about which you can be informed.

One fiction is that labeling what is wrong with you—that is, diagnosing you and describing your "mental illness"—helps you. You may gain a temporary sense of relief when you think that your therapist has grasped your condition and can proceed to "cure" you. In reality, no such process follows diagnosis. Diagnosis alone makes no difference to the success of your treatment. Whatever elation you may initially feel at being told about a diagnosis will almost certainly be succeeded by discomfort and depression as you confront the uncertainties inherent in therapy.

Nor does the act of seeking help, even with the utmost enthusiasm and "motivation," alone seem to effect ultimate success. In fact, there is evidence that an initially recalcitrant patient may progress better than one who says, "Doctor, here I am. I'm putting myself in your hands. I'll do whatever you say." You may feel a great relief when, after a long inner struggle, you finally make that first appointment or have your first interview. That is a very important step, but the hard work of changing your behavior still lies ahead—which leads us to the next fiction: that therapy is a happy experience.

In practically all instances, successful psychotherapy is hard, painful work for the patient. You enter it foolishly if you think you will enjoy your sessions. Usually they are compounded of the sweet hope that you will come to enjoy your life more and the bitter process of facing up to your faults and struggling to change them.

Strong faith in your therapist or in therapy is not likely to help you much either. It is a strange process that keeps your faith strong even when therapy is not progressing, yet that is likely to happen if you have unrealistically high hopes of your treatment. In fact, a blind faith in whatever goes on means giving up the best use of your intelligence to interact with your therapist and to find the best ways for yourself.

Nor is "insight" alone effective in changing behavior. You may enter therapy believing that discovering dramatic episodes in your past or connecting distant events with present ones will produce changes in your behavior. There is no evidence that brilliant "discoveries" or dramatic insights change your behavior at all. You still have strenuous work ahead of you to alter current bad habits. Habit change does not occur just because you have insight.

"Deeper," longer, or more intense therapy does not provide more basic improvement or more lasting gains. There is no demonstrable relationship between whatever is called depth therapy, or longer treatment, and greater or more lasting progress. Such a relationship is a bit of folklore that seemingly will not die, even among professionals. The more you talk about yourself to an analytic therapist, the more you are likely to discover about yourself—but this has nothing to do with attaining your goals of changed behavior.

Nor are there miracle drugs or dramatic new techniques which will solve your problems. Many therapists hope and expect there will be at some distant time, and even Freud considered that human problems eventually would be traced to the brain and treated directly there. But the chances are overwhelming that you in your lifetime will have to put up with today's methods, with modest improvements to which new research will contribute. You can probably improve your therapy much more by choosing wisely and utilizing well what is available.

WHAT THERAPISTS KNOW (AND DON'T KNOW)

The knowledge that therapists have about human behavior has never been measured. They must take many courses in their professional training and pass many tests on what they have learned, but this has no established relationship to their ability to answer your questions or help you with problem situations.

For example, sexual problems are among the most widespread, intense, and sensitive that come up in psychotherapy. Yet practically no training programs for social workers, psychiatrists, or psychologists require a course to educate them in the facts of sex. As a result, some therapists have less sex knowledge than some of their patients.[1]

Similar deficiencies undoubtedly occur in the handling of financial, occupational, and social problems, where your therapist may simply not know enough to help you. He usually receives no specialized training in the facts and resources to help you with such problems. Nonetheless, you may look to him for help, and he may seem to offer it, at least indirectly. Can he truly help you through indirect means to solve your problems without concrete information?

He will, of course, *try* to help you in any of these areas in which you describe serious problems. However, his efforts will usually be limited to trying to change your *feelings* about your problems, about yourself, and about others, and will be based on the hope that if you change your feelings and attitudes, you will be able to function better.

Such a conclusion may not be justified. Even when you are eager to meet girls and to experiment with sex, you may not know how to begin. Even if you want to manage your money better, you may not know how to prepare and implement a budget. Your therapist could refer you to a group social worker or a bank budget planner for such specific help, but seldom does. He might also know and refer you to social groups appropriate for you in your locality, but seldom does.

You cannot, then, depend upon your therapist for the specific information you may need to carry out the new attitudes and hopes you develop in therapy. You can, however, press him for such information.

It is important that you work with such specifics while you are in therapy, since follow-up on your new feelings and attitudes until they result in *deeds* and effective habits is vital to the continued success of your therapy. Otherwise, your good intentions will too often dribble away to nothing.

[1] D. A. Krampitz, "Sex Knowledge and the Psychotherapist" (M.A. thesis, Univ. of Minnesota, 1966).

GENERAL SUCCESS RATES

Seldom will a therapist even try to answer your questions about your chances of success in psychotherapy. Generally acceptable information is simply not available, and he can and should tell you this. The sparse data available conveys an extremely pessimistic picture—that is, as far as the contrast between improvement under any existing form of psychotherapy and improvement that occurs with no therapy at all is concerned.

It should be noted that H. J. Eysenck,[2] a leading evaluator of treatment, has concluded that techniques based upon learning-theory principles ("short methods of treatment") appear to be somewhat more effective than others. Eysenck and others have estimated that roughly two-thirds of the neurotic patients will improve markedly. About half of those seeking help will apparently improve markedly even if they don't get it, about a quarter will not improve much even with help, and a quarter are a potentially responsive group of whom around half will get effective help.

The main trouble with such surveys of results is that the various studies of improvement from psychotherapy use widely different kinds of patients, comparison ("control") groups, methods of providing therapy, combinations of circumstances, goals, criteria of success, and ways of measuring results. A mere handful of well-controlled studies has recently been done, almost all by psychologists interested in the shorter-term, more structured methods of therapy, and these have been favorable to structured methods, compared to more conventional, unstructured forms. Unstructured therapy is less easy to measure or to evaluate.

In brief, available data on results suggest that therapy generally is not dramatically better than no therapy at all. Such a conclusion should at least put you on guard against indiscriminately accepting or choosing treatment that might be available. Despite the fact that scientific findings are not available, it makes sense for you to choose therapists carefully, scrutinize your personal results, and constantly seek to improve the treatment you undertake by directing your actions to solve concrete problems. If you do so, you can substantially improve your chances of success.

This latter point is crucial. It is far easier to determine and direct

[2] *Handbook of Abnormal Psychology* (New York: Basic Books, 1961).

progress if your goals and actions are concrete rather than hazy. Thus, if therapy is not helping you to date girls, get more satisfaction at work, stay out of debt, or improve your school grades, you can change therapists or experiment with new ways to progress toward your goals more quickly. On the other hand, if you are seeking a sense of fulfillment, or relationship, or maturity, you will usually be unsure of your progress and methods and how to judge them. Research itself bogs down on the same considerations. This is why your therapist cannot cite effective rates of success—except, perhaps, in terms of his own practice if he has compiled figures on *that*.

Overall, however, regardless of the weakness cited above, around two-thirds of patients in therapy seem to improve to some degree; about one-third do not. Those patients given no treatment at all seem to improve in about the same ratio. This latter finding is why a "control" group is so vital; otherwise, what is attributed to therapy would never be known to occur equally without it. Apparently you or your environment "naturally" tend toward improvement; or perhaps this is the effect of increased time and distance away from distressing events or of your ability to get used to trying conditions or of your getting nonprofessional help.

The crucial question for research in the field, and for you personally, is how to better for yourself this general rate of improvement that does not depend upon the skill of the therapist, or indeed upon therapy at all. That is the purpose of this book—and of the most significant research in the field.

Therapy may even make you worse. In a very recent survey of psychotherapy research, Allen E. Bergin[3] lists several research studies indicating that psychotherapy may cause people to become better or worse adjusted than comparable persons not receiving treatment. There have long been suspicions that under some conditions therapy might have a negative effect. Professionals sometimes say to each other, for example, "We had better not tinker with this man's defenses or he might fall apart. He *needs* to believe such things." Sometimes, too, it is said that under the impact and pressure of examining your weaknesses, you might get worse before you get better in treatment. There are no studies to support either of these two views. Your most secure base of

---

3 "Some Implications of Psychotherapy Research for Therapeutic Practice," *Journal of Abnormal Psychology*, LXXI, no. 4 (1966), 235–246.

judgment will be to decide for yourself whether you are progressing, as directly as possible, toward concrete goals.

ON BEING A GOOD PATIENT

By coming to therapy with certain background characteristics or certain attitudes, you increase the likelihood that you will be accepted for treatment, be given a certain kind of treatment, and be judged successful in treatment—all independent of your diagnosis or symptoms. In other words, therapists, being subject to the same rules of behavior that you are, will feel comfortable or like you more or less depending upon your similarity to them, your generally likable qualities, and your ability to put them at ease. They tend to treat you accordingly, even if they do not intend to.

The most blatant example of this kind of effect has its basis in socio-economics. Hollingshead and Redlich,[4] among others, have vividly documented how poor people are usually denied psychotherapy in favor of hospitalization and drugs, while middle- and upper-class persons much more frequently get psychotherapy. They attribute this finding to the fact that most psychotherapists themselves are middle class and feel most comfortable with such patients, as well as to the obvious fact that most psychotherapy costs too much for poor people. It also seems likely that lower-class persons are less understanding of or sympathetic to the complexities of psychotherapy—at least of the intensive long-term, "depth" type. They want quicker, more direct results, whereas persons with more education are willing to go along with sophisticated theories that do not lead to obvious results.

By the standards of most psychotherapists, the Good Patient tends to be middle class and also bright, articulate, well motivated, well educated, and not very disturbed. That he also appears to need therapy the least, and to be likely to succeed in anything he undertakes, bothers many socially minded therapists. How can psychotherapy be justified when it concentrates its care on the least needy and has little to offer the most disturbed?

Certainly, if you are not articulate, well motivated, and middle-class, you should ask your prospective therapist how he would feel about working with you. If he does not refer you elsewhere, at

[4] A. B. Hollingshead and F. C. Redlich, *Social Class and Mental Illness* (New York: J. Wiley & Sons, 1958).

least he will be confronted early with possible areas of misunderstanding that may arise between you because you do not conform to the kind of patient he likes to work with. Otherwise you can try to find a therapist who is more behavior-change oriented and not as interested in plumbing your background and feelings, or try clinics that often deal with less sophisticated patients. But then if you were not a Good Patient type, you would probably not even be reading this book.

Besides, current developments are changing such conclusions. Within just the past five years, concern about the poor has grown, community mental-health clinics which treat everyone have sprung up all over the country, and behavior-change methods not concerned about patients' introspections have begun to take hold. Concepts of the Good Patient are in transition, and the cautions written in this regard will apply mainly to your choice of a relatively conventional (psychoanalytic, nondirective, and eclectic) therapist in private practice rather than to the newer services springing up.

ON BEING A GOOD THERAPIST

Most studies of therapeutic success have tried to describe the kind of patient in terms of background, motivation, diagnosis, symptoms, and personality who profits from treatment. The therapist's role and characteristics have been mainly ignored. Yet those few studies which have been done suggest that the therapist probably determines the outcome of therapy far more than does the patient. This seems logical, since he should be the prime mover of treatment, the expert who makes changes happen.

His theories do not affect success, but there is some evidence that the amount of his experience does. Also, therapists more often tend to say that improvement has occurred if patients stay in treatment longer—even though the patients do not agree. The therapist is more likely to rate his patients as "improved" if they meet his needs or conform to his beliefs. His own personality characteristics tend to determine how long he keeps patients in treatment more than do the patients' characteristics.[5]

This is not to denigrate the therapist. It is merely to say that

[5] D. R. Stieper and D. N. Wiener, "The Problem of Interminability in Outpatient Psychotherapy," *Journal of Consulting Psychology*, XXIII, no. 3 (1959), 237–242.

he is subject to the same influences and is predictable in the same ways as are other human beings. He may strive hard to gain more control and objectivity in his life than most men possess, recognizing that he must try to understand, be able to sympathize with, and become scientifically analytic about as broad a range of human behavior as possible. But ultimately his striving is confined by human limits which you would do well to discover explicitly and early. You can question him and others about him, and then judge for yourself whether the limits you can discover might seriously impede his effectiveness with you. If he is disturbed by reasonable inquiries into his skills, limits, and biases—and some will be—you would do well to discover this as early as possible and decide whether to go on with him or to change therapists.

HOW SYMPTOMS AFFECT THERAPY

The therapist or clinic you select will probably be affected by the nature of your complaints. While symptoms and diagnoses do not actually correlate with results of treatment, therapists tend to believe they do and as a result base certain decisions about your therapy upon them.

From the standpoint of symptoms, the Good Patient (the one he prefers to treat), in most therapists' eyes, has mainly nonphysical, nonbizarre neurotic symptoms and does not act impulsively. The psychotherapist tends to prefer patients who worry, are depressed, are cautious, work hard, try to please, are sensitive, and suffer. Conversely, he tends to be uncomfortable about and often shies away from patients who threaten or attempt suicide or assault, who overdrink or overuse drugs, who suffer from severe physical complaints even if on an emotional basis, or who have bizarre symptoms.

The reasons are clear. The Good Patient is not likely to cause the therapist trouble by beating up people, getting into other social trouble, turning seriously sick, or requiring hospitalization. He is likely to listen carefully to the therapist and to talk about feeling improved. His opposite is much more likely to offend the therapist with hostility, to require the therapist's intervention and time with the family, court, or social agency, to require the therapist's involvement with a general physician or internist, even not to pay his bill or admit to improvement.

Most readers of this book are likely to meet the Good Patient requisites, except perhaps for physical symptoms. Special problems involved with such symptoms will be discussed in a later chapter. Here we will note merely that many therapists are uncomfortable about treating patients with severe ulcers, colitis, asthma, and the other so-called psychosomatic disorders in the belief that those conditions may flare up during psychotherapy and that therapy may be blamed for it. Consult with your physician about a physical condition and gain his support if it should be needed with a psychotherapist.

KINDS OF GAINS LIKELY

The gains you can make in therapy may be viewed from several vantage points: Your internal one—do you feel better? Your therapist's—does he think you are better, in feeling or deed? An outsider's or other objective view—are you specifically handling your life situations better?

The kinds of gains you might make can be inferred from these viewpoints. Whether you feel better is both an eminently sensible criterion and at the same time, entirely by itself, a meaningless one for so serious and costly an enterprise as psychotherapy. Though all personal satisfaction and sense of accomplishment must ultimately be signaled by your feelings, you may gain a sense of well-being from many things which are limited or self-defeating.

Activities such as using narcotics or stealing are dangerous. Some, such as sucking a candy stick, letting off steam to a friend, or overspending impulsively are trivial. Some, such as drinking alcohol or taking tranquilizers, reduce effectiveness. Some, such as escapist movies or vacations, are transitory.

Merely feeling good may be a trivial, dangerous, transitory, interfering, or damaging "gain" from psychotherapy unless it fits in with your whole life, your longer-term goals, and your major activities. The crucial issue would seem to rest with *why* you feel good and whether the cause has a reasonable and important place in your present and future.

Therapy can make you feel better simply by providing you with a listener, by implying a hope that you can change, by giving you encouragement or affection, even though from a stranger, or by providing you with pills or relaxation. This happier feeling, sometimes even to the point of euphoria, comes on quickly, sometimes even as you approach the therapist's office or after the first session, and just as often dwindles after a few hours or weeks if unsupported by much harder-won gains achieved through changing your habits. The lasting quality of the improved feeling is a crucial factor that must stem from lasting changes you can achieve in your ways of living.

The second kind of gain is that judged by your therapist. He is often as eager as you are to see progress. After all, you can blame him if you make no gains, despite a heavy expenditure of time and money, and he must justify his time and charges by seeing gains somehow. When he cannot, however, he is quite as likely to blame you and your intransigence as you are to blame him and his incompetence.

When there are no clear-cut, concrete goals in therapy, the therapist can ingeniously and sincerely discover subtle gains. If you have come in hoping in vain to overcome sexual impotence, he may nevertheless consider you improved because you are more relaxed about your difficulty. If you continue to fight bitterly with your wife, he may note that you don't feel as guilty afterward. If you continue to function below your ability at your job or education, he may observe that you have adjusted better than before or that you have more insight.

Your therapist cannot, however, force you to agree with him, and dramatic disagreements do occur between therapist and patient about improvement.

The objective, outside view of your progress is the best for research, but it is likely to be meaningless to you. What do you care if a personality test shows improvement, or your school grades rise, or that strangers observe more congenial behavior in you if you do not feel better?

Still, it is likely that you *will* feel better when such outside judgments also indicate improvement, particularly if these objective measures indicate achievement of goals you have chosen to work for. Thus, if better grades are your goal, you are likely to feel better when you achieve them. If being more likable socially is your purpose, becoming more congenial will make you feel better. The outside measures then should merely confirm what you report.

It is your choice of goals in therapy that is crucial in determining your gains. Without clear-cut goals, you can never determine your gains in any stable, objective way. You will be at the mercy of your own transitory moods and your therapist's biases.

In any case, the gains you make are likely to be modest, even disappointing if you have had grand expectations. Gains are not likely to be related to the type of therapy or its length or intensity or "depth." Large hopes are most likely to be disappointed and small, specific ones fulfilled.

CHAPTER 3

Determining the Need for Help

THE DIFFICULTY in determining one's need for help says as much about uncertainties in the field of psychotherapy as it does about the potential client's indecision. When a physician is asked for the danger signs of cancer, he will list a number of symptoms that are also common among normal people and which by no means in themselves indicate that one has cancer. The symptoms are merely signs to be checked upon, and their value in diagnosing cancer will depend upon their intensity, patterning, chronicity, and accumulation.

When psychotherapists try to list the signs indicating a need for psychotherapy, however, they not only list many symptoms which by themselves may be common, but they can provide no clear way of checking whether the signs are pathological. If you go to a psychotherapist with mild psychological symptoms and want to pay for his services, chances are the therapist will decide you need, or at least can profit from, his therapy. He generally bases his decision more upon your expressed desire for help than upon your symptoms, and is therefore not likely to turn you away just because he thinks your symptoms may either be within normal limits or not seriously disruptive.

WHAT IS "NORMAL"?

"Normalcy" can be defined as acting and feeling as if nothing serious is the matter with you, so that neither you nor others are aware that you have problems beyond your control.

As soon as you or others start to worry about your behavior or feelings, it is likely that the fragile idea of "normalcy" will be punctured and the painful process of trying to decide whether you should seek professional help will begin. Several steps in this process will be discussed. Perhaps the most that can be said about "normalcy" is that, like health, it tends to be taken for granted, and is negatively defined as the absence of serious trouble.

Some objective signs are available. A good personality test, for example, can tell you whether your attitudes or deeds are similar to those of certain kinds of severely disturbed patients. Less objectively, teachers or employers can let you know how your behavior compares with that of other students or employees they have observed under similar conditions.

Such standards of normalcy are imprecise and tenuous, however, and ultimately you will be forced simply to judge for yourself whether you are suffering more than you are willing to and ignore questions of what is "normal"—unless, that is, simply being told by an authority that you are normal substantially reassures you and relieves your suffering.

SENSING (WHEN NOT RECOGNIZING) SERIOUS PROBLEMS

Since this book is addressed to the prospective or actual consumer of psychotherapeutic services, it is assumed that persons who totally reject the very idea of their possible need for help are not in our audience. There will be those, however, who can, through the guidelines presented, recognize a possible need. There may also be some readers who are too disturbed or disrupted to be able to make such a decision for themselves. They may be able to sense dimly that they may have a need, but by the very nature of their disturbance be unable to progress further.

Persons who are psychotic, brain-damaged through injury, disease, drugs, or aging, or disordered in character to the extent of being insensitive to social standards may vaguely feel their need for help, but be unable to translate it into making a concrete decision. In such cases—as with children—relatives, friends, or social or legal agencies may finally have to make the decision for them. If you sense that something serious is wrong with you but are unable to express it because your mind wanders, or you are too bitter against society, or you are overwhelmed with fears or bizarre thoughts, you can at least try to ask for help through relatives or agencies. You can try, however vaguely, to convey your sense of being out of kilter or simply try to draw attention to yourself.

The line between rational and irrational behavior is thin much of the time. Often your most disturbed thoughts and deeds are known only to you, and frequently only you will know how peculiar or dangerous your thoughts are. So only you can draw attention to them.

To depend entirely upon others to recognize your need will often long postpone help, since you may very well have isolated yourself from others, preferring to live a lonely life rather than face possible criticism or rebuff. No one then pays attention to you unless you can help to draw attention to yourself (choosing harmless ways).

DECIDING FOR YOURSELF

It is extremely important for you to try to decide ahead of time whether your problems are such that you need help, how you can present them clearly to permit the therapist to decide whether to try to help you, and whether his thinking and responses indicate he is able to provide what you want and need.

Making such judgments places a heavy burden upon you. Most therapists would probably prefer to have you depend upon their judgments. Yet the present state of psychotherapy suggests no course of action more reasonable than trying to make your own decisions, for reasons which will be discussed later. If you do not go to the therapist with clear problems and expectations, you may be at the mercy of his idiosyncracies and theoretical bias. Choosing a psychotherapist at random for help with depression, for example, may easily subject you to any of a variety of treatments: hospitalization, tranquilizers or "antidepressant" drugs, electro-shock therapy, psychoanalysis or nondirective therapy, or any combination of the above. If you present a more concrete problem, however, or choose a therapist with care, you will at least know what kind of treatment you are likely to receive. You can make your choice on logical grounds, which will be discussed later.

There must, of course, be exceptions to your control of your own therapy. You may be overwhelmed by emotions, be indecisive or irrational. You may have a wise friend or professional acquaintance from whose advice about psychotherapy you can profit. But you probably will gain enormously by making at least some tentative decisions about your problems, about help that appears reasonable to you, and about sources among the alternative therapies that may be available. Ideally there ought to be a kind of "personal service broker" in the community to help you choose wisely from among all forms of personal services. Until he exists, however, you need to obtain as much prior knowledge as you can in order to choose and judge such services wisely.

GUIDELINE NO. 1: Educate yourself as fully as possible about the field of psychotherapy and evaluate your need for it by any professional guidelines you can find so that you can decide wisely upon your need for help.

THE ADVANTAGE OF FEELING TROUBLED

Some people have the notion that they should never feel unhappy, miserable, or depressed. Such feelings of pain can be appropriate and useful. For instance, not to feel grief or depression over the death of a close friend would be unreasonable. When appropriate in occurrence and intensity, these reactions not only mark one as sensitive to his environment, but can in complicated situations provide useful indicators of the source of more obscure difficulties. That is, just as a fever indicates some malfunction of the body, so can a feeling of edginess or depression or anxiety indicate a source of difficulty in handling life problems. If a person is born without the nerve endings to sense pain (which does occur), he is in constant danger of damaging himself unwittingly. For instance, he can burn himself severely if he gets too close to a fire without feeling the excessive heat. The capacity to feel psychological pain or anxiety, or other discomfort, even though you cannot see its cause immediately, can help you recognize that some obscure trouble does exist which should be given careful consideration.

The need for psychological help, or for psychotherapy, can thus be detected either directly or indirectly. It is detected directly by the presence of obviously unsolved problems such as having constant arguments with a boss or spouse. Indirectly its presence may be made known through a psychological or physical (psychosomatic) sense of discomfort or pain, the cause of which is obscure, such as feeling chronically tired at work even though one is in good health and is not under pressure. The necessity for converting vague feelings of trouble into concrete, solvable problems will be discussed later. Here, feeling troubled is viewed as an indication of problems that need to be stated and then solved. It can be a useful sign of need for help, just as the feeling of physical pain would be.

GUIDELINE NO. 2: Take advantage of the presence of troubled feelings or other inner discomfort to question yourself about what problems you may have that you have not recognized or solved.

MENTAL ILLNESS VS. PROBLEMS IN LIVING

Recently in the United States, the concept of "mental illness," the name given to the presence of emotional troubles, has been challenged by the view that such troubles are really "problems in living." "Mental illness" as a counterpart of physical illness has been heavily sold to the American public. The concept implies a kind of disease for which the individual is as little responsible as he is for being attacked by a virus. His problem then logically becomes one of obtaining professional help to cure a disease, rather than to find help in solving the problems he has in handling his life.

Even in the field of physical health, however, there are significant attacks being made upon the concept of curing disease through professional treatment. René Dubos,[1] for example, writes that "the modern American is encouraged to believe that money can create drugs for the cure of heart disease, cancer, and mental disease, but he makes no worthwhile effort to recognize, let alone correct, the mismanagement of his everyday life that contributes to the high incidence of these conditions."

The concept of mental illness has been carried to its extreme in the *Manual of Mental Disorders* (1952) of the American Psychiatric Association, which lists as "mental illnesses" such diagnoses as "Adult Situational Stress," thus presumably assuming for the medical profession the treatment of "poor efficiency" and "low morale." One pernicious result of so broad a concept of mental illness is that the individual's responsibility for the maximum control and direction of his person and his environment is diminished,

[1] *The Mirage of Health* (New York: Harper & Row, 1959).

and a burden is lifted from his shoulders and placed upon a disease and the professional care of it.

Originally the concept of mental illness had the desirable goal of removing the stigma from hospitalization in mental institutions and from psychiatric diagnoses, leading to more humane attitudes toward the emotionally troubled. But the current implications for treatment have been carried to a damaging point. It seldom helps a person's efforts at change to define his problems as being beyond his control, and to claim that he has been attacked by a mental disease against which he has been helpless to protect himself. The fault for the curse society originally put on the emotionally disturbed would seem to lie as much with the nature of the diabolical-sounding diagnoses and the cruel institutionalization for which the professionals were often responsible, as with public misinterpretation of what emotional difficulties mean.

Middle- and upper-class patients in the United States today receive considerably more protection against being diagnosed as mentally ill or being put into mental hospitals than do lower-class patients.[2] Middle- and upper-class people who go to private practitioners seldom have anything more onerous put into their records than "run-down condition," "extreme fatigue," or, for insurance purposes, such innocuous diagnoses as "anxiety reaction." In the same circumstances, a poorer patient who obtains help from a public agency or public institution is much more likely to be diagnosed—without consideration of the adverse consequences for employment and other community situations—as "schizophrenia," "schizoid personality," "passive-aggressive personality," and similar dire-sounding terms. He is thus more likely to be labelled adversely in a public record, just as he is more likely to be put into a public mental hospital or ward rather than into a private general hospital, or to receive therapy outside of a hospital altogether.

In contrast, diagnosing and treating emotional difficulties in terms of problems of living can clarify and normalize the public's view of the psychologically troubled, as well as the troubled person's own conception of what and whom he needs to resolve his difficulties.

[2] A. B. Hollingshead and F. C. Redlich, *Social Class and Mental Illness* (New York: J. Wiley & Sons, 1958).

Innumerable patients ask, "Doctor, tell me what's the matter with me," or "What's my diagnosis?" or, "What's *really* the matter with me?" How reassuring it can be to be told that "what is the matter with you is what you tell me is the matter with you, and what we can discover together are your additional and concrete problems." Why should a concept such as "schizoid personality" be injected into the situation when a person's problem is that of feeling alienated from people, and not knowing how to make personal friends and perform daily tasks which will keep him constantly in touch with his environment and away from day-dreaming?

How much easier it could be to change your behavior if you viewed your problems as stemming from the way you handle your daily life, and not from "being" passive-dependent, having schizoid tendencies, or never resolving the Oedipal situation. A diagnosis may have some practical use as a shorthand way of describing a set of behavioral characteristics or for research purposes. As a way of contributing to effective psychotherapy, however, the conventional diagnosis has little value and many disadvantages.

GUIDELINE NO. 3: Consider your trouble in terms of problems in handling your daily life, which you need to learn how to master, rather than in terms of a mental illness over which you have little or no control.

VAGUE VS. SPECIFIC PROBLEMS

You may describe your problems in a great variety of ways ranging from such vague terms as "unhappy," "tied up in knots," "unfulfilled," "just plain miserable," to such specifics as "can't get along with my boss," "stomach always hurts," or "can't get an erection." But for any problem to be solved directly and efficiently, it must first be put in terms that can be seen and operated upon. It is therefore important for you to try to convert vague complaints into more concrete ones. That is, to obtain effective help you must sooner or later be able to define specifically what in your daily life makes you unhappy or miserable or depressed, so that you know what to change and how.

If you go to a therapist with vague complaints, he may very well fumble with them in an equally vague way, discussing philosophy, values, theory, or the past with you. He may be a long time getting to work on your current problems and their direct solution, or he may primarily be interested only in your feelings and not in the specific habits which get you into trouble. Or he may be interested only in an immediate solution involving not your habits and attitudes, but only ways of making you feel better, such as by prescribing drugs or recommending a vacation.

He may try to discover the "underlying causes" of your complaints in relatively inefficient ways, in extended, sometimes interminable, analyses of your past and the obscurest aspects of your feelings, dreams, and free associations. It sometimes takes a therapist years to convert his interpretations of your vague feelings of unhappiness or your psychosomatic symptoms into recognition of the concrete problems that you can attack in your daily living. Of course, this danger can be avoided by careful choice of a psychotherapist (to be discussed in a later chapter). In any case, it is well for you to be thinking in terms of relatively concrete causes and solutions, and at least to bring into your therapy the attitude that you should convert your vague complaints as soon as possible into specific ones that you can directly do something about.

You may find yourself treated by an eclectic psychotherapist who is not interested primarily in attacking your mishandling of your daily life, but only in palliating your symptoms as quickly as possible; that is, he may want to prescribe a tranquilizer, an inspirational book, or a vacation, just as a physician might hand you an aspirin for an ache. This may be sufficient for a trivial problem. If, however, you have decided you need help on a larger scale such as will be proposed later in this chapter, then to attack vague complaints such as depression with equally vague solutions such as a rest will gloss over the problems of living that bring on the depression and merely postpone a day of reckoning.

GUIDELINE NO. 4:   Try to convert vague symptoms into concrete problems in your daily life, before seeing a psychotherapist if possible, or at least early in therapy.

REMOTE VS. CURRENT CAUSES

Psychotherapy that attempts to handle your problems on a direct, current basis is considered superficial by some psychotherapists who advocate therapy in which the most remote "causes" and feelings are explored, your distant past is analyzed, your dreams, free associations, and most obscure feelings are elicited, or your values and philosophy are explored and clarified. Such approaches are an indirect way of trying to eliminate your current problems, in the belief that such "deep analysis" or "uncovering" of your feelings or values and philosophy will have more profound and lasting advantages than attacking immediate problems.

A newer kind of psychotherapy, based upon recent research into the processes by which persons learn and change, treats problems as they arise, and as directly as possible. This view will be elaborated later.

Symptoms, causes, and solutions can refer to specific problems in current living as well as to those in the remote past. A headache can be related to the immediate events that bring it on more easily than to distant events in your upbringing even if such earlier events originally precipitated it. It can be cured in the present by trying to change your way of handling yourself at a party if that is where you now have your headache, or of handling your spouse differently if his presence brings on your headache. Analyzing your behavior as a child may contribute little that is useful to effective therapy for current problems. You can cure symptoms that arise from being with a husband as well or better by learning directly how to handle your husband if he, rather than your father, is now the most important adult male in your life. Although it is often more difficult to face current problems than past ones, available research suggests that handling matters on a current basis produces at least as good and probably better results than trying to analyze "original" causes.[3]

Of course, it is by no means simple to analyze and change your current ways of handling yourself. To change your way of handling your husband may very well involve facing and resolving a fear of him as if he were a domineering father, or learning to treat him as an equal, or setting limits on him, or disregarding his unreasonable complaints. But all of these conditions can be viewed as current problems, to be resolved in the present. They do not require that you ignore or temporarily defer work on present causes in favor

[3] See Phillips and Wiener, *Short-term Psychotherapy and Structured Behavior Change* (New York: McGraw-Hill, 1966).

of a search for distant causes which must then be brought up to date after many hours of discussion.

GUIDELINE NO. 5: To obtain help most efficiently you should try to put your problems in terms of the most directly observable current causes, and try to solve them by changes in your current behavior before analyzing more distant causes and using more indirect ways of trying to change.

SERIOUS PROBLEMS—OR SERIOUS WORRY ABOUT UNIMPORTANT PROBLEMS?

You may have great difficulty in deciding whether you truly have a serious problem or whether you are unduly worried about a minor, or "normal," difficulty. In other words, is it the problem that bothers you or excessive worry about something that should not trouble you so much? This situation can most usefully be put in terms of its *effect* on you—the effect of the problem or the effect of the worry about it—rather than whether it is a serious problem by some general standard.

You may be extremely worried about losing your job, for example. You may truly be in imminent danger of losing your job, or you may simply be excessively insecure about this, or any job, even if you are in no actual danger of losing it, or even if you could easily obtain an equally good or better job if you did lose your present one. A serious problem can exist for you in either form. In the first case, it would be a realistic question of how to handle the loss of a job with as little damage or as much gain to your life as possible. You might very well solve the problem by doing what many people have done in such a situation: look efficiently for a good new job. The problem would be defined as serious, for purposes of this chapter, only if it produced some disorganization in your habits of living and you were not taking steps likely to solve it.

Or you may have a family living next to you which bothers you and your children by quarrelsome or boisterous behavior. You can take realistic steps to solve this problem by moving, or by confronting your neighbor with the situation and trying to arrive at amicable solutions, or seeking out arbitration through a minister or other third party. Or you may not take any direct effective action at all, but simply worry about what to do. In this case, it would not matter whether the problem were objectively large or small. The factor defining your problem would be the degree of disruption the unresolved situation introduced into your life.

The criterion of seriousness, then, would be what you are making of the problem and what you are doing to solve it. Any problem, no matter how trivial, is capable of triggering intense worry and disorganization in your life in terms of extreme sleeplessness, nervousness, irritability, headaches, stomach-aches, suspiciousness, or whatever. It does not matter whether the problem is serious, or if it is only the worry about it that is serious.

GUIDELINE NO. 6:   Any problem is serious enough to require help if it seriously disrupts your life, and attempts to rate problems as major or minor have little to do with your need for help.

DO YOU HAVE TO BE MOTIVATED FOR PSYCHOTHERAPY?

Most psychotherapists believe that you must be "motivated" in order to profit from psychotherapy. It does seem to be true that if you are not eager to talk about yourself and your problems, or otherwise to act as the therapist thinks you should in the therapy interview and outside, the rather passive ways of most therapists will probably not change you.

The result is that most therapists (outside of public agencies, which may be compelled to take stronger action in acute community-problem cases such as psychotics, wife-beaters, or school truants) select their patients according to the treatment they practice— which is, in the perspective of social needs, a backward way of operating. Thus, as we pointed out, the most seriously disturbed persons are usually ruled out of private psychotherapeutic treatment. Those persons who are most out of touch with reality (psychotics), and those who are most anti-social (psychopaths), are not ordinarily accepted for private psychotherapy.

Of course, if good alternatives to psychotherapy were available, the therapist could simply say that their kind of treatment is wrong for the "unmotivated" and that other kinds should be provided. The trouble is that there are no good alternatives available if you believe that psychological problems must be solved through changes in behavior.

Most psychotherapists consider that they cannot work effectively to change "unmotivated" persons through ordinary interview methods. But the methods of psychotherapy, as will be discussed in later chapters, can be far more aggressive than they conventionally are. The psychotherapist can work to convince the "unmotivated" patient of the advantages to him of acting in certain ways and not in others. He can utilize social forces to encourage, to reinforce, or to prompt change in the "unmotivated" patient. He can increase the effective impact of parents upon children, of one spouse upon another, of relatives upon the patient, or of an employer upon an employee. The psychotherapist can use many such outside forces to help change the behavior of poorly motivated patients, as well as make more aggressive use of his own powers of influence and persuasion in the interview.

Hospitalization, shock treatment, massive drug dosages, and other physical means are the forms of treatment used with the most seriously disturbed persons, but not because these methods are considered to be better than direct efforts at changing behavior. If they were considered effective ways of helping people to solve serious psychological problems, they would be used to help everyone, neurotics as well as psychotics and psychopaths. Instead, such methods are usually considered last resorts or all that can be done with people who are not accessible to psychotherapy.

For greater efficiency, the therapist may well *prefer* to work directly with the patient, or he may *prefer* at least that the patient be present. The patient need neither be eager to be present, nor be at all interested in psychotherapy, nor like the therapist, nor show any other signs of "motivation" for a change in him to occur. The patient may be present only because his spouse has said that she will divorce him otherwise, or because an employer has threatened to fire him, or because a friend has insisted that he desperately needs help and should try at least one session. In other words, you need not be "motivated" in order to profit from psychotherapy, as long as your therapist is willing to take the initiative to convince you of the possible advantages of treatment, at least on a trial basis, or is willing to try to help you gain some quick, encouraging rewards if longer, harder work is necessary to solve more important or tougher problems.

When you are not highly "motivated," it may be necessary either to find a therapist who is willing to work with "unmotivated" persons or to let others such as your wife obtain help for you. This, too, can be an effective form of therapy, and may change your behavior even when you are not present at the sessions.[4]

GUIDELINE NO. 7: Since most therapists consider your "motivation" in deciding whether you need or can profit from their help, you should be prepared either to express fairly strong motivation to your proposed therapist or to seek out one who does not consider motivation vital.

TAKING RESPONSIBILITY

Woven throughout these sections on determining need is the concept of your taking responsibility for determining your need. Nonprofessional as well as professional persons can help you with the process, but unless you are mentally incompetent, the ultimate decisions must rest with you.

Motivation is not necessary for successful behavior change. Neither is taking responsibility, but it will vastly accelerate the process of determining need if you can assume an active role. Otherwise others may be forced into making decisions for you should you get into trouble with the law, become a danger to yourself or to others, or act so oddly as to come to public attention.

The educated consumer is the best judge of his own needs and aid, and becoming educated as a consumer requires that you take an active role in studying your problems and community services.

There is a distinction between motivation for therapy and assuming responsibility for one's behavior. In the therapist's eyes, motivation for therapy too often is interpreted as a relatively uncritical, eager, perhaps even dependent attitude toward his services. More helpful would be a critical, inquiring attitude toward therapy. Such an approach might easily suggest that you are poorly motivated. Yet it is consistent with taking responsibility for finding the listener to your problems, for the decision to try professional

[4] Since this is a guide for you as the direct consumer of psychotherapeutic services, you should, for further development of this concept of indirect therapy, refer to the book *Short-term Psychotherapy and Structured Behavior Change* by Phillips and Wiener. (New York: McGraw-Hill, 1966.)

help, for the choice of help, and in substantial part for the progress of the therapy.

GUIDELINE NO. 8: *Taking responsibility for your psychotherapy with active and critical attitudes will probably improve your chances to obtain outcomes satisfactory to you.*

CAN YOU GET PREVENTIVE HELP?

The concept of preventive help is widely talked about, but with very uncertain knowledge. There is no evidence that any program of personal or professional help, child-rearing services, or public education reduces the subsequent incidence of psychological disturbance. The idea that by taking an extensive course of psychotherapy you can somehow stave off subsequent trouble is wholly untested. Yet many professional persons in the mental-health area undergo psychotherapy partly on the assumption that they will somehow better be able to cope with their own problems for having had this kind of professional help. Similarly, many middle-class and upper-class persons who live in cities where psychoanalysis particularly is much talked about and widely available, go into psychotherapy as if it would help them become more creative, stable, and insightful persons, even if they have no pressing problems.

To seek help for such vague goals seems to invite a kind of psychotherapy that is relatively aimless, interminable, and unmeasurable. It might well be *interesting*, and if that is enough for you, well and good. You cannot expect such a course, however, to improve your future stability, creativity, happiness, or problem-solving ability *unless* it is specifically focused upon problems you now have in these areas, upon specific ways of enhancing your accomplishments in these areas, and upon ways of determining your progress toward achievement of such goals.

Preventive help can be considered a matter of learning efficient habits that can be useful in solving future problems. But large numbers of people cannot be served through individual psychotherapy in any case. The time and personnel are not available. Besides families, the mass institutions of society such as schools, churches, and social agencies would seem to be the most feasible units through which experts could teach effective methods of problem-solving. Such methods would probably involve learning how to apply the rules of science in your life for you to see matters as they really are, how to analyze events and human beings objectively, how best to learn about and to solve problems, how to develop habits of discipline, study, and productivity that permit you to gain satisfactions in life and progress toward your goals—all in ways advantageous to you and society rather than to the detriment of either.

GUIDELINE NO. 9: Do not expect psychotherapy to help prevent future problems unless it is also specifically directed to help you develop habits to handle concrete, current situations successfully.

SHOULD YOU ANALYZE YOUR PAST?

Analysis of the past is a popular pursuit in psychotherapy. The assumption is that you can in this way learn what made you what you are and what brought on your current troubles. Gathering such historical material would seem to be useful if it provides clues to the troublesome factors in the current situation. Even in this limited regard, however, research has discovered very little in past personal histories that relates to current behavior—certainly far less than most therapists and patients assume and act upon.

If it works, trying to solve problems in the present is obviously more efficient than first analyzing the past and then applying any findings to the present. Spending months, even years, discussing the past without having clear ways of judging the results means that you cannot very well know when to quit doing it. There is no scientific evidence that uncovering, analyzing, and interpreting the past is by itself therapeutic. Freud himself turned away from psychoanalysis as a therapeutic method that would produce behavior change and came to consider it instead as a scientific tool in the study of human behavior.[5]

Having yourself and your history analyzed by a wise man can provide you with many insights about yourself, just as an archaeological exploration can provide data about a culture. You may learn about the roots of your habits, attitudes, and values provided you have a wise man for a psychotherapist and one who is willing

[5] S. Freud, "Psychoanalysis," *Encyclopaedia Britannica*, 14th ed., XVIII, 721–722.

to explore and establish the facts of your background. To do such analysis *accurately* would require the application of the most precise methods of science in a way which no therapists do. For example, if you were trying to establish the nature of your attitudes and activities in your childhood relative to your parents, the therapist or you should interview as many people and study as many documents from that period as could be obtained. To depend upon your loose retrospections about that time from your disadvantaged position as an adult, or to explore your free associations about that period, is not at all scientific and does not reveal the true past. At best it could only provide some data about your current interpretations of the past, and this may be useful to therapy. Perhaps a new kind of psychotherapy could be developed —better called autobiographical exploration or an archaeology of the self—which would not be confused with the aim of changing your behavior.

GUIDELINE NO. 10: Do not expect to get efficient help from psychotherapy with current problems through an analysis of your past life unless you focus specifically upon your current problems and the direct application of knowledge of your past to the present.

IS THERAPY ELABORATE, ARE RESULTS PERMANENT?

The decision to seek help is often affected by a view of psychotherapy as an elaborate, once-in-a-lifetime enterprise. In a later chapter, we will discuss present-day psychotherapy as, for the most part, a long-term and costly procedure. Even free or inexpensive service from a public agency will often make it necessary for you to take off time from work and may stretch out for months or years. In private psychotherapy, of course, the problem is not only that of time but also of heavy cost. At the extreme, it may cover forty-five or fifty-minute sessions three to five times a week for several years, and would seldom, at least in "depth" psychotherapy, run less than one or two interviews a week for one to three years.

In addition to the time and cost involved, other factors also contribute to the idea that therapy is an "all-or-nothing" proposition, a struggle to solve all your problems and to change your personality so that you should have no need for help ever again.

One fact that challenges this notion is that most people currently in psychotherapy have had previous therapy with different therapists. This seems to be true regardless of whether the patient has had prior psychoanalysis—which is presumably directed to the most basic kind of change on a permanent basis—or more "superficial" forms of help. Yet most theoretical approaches to therapy at least imply that it should be a "once-and-for-all" thing where you learn how to cope with yourself and your environment on a permanently enlightened and successful basis.

The idea presented here, however, is that there is no good reason why therapy must be considered a permanently successful (or unsuccessful) enterprise. If it is viewed simply as a matter of learning how to cope with problems, in as short a time of treatment as possible, then the formidability of seeking help can be vastly reduced. You can seek help for problems that you learn to solve directly and quickly. While the very process of solving any one problem should and usually does contribute to the development of habits which will help to solve subsequent problems, permanent solutions to all present and future problems need not be sought or expected. Nor should therapy be considered a failure if, after finishing it, you develop problems for which you need help later.

If psychotherapists could take the curse of failure off any psychotherapy which does not permanently solve all problems, and reduce the time and cost involved in facing, solving, and getting help with problems as they intermittently arise, then the enterprise can be made far more modest and less fearsome than it is usually considered. You could experiment with it more freely for problems whose seriousness you are not sure about, or when your attitude or financial position rule out long or costly help.

GUIDELINE NO. 11: If you begin psychotherapy viewing it as a modest enterprise from which you can seek and obtain fairly direct, efficient help which need not be elaborate or permanent, you can reduce your doubts about seeking and using help at any time.

TECHNICAL HELP FOR TECHNICAL PROBLEMS IN LIVING

There are several different methods of psychotherapy (these will be discussed in a later chapter), and to determine your need for help you must know the possible forms help can take. For our present purpose, the most modest view of psychotherapy will be presented. This is the view of therapy as technical help for troublesome problems in living—a view that can serve as a screen to try before you move on to more elaborate, expensive, or radical forms of help. It is consistent with the view that you should obtain the least expensive help, in terms of time and money, that will solve your problems.

Although any problem may become formidable, it need not be any more difficult to consult a psychotherapist than it would be to consult a lawyer, physician, or engineer. Good practitioners of any profession can help you to decide whether you have a technical problem for which they can provide help. Incidentally, no other professional person needs to investigate your "motivation" in order to practice his profession skillfully, although it is always pleasant to have a client who is eager and enthusiastic about the practitioner and his services. But the technically helpful skills and knowledge can be effective despite the client's personality and attitudes; this can also be the case in treating someone with problems in living.

Psychotherapists often do not take to this role of trying to practice their skills gracefully regardless of client motivation. If you are not eager to talk with them, they may not see you at all, or they may transfer you to someone else. If they must see you, they may not want to work directly with you on current problems, but may elect first to discuss your feelings and your past. Many, for example, may not want to discuss solutions to your immediate problems of how to budget, handle your children, choose a neighborhood, develop friends. They may take the view that if they can get at certain features of your personality and change some deepseated attitudes, you will then more or less automatically solve the more concrete problems of your daily life.

Many therapists take the view that psychotherapy never hurts anyone, that even though half a dozen therapists chosen at random will almost certainly take several different directions in their discussions with you, you will end up receiving the help you need. But help for what? If you do not help to determine the goals, your therapist certainly should contribute to the clarification of your vague complaints, the sharpening of the problems you present, and the conversion of your distortions into more realistic views. But you are likely to have to set the pace yourself for solving your problems. He will seldom be as intensely concerned as you are about the time or money involved.

GUIDELINE NO. 12: Unless you want your therapist to set your goals and problems according to his theory, which may result in long-term or expensive treatment with results that do not satisfy you, you should try to use him as a technician whose help you are soliciting for the most direct solutions to technical problems you have in handling your life.

A SCALE FOR CONSIDERING NEED FOR HELP

There is no precise way to determine your need for help, and every practitioner if asked would probably present a different method of doing so. Even psychological testing, which is the most precise and scientific way of measuring the attitudes and behavioral tendencies of human beings, is of little use to you in determining your need for help. Most psychologists practicing psychotherapy privately apparently do not use tests to determine the problems of their clients. While psychological tests, psychiatric exams, or social-work interviews can help to make diagnoses for legal or administrative purposes, to provide clues to problems which can then be discussed, or for research purposes, they have no demonstrable value in helping you to determine your need for psychotherapy or in facilitating your treatment. They do, however, often take a great deal of time and expense that might be put to better use in beginning therapy directly and immediately. The problem of lengthy preliminaries will be discussed in a later chapter. Suffice to say here that while tests may help to tell you whether you have extreme tendencies toward depression, for example, compared with other people, they do not say how you are feeling or handling your daily problems, what kind of therapy would help you most, or what kind of therapist you could best work with.

What is suggested for use here is a rough scale, developed in keeping with other views expressed in this book, to help you to examine yourself and your need for psychotherapy, and to make the important decisions about whether, in what form, and with whom to seek help.

Need-for-Help Scale

STEP A: Problem under control; no major disrupting effects from it in your life.

STEP B: Problem not under control; major disrupting effects; you know possible solutions to try out.

STEP C: Problem not under control; major disrupting effects; possible solutions not in view; you seek help to find solutions.

STEP D: Problem not under control; major disrupting effects; possible solutions not in view; you do not seek help to find solutions.

These steps are scaled in increasing order of seriousness. Steps A and B would rule out the immediate need for psychotherapy, while Steps C and D suggest immediate need: C on a voluntary basis, and D only through pressure from others.

A problem "under control" is one that has no major adverse effects upon your life. The housewife, for example, who uses a drink to prepare herself for her children's return from school, but who stops with one drink which does not subsequently impair her ability to handle them or her problems, would not solely on the ground of drinking have a problem needing help. If she could afford the luxury of professional help, she might learn to get along without the one drink, but she does not *need* therapy. The man who sleeps very little one night out of every three or four, and must live through the subsequent working day operating at only two-thirds of his usual efficiency but well enough to get by, may have his problem under reasonably good control; unless he shows further disruption or begins to take pills for sleeplessness which themselves subsequently impair his effectiveness, he does not *need* help.

Unless you consider golfing success to be a major part of your life, impairment of your game or inability to achieve your full potential because of anxiety would not seem to be an adequate basis for seeking psychotherapy. Nor would a student's getting "B" grades rather than the "A's" he is capable of seem to be adequate grounds to seek therapy—unless he or his parents suffer considerable misery as a result of the slight underachievement, which is a different problem in itself.

Even if the problem is not under control and does produce major disrupting effects in your life, if you have a plan of attack which offers reasonable hope for a solution, there would as yet seem to be no need for professional help. Of course, many people postpone working on a problem in the vague hope that it will simply go away by itself, will be "outgrown," or will be solved by some unpredictable event. This kind of temporizing is self-defeating, for such solutions cannot be depended upon to occur spontaneously, and if by chance they do they teach you nothing useful for the future control and solution of your problems. But if one has a plan in mind for sleeping better or for handling the return of the children from school, it is obviously worthwhile to try it before seeking professional help. In fact, the frame of mind that formulates and executes various attacks on troublesome problems would seem to be the major medium for achieving a satisfying life. Such a frame of mind is probably the best result that successful psychotherapy can accomplish, and it is most likely how most people handle their problems without outside help. It is a goal to be worked toward whenever possible before trying professional help, as well as a goal for professional help when that becomes necessary.

The third step in the scale involves a situation in which there is no possible solution in sight, and you voluntarily seek help. Between Steps B and C on this scale is where treatment becomes necessary or highly desirable; otherwise you are simply waiting, probably in vain, for something to happen. While events beyond your control—such as being fired from a job, being moved to a different part of the country, being sued for divorce, or being proposed to for marriage—sometimes do happen and provide a solution, to depend upon such events puts you at the mercy of unlikely occurrences. The very stance of waiting for something to happen or to feel better is self-defeating. It is at Step C that seeking professional help which offers a plan for solving your problems becomes logical.

The final step in the scale adds the factor of "not seeking help" even though no solution is in sight. Here are to be found the most passive and depressed, as well as the psychotic and anti-social persons. It is at this point that the dependency of conventional psychotherapy upon "motivation" bogs down, since these persons are too overwhelmed, insensitive, or withdrawn to perceive their problems. Newer forms of psychotherapy can, however, cope with people who have problems even when they do not recognize or want help with them. In Step D, one finds the most seriously disturbed persons. The best resources of society and of the profession should be mobilized to treat them, through relatives, friends, supervisors, political and legal agencies, and whoever else may be available to influence them. If a person presents legal problems and is hospitalized, he is already in a sense being involuntarily treated. But psychotherapeutic techniques themselves seldom come to grips with the problems of the involuntary groups. This problem also involves very important questions about conformity, and will be discussed in a later chapter.

CONVERTING VAGUE OR INDIRECT COMPLAINTS INTO CONCRETE PROBLEMS

Use of the above scale as well as the related views of this book depends upon translating vague complaints into concrete problems of living. Vague complaints, whether psychological, psychosomatic, or philosophical, can seldom be "solved" by any known techniques of psychotherapy. If they are considered valid by themselves and not merely conversions of other problems into a form more acceptable to the person or public, they could then be directly and successfully attacked with drugs, hypnosis, or direct suggestion.

If they stand by themselves as relics of earlier bad times with no important ties to the present, they need not concern the psychotherapist, but can and should be eliminated by the simplest educational devices, such as an alarm clock for oversleeping or bedwetting, or hypnosis for smoking or nail-biting. In keeping with a major theme of this book, it would seem desirable to try the simplest, most direct methods first before turning to psychotherapy. The often-mentioned fear that curing one symptom causes worse ones has never been borne out in research.

Vague or indirect complaints would not be cured by direct methods if you have self-defeating ways of handling your life which are not touched by such methods. Psychotherapy clients often have more than simple, obscure symptoms; frequently they seem to have fairly large systems of poor habits which interfere with important segments of their lives. The question here is how psychotherapy can best convert such vague or indirect complaints as, "life seems meaningless," "I have these bad headaches a lot of the time," "I'm afraid of almost everybody," into the concrete ways you mishandle yourself, which can be changed.

The conversion of vague problems and indirect complaints into concrete behavior is thus necessary to make the above scale most useful. For example, the person who says, "I have these bad headaches a lot of the time," should be asked for details about when he gets the headaches and how they stop him from doing things he feels he should do to reach his goals.

This is not the same as saying that you cannot treat symptoms effectively but must get at "underlying causes." For one thing, a symptom can be considered to be the main problem and be attacked through very simple, direct means—if widespread, self-defeating habit patterns are not obvious. For another thing, the view presented here would not try to get at any deep-seated, underlying causes of the symptoms lying in the past, but would instead determine the exact current circumstances that give rise to the symptom and then proceed as directly as possible to the solution of current problems.

CHAPTER 4 *Alternatives to Professional Help*

THERE ARE many alternatives to professional psychotherapy. They include persons and organizations willing and able to provide help ranging from the superficial and ineffectual to devoted, sustained, and, at times, even more effective help than professionals can offer.

There are many special problems in using nonprofessional help. You may analyze yourself interminably for years with no effect whatsoever. You may withdraw from society to such an extent that you are simply not exposed to the kinds of help that ordinarily are made available to or imposed upon people, such as friendly criticism from a friend or boss. You may make abortive efforts to get nonprofessional help, retracting when it begins to have painful impact.

The various alternatives to psychotherapy will be discussed in four categories: unstructured self-help, nonprofessional outside aids, mutual-help groups, and finally structured *systematic* self-help, listed in probably increasing order of effectiveness.

Unstructured self-help is the most common way by which people attempt to solve their problems. It usually serves as a screening device before you seek help from others, but it is often not sufficient to help solve any but minor problems. You might be able to think of what your problems are and even to figure out possible solutions, but if you withdraw from your environment, you will be unable to translate your thinking into effective action. Ordinarily, with serious problems, you must advance to the next step, the use of conventional outside aids.

Relatives, friends, ministers, teachers, co-workers, and physicians all provide help, often without being asked to do so. They are a natural part of the problem-solving process for most people and are used in this way even when you might be practically unaware of so using them. You might appreciate this fact only if you are cut off from them.

It is only when these first two steps fail, and your problems slip through the screen of these everyday methods, that you feel the need to make a special, concerted effort at a solution. Certain groups seem to have developed naturally to provide some self-help. Church groups, charitable groups, study groups, activity and hobby groups all answer human needs in certain interest or problem areas and provide good opportunities to test yourself and your problems against the views of others, even to the point of asking for their help. In recent years, self-help groups have become more specifically focused upon personal problems, and patient groups of various types have been started by professionals, as well as by patients, for the purpose of helping each other.

Finally, when these three steps fail, a system can be applied which is directed at helping you solve your problems in the structured, systematic ways of effective psychotherapy. In some instances, such a system can, at least in part, be used without your having to go through professional psychotherapy. It will be outlined briefly in this chapter.

UNSTRUCTURED SELF-HELP

It is only too easy to get hung up on unstructured conventional forms of self-help. By "unstructured" is meant unsystematic or hit-or-miss kinds of therapy which are not directed consistently by a theory or organized effort. To determine their effectiveness, you need to apply critically the standards described in Chapter 1. The danger in trying to guide yourself in this way lies in the possibility that you may temporize for months or years while your problems gradually become worse, somehow deluding yourself into believing that thinking or reading about them is tantamount to handling them.

An obese man, to take a true example, read voraciously on psychology and mental health and discussed himself and his reading at length with anyone who would listen. Meanwhile, he continued to get fatter and finally, at a relatively young age, after a minor accident died of an embolism because of his obesity.

You may find inspiration in sermons, in public lectures, in church retreats, in books, and may momentarily be resolved to attack your problems with vigor, yet end up a day or week or month later without having accomplished anything permanent toward solving your problems. Inspiration can be useful, and it can lead to deeds which can blossom into many desirable effects, yet it must be measured against effective actions. Otherwise it is merely a kick that could get a stone rolling—but often does not. You can become involved in situations or with people inspiring you to effective deeds, even while remembering that the value of the inspiration should lie in whether the behavior that follows can be sustained for weeks and months and not merely hours.

A man in serious marital trouble left his wife for a month to try to get a clearer picture on how he could improve their marriage. During the separation he decided to improve his behavior toward her, to try to do everything she wanted him to do, to take the initiative in suggesting dates and sexual relations. Yet as soon as he returned, her manner of talking and looking at him still wilted him, and he lost all the resolution and courage that had flourished in the greenhouse of separation.

You can seek further self-help in systematic reading, night-school and college courses, and lecture and study-group series. Such stimuli may inspire you to do something about your sexual difficulties, marital problems, child-rearing dilemmas, self-understanding, and social effectiveness. Programs like these do have some advantages over one-shot exposures: they last longer, take into account more factors, and require somewhat better follow-up on results. However, you can still easily postpone taking action based upon the additional knowledge you gain and the hope stirred in you. The effectiveness must be measured by the results in your daily life. You may become very well educated on the facts and theories of mental health, yet lead an utterly miserable personal existence. There are professional persons practicing in the mental-health field who are alcoholics, homosexuals, psychotics, severe neurotics, maritally in turmoil, or terrible parents. Self-knowledge is no guarantee whatsoever of effective problem-solving, and may not even be necessary for it.

You should, of course, explore all forms of self-help. Much of it probably can screen out and help you to solve most of your problems so that you need not move on to the other forms of help —except perhaps for conventional outside helps, which will be discussed next. Surely you should not overlook a source of help which is simple and cheap and may be sufficiently effective for you. Neither should you go on with such a source for months while at the same time realizing you are not solving your problems.

Another problem in using unstructured self-help methods is that you may mislead yourself in your "thinking." The word *think* implies a positive effort to formulate, evaluate, and resolve problems. It suggests an ongoing process by which you shape impressions toward some rational use. But what is often called "thinking" by persons with serious problems is a circular process in which they review many impressions over and over without moving ahead or shaping constructive solutions.

We therefore again urge you to have objective, practical criteria by which to judge the effectiveness of whatever help you may use, whether it is from within you or from outside sources. Standards for judging can come from people whose opinions you respect or from measures you may respect in your environment such as grades, promotions, or group approval.

NONPROFESSIONAL OUTSIDE AIDS

Except for the most extremely withdrawn persons, we all must interact with groups and other individuals; most people look forward to doing so. From such contacts we derive a sense of our standing relative to others. We observe how others solve problems similar to ours and how they react to us. We obtain hints of how we can go about getting from groups and others what we want or need, and the pleasure of discovering others who enjoy things as we do. There is an almost infinite variety of other ways in which we gain help from others in making life more satisfactory.

The individual in trouble tends to restrict his outside contacts, often limiting them to the bare necessities involved in making a living, eating and sleeping, or navigating through life in the most primitive way. It is an unfortunate paradox that the more unresolved or disturbing problems you have, the less likely you are to use the conventional outside aids available for help. In isolation, your problems increase, and as they increase, your opportunities to obtain and use outside help in natural ways tend to decline further. Yet that help is available.

Churches are increasingly providing help for persons with difficult personal problems; yet how they do it is difficult to ascertain. Churchmen may give advice based upon personal experience or upon reading the literature of mental health. They may variously advise a member to turn to religion, to pray harder, to participate more in church affairs, to read the Bible more assiduously, to take a vacation, or to seek personal help elsewhere. As professionalism in the field of mental health becomes more prevalent, so are there more ministers who are at least partially trained in various principles and practices that professional therapists have learned. Such professionalism contrasts sharply with the more historical function of the minister in helping people, and it is the distinctive contributions of the minister-counselor as a religionist that interests us here, rather than what he merely shares with other trained or semi-trained psychotherapists.

A person who is seriously disturbed might gain help from the church most readily and distinctively in the form of inspiration, moral principles, leadership, and the aid and comfort to be derived from interacting with others who share one's values, interests, or ritual preferences. One may also use his church as the most convenient and reasonable place to admit to his problems, to expose himself to the suggestions of others for possible solutions, to obtain follow-up from others who are interested enough in him to ask questions about what he has been doing about his problems. These uses of the church environment are, of course, not different from the uses to which any group may be put, but this does not lessen the advantages of associating with so widespread, convenient, and accepting a social institution as the church.

Along with the church, the educational system is a major institution of society which provides help in problem-solving to masses of people. More children are exposed to intensive human contacts in schools than in any other institution in the country, and schools are increasingly taking fairly close aim at the problems of their children. While counseling in schools at all levels is becoming professionalized, the bulk of the help rendered to children and young adults in schools tends to be an inherent part of the educational process operating through classrooms and ordinary teachers, and it is likely to remain so.

The classroom teacher is becoming increasingly trained (as are the minister and the general physician) in principles utilized by the professional psychotherapist, but his role as a resource for children and young adults is traditional and far transcends the effect of school mental-hygiene courses. As an esteemed member of the community, the teacher has often been consulted by parents of children with personal problems centered around the learning process, but which undoubtedly also have their effect in other areas of the child's life. The teacher may be an excellent source of objective information about the child's behavior, social relationships, potentialities, and problems. To the child or young adult who is interested in getting help for himself, the teacher can be useful as an objective source of information about this relationship to his peers.

Other persons whom you respect—physicians, friends, colleagues —may be used as sounding boards about your problems and views, for suggestions on handling your difficulties, and for opinions on how you are getting along. You may have no one whom you can use in this way, and this may be one of your problems. If you can find someone whose judgment you trust, however, you may be able, with considerable effort, to open a helping relationship. If you cannot do so now, such a relationship might itself constitute an important goal for professional therapy.

Discussing one's personal problems with friends is probably the most universal way of trying to solve them. But when this obvious method fails, and before professional methods are sought, a mutual self-help group might well be tried.

MUTUAL-HELP GROUPS

The idea and function of mutual-help groups is very old, but only in recent decades have such groups been organized and studied by the professionals in psychotherapy. Hobart Mowrer, whose ideas about learning theory and psychotherapy have attracted wide professional attention, and whose recent views are labeled "Integrity Therapy," has turned increasingly for inspiration to a model of early Christian groups, which banded together to help each other and worked toward common goals for a good life.

Groups interested in forming Utopias have joined together for centuries, and while they have tried to apply their views to all society, basically they have succeeded only in creating a small, satisfying, and short-lived group for themselves.

The modern self-help groups referred to here, however, are organized specifically to deal with personal problems. They apply themselves to almost all areas of human troubles, but among the most conspicuous are those groups that offer help with problems of alcoholism, suicide, readjustment after a mental-hospital sojourn, obesity, drugs, single parenthood, old age, marriage, and young parenthood. They go under a great variety of names such as Alcoholics Anonymous, Samaritans, TOPPS, Neurotics Anonymous, Golden Age, Fellowship Club, Addicts Anonymous, and Synanon.

Besides the distinctive character of their membership, their major feature is the spirit and practice of mutual help. Professional group therapy, as we will discuss it elsewhere, is something else. It is organized and led by professionals, and while it attempts to imitate the self-help groups, which have often blazed the way, it can never capture the vital aspect of self-help groups—the complete sense of responsibility and humanitarianism their members share—which a professional leader usually abridges even if he tries hard not to.

How this vital difference affects group results is not known, although it is an important question for study. Imagine, for example, that you have been feeling extremely depressed and all evening have been thinking about taking an overdose of sleeping pills or breathing carbon monoxide. Finally you decide to make an emergency call to someone for help. You may have this choice: a suicide prevention center, staffed by professionals, where the professional person answering the phone will try to make you feel better about your prospects and urge you to come in the next day for professional help; or a Samaritan affiliate, staffed by volunteers, where a nonprofessional person (who, like you, has considered an attempted suicide) will try to reassure you and offer you the help of fellow sufferers.

There are arguments on both sides. Some favor the superior technical competence of the professional expert; others favor the superior humanitarianism and understanding of the volunteer fellow sufferer. But with the almost universally respected example of Alcoholics Anonymous before them, professionals need to prove the superiority of their approach to justify the heavy expenditures required. It seems simply logical otherwise for society in general and you in particular to turn wherever possible to self-help groups instead. Besides the savings involved, the spirit seems better: that is, doing for yourself, assuming responsibility, and learning to gain the satisfaction of doing good deeds with others.

One other advantage is that the self-help group usually requires that its members be open with one another. This removes the stigma from problems that have been kept secret and permits the feedback from the environment which is required to solve problems. While this can also happen in professional group therapy, it seems less likely to do so there since such candor is *requisite* in the self-help groups, while other methods can be substituted in professional groups.

The most practical argument against staying solely with self-help groups has to do with the difficulty of deciding that non-professional help has failed and that it is time to try professional help instead.

The presumed purpose for the group, focused on a particular kind of problem, is of secondary importance. Almost any kind of group can be formed, whatever the excuse, and its members can profit from discussing problems candidly and helping one another. Prophets who warn of danger from attempts by nonexperts to extend help can never cite figures to support their case, except for an extremely rare instance here and there.

Such groups, in fact, can hardly *not* help one another. They can be as randomly composed as they are for group air-travel fares—simply as a social convenience or as an excuse to take advantage of a "good deal." "Sensitivity" training, a kind of mutual revelation and self-help group procedure, is widely used now among groups of executives, employees, and students in a wide range of situations. You can, for example, organize a group of church members, neighbors, school parents, or fellow workers simply to discuss problems of religion, neighborhood living, rearing children, or coping with the work environment. Such a group can hardly avoid discussing personal problems of the broadest scope if its members are candid.

STRUCTURED SELF-HELP

If you could successfully apply the same procedures the professional therapist uses to yourself to change your behavior, you would not need professional help. If you have not been able to do so, several reasons may be involved.

First, the way by which therapists get you to change seldom are clear to them or to anyone else. A few therapists of what is called the "behavior-change" viewpoint are beginning to make their methods explicit enough so that anyone can apply them. They speak of scheduling yourself, making rewards and penalties explicit, and setting concrete goals. Otherwise you will generally have to contend with the vaguest of directions from professionals on how you can apply principles of therapy yourself through such procedures as "analyzing your relationship with 'significant' people in your past," "clarifying your values," and "keeping busy." Without knowing how, what, when, and why more concretely, however, you are not likely to be able to proceed effectively on your own.

Secondly, unless you set clear goals ahead of time and have objective checks made on your progress, you are not likely to know how you are getting along with your self-help. Of course this difficulty is also often encountered in professional therapy, but there at least you have help from an experienced person as you fumble for answers about goals and progress.

As with any form of entirely self-controlled effort—from calisthenics to correspondence courses—a third obstacle to effective self-help lies in the fact that it is exceptionally difficult to sustain effort over a period of months and exceptionally easy to quit prematurely, as compared with when organized programs and other persons are involved.

If, however, you are willing to make the effort to help yourself as systematically as possible, you can apply reasonable guidelines and utilize certain outside aids to make a self-help program effective. At least it is worth the try, for you may succeed.

The steps are the same as in any form of professional therapy: to define the problem, to recognize and block bad (i.e., self-defeating) habits, to substitute new behavior on a trial basis, to observe results as objectively as possible, to continue the work that moves you toward your goals and to quit whatever does not help, and to try other solutions if current efforts are not useful. You would assume that bad feelings about, for example, your job or your marriage would point up a problem, and that good feelings would indicate progress in the right direction.

One way to help determine your progress and to sustain your effort is to involve others around you in your endeavor. If your wife, co-workers, employer, children, or neighbors know what you are trying to do, they will be more likely to comment to you on any changes they notice. Furthermore, involving them makes your commitment to follow through somewhat stronger. At least you are more likely to have second thoughts about giving up if you have declared to others your intention to change, and if you know that they are likely to bring up this fact—or at least to think of it—if you quit trying.

If you are not well-organized or disciplined, you can also try to firm up an hour-by-hour schedule for a few days ahead after listing your goals, modifying them if they are unreasonable, deciding what you need to do to reach them, and budgeting your time accordingly.[1]

Many helpful outside resources can be found in programmed education. The Human Development Institute,[2] for example, publishes well-considered, step-by-step programmed instructions in how to get along better in marriage and in other personal relationships. Many other programs are being developed in this area.

There are also a number of self-help books, but our topic here is *systematic* self-help and rarely are such books systematic. Some of the books do, however, make suggestions that you may find useful, and are listed in an appendix to this book. In this section we are trying to convey the view that there is a substantial difference between random and disconnected efforts to gain help from the many sources available all around you, and efforts which require greater discipline, follow-up, and planning on your part in applying a systematic approach.

INFORMATION AND PLANNING SOURCES

Many sources of information and planning that can help you to solve problems in living without psychotherapy are available in every city. Perhaps thousands of persons whom therapists try to treat could solve their problems much more simply by learning

---

[1] This and other methods you might find useful are described in *Short-term Psychotherapy and Structured Behavior Change*, by E. L. Phillips and D. N. Wiener (New York: McGraw-Hill, 1966).

[2] 1299 West Peachtree Street N.E., Atlanta, Georgia.

some basic facts about how to manage money, find a good job, use legal help wisely, or handle other complexities of living.[3]

Therapists often struggle for months with problems of finances, birth control, legal difficulties, vocational and educational adjustment, homemaking, recreation and the like *as if* they were psychological and required extensive psychological treatment. Why not *try* to use simpler information and planning resources in the community first—since most therapists are not good at providing such information and planning anyway—and resort to psychological help only if your problems pass through the screen of the more direct services?

State employment services with offices in most cities are a fertile source of occupational and employment information. The latest edition of the *Occupational Handbook,*[4] available at those offices, is a rich mine of information about vocational fields, training required, pay, prospects, and duties. These offices can also often provide free vocational testing and counseling. Their placement services may not be as good for some specialized purposes as those provided by a private agency,[5] nor do as well as you can do for yourself if you are thorough and persistent, but they can give you leads in your own locality as well as nationally.

Financial-planning advice is often available at banks and also at family-service agencies supported by voluntary community funds. Many persons are helped simply by a chart available at such places which shows how "average" people at different income levels spend their money—the percentages allotted, for example, for food, clothing, shelter, entertainment, medical care, donations, and gifts. Money problems may be a source or a symptom of marital trouble. There is good reason, in any case, to try out financial advisory services before assuming that money problems are only a symptom of deeper disturbance. You may discover how to solve a serious

[3] Research is needed to investigate this possibility. It would basically consist of testing whether persons obtaining such practical help are less likely to need psychotherapy.

[4] U.S. Government Printing Office, Washington, D.C.

[5] But first you must figure out how to choose a private agent well, a procedure which involves principles similar to those described for choosing a psychotherapist. There is a serious problem in choosing well of the services listed in this section, and each could probably be served by a book similar to this one.

problem through the use of direct factual and planning aids, but may find that you do not put the solution into effect. Then it is time to seek other sources of help.

Ignorance of birth-control methods is a source of trouble in many marriages; yet there are excellent sources of information available. Many physicians provide it, as do all Planned Parenthood Associations (listed in phone books), and such authoritative pamphlets as "Family Planning."[6] You can become involved in interminable bickering and misunderstanding when you unnecessarily limit yourself to certain times of the month (unless you do so on religious grounds), to mechanical devices (if objectionable to either party), or to "the pill" when it produces objectionable side effects. The mere fact that you are able to label this openly as a problem and then seek accurate information may be a very useful step and model for handling future problems in your marriage.

Most other home- and family-management information and planning services you need can be obtained directly or indirectly from the family-service agencies in your community. They can help you to obtain competent homemaking help and financial aid. They usually have lists of community groups that might attract your interest and reduce your loneliness. There are free legal-aid societies in many cities to help with legal problems. And most large colleges provide vocational literature in their libraries and informational literature in many other areas.

The Federal Government, through the Government Printing Office, gives away or sells cheaply many excellent informational pamphlets in practically all problem areas. You can often get this material free by writing to your Congressman for it. In the area of consumer information and life-management problems the Federal Government is increasingly becoming the pre-eminent public educator. It is easy to imagine that, eventually, the community mental-health center or a public information and planning center could offer all of the informational and planning services—social, familial, legal, hygienic, financial—which could make your life more effective. Such a center might in this way become a truly preventive service from the standpoint of severe behavioral problems.

[6] Mt. Vernon, N.Y.: Consumers' Union, 1966.

It could show you how to handle your realistic problems of living successfully and if you could learn to approach and handle your difficulties through the use of such resources, you would save yourself from much subsequent grief and perhaps from the need of psychotherapy.

WHEN TO GIVE UP ON NONPROFESSIONAL HELP

Literally, you should never abandon nonprofessional help, since it should always be a useful aid in the management of your daily problems. One way of viewing professional help is that it prepares you to make better use of nonprofessional resources to solve your continuous problems in living.

A time may come, however, when you might seek out a more expert kind of aid for your particular problems of the moment.

Many therapists believe that you would not have serious difficulties if you "merely" had to get some concrete information or nonprofessional help, for presumably this has been thrown at you all of your life without effect. Often, however, the person in trouble has withdrawn from the company of people who could help him. He is afraid to visit places and consult with nonprofessional persons who could help, is ignorant of common sources of simple help, is prejudiced against utilizing aid, or is fearful of becoming dependent. So, at the outset, an open, experimental attitude toward the use of these sources as suggested in this chapter can make a big difference to you if that has not been your attitude, or if you have for some other reason not used them.

Once you begin to try them, you should give them an adequate chance to work. If you try only for a week, or allow the frown of a social worker or office clerk to discourage you, or expect to listen and have things done to you, but not to have to work hard to put suggestions into effect—then you have given up nonprofessional help prematurely. Such responses would also make the most expensive professional therapy a failure, although therapy provides more follow-up and more pressure. In your individual effort, as in therapy, you must push yourself to gain the most from it.

If you have, however, continued your efforts for several weeks and have tried hard but unsuccessfully to fulfill various plans for change, or have found that you could think of nothing further to do, it then may be time to change. You should consider changing professional therapy on the same grounds. It then makes sense to go on to more complex or sophisticated methods that may help you to overcome your self-defeating ways.

Part II

*CHOOSING A
PSYCHOTHERAPIST*

CHAPTER 5

Forms of Psychotherapy

THE MAJOR FORMS OF PSYCHOTHERAPY

SINCE THE most ancient past, there have been many kinds of psychotherapy. Religious men were the first psychotherapists in that they attempted to cure mental afflictions by calling upon the help of divine or magical powers.

Psychotherapy today is essentially the effort of a socially designated, acceptably educated group of men to cure their fellow men of complaints about themselves and their world through psychological means. By such definition, one can rule out such groups as the followers of Dianetics, who are not designated by an agency of government and trained by accredited institutions; general physicians and those psychiatrists who treat through physical means (such as drugs and shock); ministers and teachers, who are not socially designated nor primarily trained as psychotherapists.

Many respected professional persons such as ministers, teachers, physicians, and lawyers do work quite similar to that of the psychotherapist, and only two states have laws that come even close to limiting the practice of psychotherapy to any one group. No such regulations have ever been enforced. Most people actually go to professional people other than psychotherapists for help with their personal problems. A survey of American adults by the Joint Commission on Mental Illness and Health (1960) revealed that 42 per cent of a general adult group sought professional help for a personal problem from clergymen, 29 per cent from doctors, 11 per cent from lawyers, and only 21 to 31 per cent at most from persons who were likely to be designated as psychotherapists.

Only a minority within each of the three major professions embracing almost all psychotherapists practice mainly psychotherapy. Only about a third of the psychiatrists and an even smaller proportion of psychologists and social workers appear to concentrate on it.

Thus, when theories or types of psychotherapy are discussed, they refer directly to no clearly delineated professional groups. Psychiatrists may practice psychoanalytic, eclectic ("common sense"), or little or no psychotherapy. They may use drugs, rest, or shock treatment almost exclusively rather than psychotherapy. Similarly, social workers and psychologists may practice any form of psychotherapy—or none at all. The professional designation provides little indication of what the professional man would do to try to help you to solve your problems.

Nor does the nature of your problem provide any clear indication of the kind of profession, among the three major disciplines devoted to help with personal problems, that can best provide help, nor the type of help that would be most effective. Most psychotherapists tend to treat all their patients, regardless of their problems, in roughly the same particular way, more in accordance with their beliefs in the best ways to help people rather than according to the nature of the problem presented. Thus, most psychologists who believe in nondirective therapy will apply that method to most of their cases; most social workers who believe in psychoanalysis will use that approach with most of their clients; and most psychiatrists who believe in drugs will tend to prescribe them for most of their patients.

There are many exceptions to these generalizations. Very psychotic, depressed, and financially poor patients are more likely than others to be given shock or drug treatment. Patients who are extremely passive are more likely to be talked to than be given drugs. Those who tend to act impulsively by stealing, fighting, getting drunk, or acting sexually promiscuous are more likely to be rejected for psychotherapy, or to be hospitalized or required to demonstrate control of their misbehavior before being accepted for therapy.

Furthermore, psychiatrists alone among the three professions are legally allowed to give drugs and electric shock; members of the American Psychoanalytic Association claim that they alone can practice genuine psychoanalysis; and marriage counselors are organized to treat with marital problems only. However, competent and popular practitioners of any major type of psychotherapy legally can and do practice in each of the different professions; the name of the profession is no indication of the form of psychotherapy that will be used.

Any designation of types of psychotherapy is bound to be arbitrary, but the classification used here can be applied to encompass all the major current forms, and should at least make it fairly easy for you to communicate with professionals in the field when you seek help. The four major categories are: Eclectic, Psychoanalytic, Nondirective, and Behavior Change.

There are many variations of each of these forms, and devotees of the various therapeutic creeds tend to consider their approaches —such as Jungian, existential, rational, and hypnotic therapy— unique. But in the discussion to follow, it is hoped that the system of classification will be sufficiently clear and comprehensive, so that you can roughly fit any form of therapy you may encounter into one of the four categories.

The order of listing reflects the historical development of the field. "Eclectic" refers simply to the gathering of methods from any available systems, theories, and practical experiences, and applying them however they may be useful, with no attempt to be systematic. It may also be called "common sense," or "practical," or "the best-at-hand" way of helping people. Eclectic therapy today little resembles its form of fifty years ago. Inevitably it changes most with the times, since it reflects a potpourri of theories and practical experience current at any time.

Psychoanalytic therapy was fathered by Sigmund Freud, and its followers revere, dogmatically quote, and elaborate on his views. Freud's views were developed primarily in Austria in the early twentieth century, and provided the first comprehensive, widely accepted theory and practice of psychotherapy, with the most pervasive effect any theory has ever had on psychotherapists. While there have been many intense and popular schisms from orthodoxy, Freud's views still underlie and provide the major generally accepted tenets of psychoanalysis.

In the mid-twentieth century, Carl Rogers formulated systematically the next distinctive and widely accepted method of practicing psychotherapy. Nondirective therapy has a solid role in the thinking and practice of most therapists even if they do not accept it as their primary method. It has seemed to shade into existential psychotherapy in more recent years, following the progression of Rogers' own views. Basically, it assumes that psychotherapy can be successful when the client, through self-searching, encouraged but not directed by the therapist, understands and fulfills himself.

Behavior-change therapy is the broad name usually given to still newer forms of treatment. The label could of course be applied to any form of therapy, since all profess to change behavior. Yet to most professionals in the field, the term indicates a specific approach which is distinctively based upon learning theory and applied directly to change external behavior without primary consideration to the internal feelings of the patient. This form has flowered only in the past several years, but has currently become the most active and exciting form in research and practice.

Distinctions have been made among these forms only for your convenience in making comparisons and decisions. Most therapists, while they may classify themselves primarily under one of the four categories, or may be unwillingly so classified by an outside observer, do mix in bits of other forms. Thus a nondirective therapist may sometimes give advice when it is badly needed, a behavior-change therapist may ask for the details of a vivid dream when the patient mentions one, and an analyst may directly suggest that you take dancing lessons to help you meet or get along with a mate. As therapists become more experienced, they tend to become more relaxed about practicing any method and come to practice more like other equally experienced therapists regardless of differences in theory.

PSYCHOANALYTIC PSYCHOTHERAPY (PSYCHOANALYSIS)

The terms "psychoanalysis" and "psychoanalytic psychotherapy" will be used interchangeably here despite a certain touchiness in psychoanalytic circles about maintaining a distinction between them. Analysts (psychoanalysts) have gone through the most orthodox and longest training and belong to the most select society, the American Psychoanalytic Association; they tend to view only themselves as practicing "real" psychoanalysis. To them, psychoanalytic psychotherapy connotes a diluted—possibly even distorted—process, practiced by pallid imitators.

To you as a potential consumer of such services, however, these distinctions would probably be imperceptible, and since no such fine differentiations are made within the other forms of therapy, they will not be made here. From your standpoint, the therapist's designation is best made by what he does; if he practices according to the methods and theories of psychoanalysis, that should be your major concern here. Even when he says he practices psychoanalysis (rather than "psychoanalytic psychotherapy"), he will still differ so widely from his colleagues on such matters as number of interviews a week, interpretation of material, use of dreams, and emphasis on various concepts that these differences are likely to be broader than any distinctions that might be made between psychoanalysis and psychoanalytic psychotherapy.

Psychoanalysis has always had the most comprehensive rules of practice of the contemporary theories. Freud remains so preeminent a figure that his views guide the field—at least in public presentations. In private practices, deviations often occur, for since the early years there have been many variations in psychoanalysis from Freud's views. Yet he has remained the touchstone.

The basic structure officially remains as Freud enunciated it, involving frequent sessions, lying on a couch looking away from the therapist, discussing dreams and free associations, paying for treatment, and developing and expressing love and hate for the therapist. Whatever it is that binds analysts together seems to lie in Freud's views; no one else's have achieved the same degree of acceptance.

For example, Freud's original view of the id (instinctual desire) as clashing with the superego (cultural structure) and being integrated into or by the ego has been interpreted and modified by analysts in innumerable ways, but his concept remains a basically recognizable scheme in most analysis. Many analysts are no longer totally committed to years of intensive analysis of their patients, and are willing to apply their methods on shorter bases toward limited goals, to the point of using drugs as supplements to psychotherapy. Even the stated goals of psychoanalysis are highly variable. Glover's[1] study of all the psychoanalysts in England yielded

[1] E. Glover, *The Technique of Psychoanalysis* (New York: International University Press, 1955).

no consensus of what the goals of analysis should be—whether personal fulfillment, sexual maturity, creative output, or whatever.

Still, a psychoanalyst is the most likely of all therapists to throw a predictable mantle of practices, interpretation, and theory over his interaction with you. He is the least likely to bend his views and methods in response to your ideas. He will in all probability set goals for you growing out of his theory, and will interpret your objections and adverse reactions to his work as "resistance" to change, rather than accept them as rational. He will be prone to interpret your setbacks as temporary and necessary to your progress toward deeper exploration and character alteration.

Because psychoanalysis usually has demanded a heavy commitment from the patient in terms of time, money, and anxiety, analysts commonly used to have a trial period to see whether they and their patients could become properly involved with each other. This excellent practice—which could be beneficial in any but the shortest form of therapy—seems to have been neglected in recent years, as a wider variety of nonorthodox analysts have taken up analytic work. You can still ask that there be a trial period, however, with the hope that your request will not be interpreted as "resistance."

Chances are that by the time you arrive at the analyst's office, you will have decided you want to be "psychoanalyzed" so that you may "understand" yourself "in depth," rather than wanting simply to solve your problems as quickly as possible regardless of method. Your expectations are likely to be fulfilled. Whatever their later practices may be, most therapists who early in their training or practice want to learn more about themselves also go to psychoanalytic therapists for personal therapy. Psychoanalysis seems to offer knowledge about human behavior, as applied particularly to one's self, which educates them to become sophisticated psychologically.

You are likely to learn about various psychological concepts, terms, and conditions from the inside, such as your "oedipal attachment" to your mother, your "infantile sexuality," your "id strivings," your "weak ego," your "infantile regressive tendencies," and so on. You are also likely to learn something about how to interpret dreams which, uninterpreted, have been called "unopened letters" and "windows into the unconscious."

The relationship between such informative interpretations and solving particular problems has, however, never been established. Contemporary behavior-change therapists consider that the analytic method is certain to be inefficient at best and damaging at worst, because it diverts you from direct practical attacks upon your current difficulties and involves you instead in almost interminable ruminations about your feelings and past life. The psychoanalysts counter by saying that your coming for analysis means that direct attacks upon your problems have proven futile and that therefore a deeper, more subtle approach is necessary. Behavior-change therapists rebut this argument with the view that well-conceived direct attacks in the past have *not* been made, and that what has occurred has been poorly conceived and misdirected. You might, for example, have divorced two wives and now be worried about remarrying, which would lead to the conclusion that your past attacks on the problem—simply getting a divorce and remarrying—were misdirected, and that you need to learn how to get along with a spouse, overcoming en route those self-defeating habits you have developed. The analyst would assume that you need to probe at length your early attitudes and feelings toward your mother, women in general, and sex before you could come to effective action in the present.

Almost all analysts will at length "analyze," that is, probe, discuss, and interpret your past and present feelings, your history, your free associations, and your dreams. Most of them will concentrate heavily on your past. They will talk little and expect you to (learn to) talk freely about anything that occurs to you. Your analyst will occasionally make interpretations based upon his theory, and make connections among various kinds of material you bring up.

A smaller proportion of psychoanalysts, perhaps a minority, will insist that all of their patients comply with the trappings of orthodox analysis, such as sessions three or more times a week, lying on a couch, and making no major decisions until the end of treatment.

Analysts are more likely than other therapists to be irked at and analyze at length the reasons for your being late, for calling in sick or for trying to cancel a session, considering your deviation from the schedule an expression of resistance or hostility toward the therapy or therapist. They are more prone to ask you to schedule your vacation to coincide with theirs. They have a stronger tendency to ask that you pay heavily and currently, at more sacrifice to your current standard of living, in order to ensure your commitment to treatment and to reduce the secondary gain from and dependence on therapy. They especially want you to like them, to believe their interpretations, to act on their advice, and to judge any conflicts between you and them as stemming from your neurosis. The relationship between analyst and patient tends to be the very opposite of democratic and experimental, or indeed of what is usually considered in this country as good teaching practice.

Psychoanalysis is likely to produce a more intense kind of personal relationship ("transference") with your therapist, and calls for stronger emotional reactions than do the other therapies. Analysis tends to rouse stronger feelings of love and hate, of fear and anxiety because of the way in which the therapist talks to you and encourages you to talk to him. You may therefore come to believe that this form of therapy is deeper, richer, more pervasive, and more effective than forms which arouse less emotionality or which depend upon your controlled thinking or supervised efforts to change your behavior outside of therapy. Certainly it does tend to be a more intensely emotional experience, but whether you end up more satisfied or effective as a result is an entirely separate question. Therapy is not necessary for you to have deep and significant emotional relationships in your life. Such relationships in your life outside of therapy may serve even more effectively to enrich you emotionally, and another form of therapy may move you into them. The test is not what happens in therapy, but what results outside of therapy. The therapeutic experience itself is not the goal, nor is its similarity to a desired life-experience a measure of its effectiveness. As a scientific treatment, psychoanalysis must, like all other therapies, be judged in the market place by its success in helping you to achieve the goals you set for it.

The body of knowledge utilized by psychoanalysts is known and taught widely in psychology departments, schools of social work, medical schools, and special schools run by analysts and others.

Although the American Psychoanalytic Association sets the most lengthy and rigorous standards of training and experience,[2] and now admits only physicians, there are other associations and training centers which accept social workers, psychologists, and physicians and which conduct shorter training programs. The analysts belonging to the American Psychoanalytic Association are far outnumbered by others who practice psychoanalytic therapy in the United States today, but to the public, the two groups are largely indistinguishable in their practices. Intraprofessional hostilities are at their most intense in this field, and none of the probably three best-known psychoanalysts in the world today, Anna Freud, Eric Fromm, and Theodor Reik, was acceptable for membership in the orthodox association.

To find a psychoanalyst, you can call any of the psychoanalytic training centers listed in the telephone books of the several largest cities in the United States. In some cities, social workers, physicians, and psychologists who practice psychoanalysis list that fact along with their name. The rules listed for choosing the best therapist for you apply. Psychoanalysts, although practicing in the most unified way of any group, are highly variable in competence, methods, demands, personality, background, and training; you should never choose one with no more information than names given out at an institute, listed in a telephone book or professional directory, or given to you by casual reference.

NONDIRECTIVE PSYCHOTHERAPY (AND EXISTENTIAL PSYCHOTHERAPY)

Nondirective (or Rogerian) psychotherapy has nowhere near the strength in number of practitioners, public attention, or organization that the three other forms have. Yet it has exercised a powerful effect upon the practice of many therapists since the 1930's. It has contributed an enduring technique of viewing and practicing therapy and has gradually melded, with Carl Rogers as its chief spokesman, with the newer field of "existential psychotherapy." Its passive, reflective technique is concrete and useful,

---

[2] It has been observed that an Association member on the average spends more years completing his training than he has years left thereafter to practice.

and its research on psychotherapy is outstanding. There is almost a complete lack of research in existentialist therapy, although the latter school is now attracting considerably more attention.

Nondirective therapy developed primarily at the University of Chicago in the 1930's and 1940's. It concentrated heavily on getting clients to talk about their views of themselves and others, and what sort of person they wanted to be. Originally the therapist talked little, and then only to encourage the client to speak more freely about himself. His method was to direct the patient's attention to select material the patient may have mentioned and to indicate support for such self-searching. Nondirective therapists were caricatured as saying nothing at all for interview after interview, except for an occasional "hmmm" or "I understand," or giving nearly verbatim repetitions of what the patient had already said.

Within a short time, however, nondirective therapists began to say that it was not the therapist's silence or literal spoken reflections that were important, but rather his efforts to get the client to think about himself and his world. With the support and understanding of the therapist, the patient was to progress toward greater personal achievement and deeper relationships with others. His basically good nature would find freedom and support to bloom.

The most recent movement in the field tends toward an emphasis upon the individual's subjective behavior (attitudes, feelings, basic good nature), and to his discovery or acceptance of values which he can use in getting along intensely and successfully with other people. In this equation, society is of only secondary importance; social values and structures are largely ignored; the touchstone of humanity within and between individuals is stressed.

In significant ways, nondirective and existential therapies are similar to psychoanalysis, except that they tend to concentrate upon the present and future more than upon the past. Like psychoanalysis, however, these therapies give special attention to what is going on inside a person. Also, like psychoanalysis, they are relatively uninterested in or even antagonistic to conventional social demands and to immediate, direct action toward relieving anxiety. They are again similar to psychoanalysis in that they are more interested in the practice and application of the theory that man must find himself through a belief in and practice of personal values, and that therapy should be directed primarily toward this purpose. The practitioners of these therapies, like the psychoanalysts, operate in the belief that they need not teach the client to devise goals and to apply means to act more effectively. Instead, they feel that the desired ingredients for feeling better already lie wthin the client, and need only to be freed, expressed, and used.

As with other forms of therapy, you should always find out ahead of time, or at least during your first interview, what kind of treatment your therapist will practice. You can expect that a nondirectivist will talk and advise relatively little, and that both he and the existential therapist will seldom make concrete suggestions as to how you may solve your immediate problems. They will concern themselves more with your feelings and values. Their practices are likely to be the most variable of any of the groups. Neither their theory nor their writings tell you how, specifically, they as a group are likely to work with you—except for concentration on what you are thinking and feeling now, and what place you can find for yourself and with others in the world. This kind of therapy seems likely to be primarily a philosophical and an attitudinal education for you more than efficient training in solving your specific daily problems.

You are not likely to find nondirective therapists operating under that label outside of college campuses, where the movement has particularly flourished, where the clientele was most verbal and goal-directed, and where no payment for help was involved. Many therapists use the nondirective method a good deal without considering themselves committed to the theory. Existential psychotherapists, labeled by and committed to this theory, do practice outside of colleges to a larger extent.

You will have a harder time locating nondirective or existential therapists than others, for they are likely to be found only in big cities and on college campuses. The University of Chicago Counseling Center has been the major training place for nondirective therapists and can be consulted for names. Neither nondirective nor existential therapists are likely to be designated as such in telephone books, nor are there professional directories indicating formally trained practitioners. The general rules given earlier for finding a good therapist can be your only guide.

ECLECTIC PSYCHOTHERAPY

This is any therapy which does not clearly follow an identifiable form. The eclectic therapist may simply say, "I don't practice any special theory. I just do what seems to work." He may even think he owes little to any theory, that he has made up his own methods out of his experience, and that he continues to feel his way along with each patient individually. Yet his views are not likely to be unusual; they are certain to reflect his education, his interaction with colleagues, and the professional literature he reads. Besides, his methods, no matter how variable he thinks they are according to the particular problem or patient, could probably be characterized by an outside observer if he could see what the therapist usually does, rather than what the therapist *says* he does.

Most eclectic therapy changes from one decade to another according to currently popular or provocative theories and techniques. In the 1920's and 1930's, for example, psychoanalytic views had great initial impact on the mental-health professions, as did experimental treatment with insulin and electric shock. In the 1950's and 1960's, tranquilizer drugs have had a strong influence on eclectic therapists. Nondirective views in the forties and behavior-change views today also affect the eclectics as they try the newer methods and shape or reject them according to their other ideas.

Eclectic therapists appear more likely than others to try out enlightened or hopeful new ways and also to succumb to passing fads and poorly founded pressures by their patients to try the latest methods. At best, they act as a filter for society, screening out pretentious or wildly unscientific methods which do no practical good. At worst, they may cynically or insensitively reject new views without studying critically their full possibilities and implications, thereby blocking a fair trial for the patient and society of a hopeful approach.

In the primitive state of the science of human behavior change, outcomes in psychotherapy usually hinge much more upon the nature of the therapist than upon his profession or practice of a treatment theory. The therapist, eclectic or otherwise, may be in various degrees rigid or flexible, Promethean or Epimethean, humble or arrogant, knowledgeable or ignorant about ways of changing behavior.

The wise, flexible eclectic represents a relatively safe compromise among therapists, a modest kind of insurance against the rigid practice of theoretical views which are not well adapted to you or your problems. He seems unlikely to carry you as far, however, as would the equally wise, equally flexible therapist who practices systematically the most effective behavior-change methods within a democratic structure, and who can continuously measure your progress toward and help you reach the goals you define. Eclectic therapy tends to lag behind the most advanced scientific views and research.

What, then, will confront you if you enter the office of a therapist who, according to the best information you have been able to gather, practices no particular method or theory of psychotherapy?

First, you are likely to face the widest variety of practices and to be least able to anticipate what you will get. It is therefore even more desirable than usual that you find out ahead of time as much as possible about the man, his views, and his practices.

He is likely to ask you for a description of your problem and a history of your life. Beyond this, a majority of the eclectics who are psychiatrists would probably prescribe a tranquilizer as the primary or secondary therapeutic device, hoping thereby to control your symptoms while discussing your problems with you, and hoping further that after some weeks or months of discussion you might quit taking drugs. The only other courses which a majority of eclectic therapists are likely to follow are to see you once a week or less often, and to refer you to someone or some place else if you are financially poor, are in or are likely to be in legal trouble because of impulsive acts, or are acting or thinking out of touch with reality.

Some eclectic therapists will verge on practicing particular approaches. Some act half-way like psychoanalysts, probing at length your feelings, memories, dreams, and associations. Others act nondirectively, trying to help you to "clarify" your views of yourself and others and hoping that you will then improve your behavior more or less automatically. More, perhaps, will give direct advice and try to convince you to take concrete steps which they think might improve your condition.

You are probably better able to affect the practices of the eclectic than those of other therapists. He is, after all, less committed to any one approach; the more flexible among them therefore have less at stake in practicing a particular way, and are less likely to impose a method upon their interaction with you in the face of demurrers from you. He may be more susceptible both to your irrational arguments against what he is trying to do, as well as to your reasonable arguments. You will probably have a better chance to sway him to your views of what he should try with you, and it is therefore especially desirable for you to be as wise as possible in making your requests.

His main failing will probably be his lack of consistency in answering your questions about what to do, why you should try this or that, and why it may work for you. He may sometimes speak as if, once recognizing a situation as he interprets it, or your feelings about it, you should change automatically because you have that knowledge or "insight." Other times he may simply say, "Try this because I think it might make you feel better." On still other occasions he may remain silent, letting you describe your strong feelings at length, as if you would be better off simply for having let them out.

At the end, then, what will you have learned from eclectic therapy that you can put to use in solving current problems or future problems that may arise—what principles and procedures?

You may gain fresh views about yourself and your habits which might change your ways of handling yourself and affecting others. Your therapist may propose concrete courses of action, which you might find helpful, toward changing a job, a wife, or housing, or taking a vacation, making dates, or trying hobbies. You may come to enjoy and relax with a friendly person to talk to openly and to use as a foil against which you try out new ideas.

You are not likely to hear or to develop a coherent system or approach to the solution of your future problems. You will not have the confidence or comfort that may come from believing that systematic ways of handling any future problem are likely to produce good results for you. The eclectic therapist is not likely to say to you: "It is because you take such and such an approach when faced with problems that you have solved your current problems and can solve your future ones." This is what a more systematic therapist is likely to be able to say to you at the end—or for you to be able to say to yourself. Whether this is *true* in a scientifically provable way is another matter; it is probably not yet true for any system. But you may at least believe it and actually have learned something that you can apply as future problems arise, instead of feeling helpless, in need of immediate professional help, or groping aimlessly for a method to try out.

One other advantage of the eclectic (and also of the behavior-change) approach: It is more likely than analytic or nondirective forms to provide you with a kind of emergency help. If you want immediate relief for grief following a death, for panic from losing a job, for depression attending a divorce, an illness, or an accident—and that is all you want—the eclectic therapist is more likely to work with you, on your terms, for such limited goals. He thus fills a substantial social need in a way that neither the analytic nor the nondirective approach is likely to accept as readily. In such circumstances, he will usually be consoling or sympathetic, advising a vacation, busy work, social activity, or conversation with friends—or anything he thinks might relieve you, however temporary or superficial this may seem from other theoretical viewpoints. Some other therapists also may do this, but except for the behavior-change therapists, they will not do so with zest or pride; they seldom view such limited objectives as their major treatment goal, and often consider them irrelevant or distracting.

A major difficulty in choosing a good eclectic therapist stems from the widely different practices encompassed in this group. One eclectic may run three patients through therapy simultaneously, having them lie down in separate rooms drowsing under the influence of sodium pentothal, while he moves among them asking what they are thinking. Another may be teaching patients how to relax so that they can get through the children's return from school or the working day more tranquilly. A third may, with a single interview, briefly analyze a dream, advise a change of jobs, suggest buying a quiet little dog to get over a dog phobia, or ask you to express freely your childhood feelings toward your mother.

Usually the best you can do in choosing such a therapist is to find out from his patients or their friends as much as you can about what he does, placing particular emphasis on whether he uses good sense, practical judgment, and offers useful advice for concrete problems. That, after all, should be his forte: useful concrete advice. He is not likely to be competent at practicing a particular theory or a new method, or in helping you to develop systematic ways of coping with future problems.

BEHAVIOR-CHANGE THERAPY

As a systematic theory, behavior-change therapy is of most recent origin. One of its pioneers was E. Lakin Phillips, who defined the position of the therapist who would work primarily to change external behavior directly (through the patient's assertions and actions), rather than to change internalized feelings and attitudes in the hope that external behavior would then change automatically.[3] A recent book by Phillips and Wiener, cited in Chapter 3, develops more concretely the theory and ways of changing ineffectual or self-defeating human behavior, following a model from learning and cybernetic theory which is applicable equally to individual psychotherapy and to social organization.

The roots of behavior-change psychotherapy lie in the laboratory science of how *all* animal life, from the lowest forms through to man, learns. Siamese fighting fish, Venus's-flytrap plants, worms, and mice—and many more living organisms—have been the subjects of learning studies. Pigeons, chickens, and dolphins have been trained to play games before audiences by being fed (reinforced) at just the right times; and any man, through carefully chosen and spaced rewards and punishments, can be trained during his lifetime to act in certain ways, even if he is not aware of the rewards or punishments. B. F. Skinner pioneered the animal methods and theory, and Norbert Wiener pioneered the cybernetic machine theory that underlie behavior-change therapy.

The primary issue between the behavior-change therapists and most other therapists lies in the way the former view the connection between internal feelings and external behavior. The nondirective and existential therapists, the psychoanalysts, and most eclectics would say that through free communication with the psychotherapist the patient changes his feelings about himself and others

[3] E. L. Phillips, *Psychotherapy: A Modern Theory and Practice* (Englewood Cliffs, N.J.: Prentice-Hall, 1956).

and that he then naturally changes his external behavior. "Understanding" or "insight" appears to be the prime goal of most therapists, although they will acknowledge that many bright, sophisticated people manage their lives stupidly even after years of insightful psychotherapy.

If, from the beginning of therapy, the emphasis is placed upon external behavior change rather than upon prior understanding and insight, a wide range of methods can be tried to advance the patient directly toward his goals outside of therapy. That is the operating method of behavior-change therapy. Whatever, within reason, advances the patient most effectively toward his goals will be attempted, subjected to study, and maintained or discarded according to objective, scientific standards of judgment.

It is not assumed that analysis of the past or of the self is essential to solving problems. Obviously many people get along well in life practically without any introspection. Research indicates little relationship between understanding and behavior change. If, however, certain kinds of understanding did help patients to reach their goals efficiently, it would be used by the behavior-change therapist. Yet he would also try direct advice to see if that worked. He would try interrupting bad habits and enhancing useful new habits in the widest variety of ways that held promise of moving the patient toward his chosen goals.

Behavior-change therapists are sometimes accused of being nefarious manipulators, of making people do things without realizing how they are being directed, as in advertising, and this can be true. The story is now classic in the profession about the classroom of students who practiced reinforcement theory by nodding approval whenever their professor moved toward the edge of his lecture platform, and indicating boredom whenever he moved away from the edge. Without realizing what he was doing or why, the professor was soon teetering on the edge of the platform as the class indicated vigorous approval.

But the idea of changing human behavior through psychotherapy, and the problem of who chooses the goals and how, is no more present in the behavior-change form than the others. The basic question concerns the patient's freedom to choose and pursue his own goals, with as much information as possible to make a wise selection of his therapist and therapy; maximum flexibility, humility, and a respectful attitude by the therapist; and ready opportunity for the patient to modify or withdraw from therapy at any time. Since behavior change is essentially *goal*-centered rather than *relationship*-centered, the patient is least likely to become emotionally involved and upset and most likely to feel comfortable about changing his goals, therapy, or therapist at any time *provided he knows at all times what is going on and why*—which is the vital safeguard he should have in any form of treatment.

The behavior-change therapist will concentrate upon changing your behavior as efficiently as possible—to block your self-defeating habits and to help you achieve your goals. If you are anxious or depressed because you are getting nowhere on your job, he may want to analyze with you what your expectations are, whether they are realistic, how they are not being fulfilled, and what you must do to achieve satisfaction. You may need to change your expectations if you lack the necessary ability or opportunity for goals you have cherished, or if they clash with other goals or values you also hold. Or you may need to beef up your work habits or to modify your social behavior if you are to succeed as you want to. In either case, the behavior-change therapist can lead you to assess and set compatible goals, and to develop the habits necessary to achieve them.

His assumption will be that your feelings and attitudes will change through this process, following change in your external behavior, and that feelings and attitudes need not change first, before action. He assumes that the rewards you will obtain by achieving your goals, however small the steps, will continuously provide you with what you need to continue with more effective activity. To *begin* to move this way, you may need only a nudge of encouragement and confidence from a therapist who knows what he is about, or the hope of a concrete plan he presents to you.

You will not find a behavior-change therapist easily. The field is the newest of all, and its practitioners are most likely to be found in the research settings of hospitals, universities, and public clinics, or among the younger therapists. Psychologists are most likely to favor this kind of therapy because almost alone they are systematically trained in learning theory, and because they most frequently do behavioral research. Thus psychology departments of treatment institutions and universities are often the best sources of information and referral if you are interested in behavior-change therapy.

A special type of therapy, which is included in this section with reservations, is that of Albert Ellis, founder of the Institute for Rational Living in New York City. He is a prolific writer on what he calls "rational therapy." Rational therapists believe that it is what a man tells himself about himself and others that gets him into trouble—and can get him out of it. They therefore analyze what it is that their patients say to themselves that makes their behavior self-defeating, and then try to get them to substitute more rational statements for the irrational ones.

By itself, this practice smacks more of changing internal attitudes as a requisite to changing external behavior than vice-versa. Rational therapists, however, combine this technique with vigorous recommendations for action to combat false beliefs about what might happen with what actually does happen when patients do what they have been afraid of. In this latter sense, the rational therapists belong to this section. Their major difference with (other) behavior-change therapists lies in the precedence they may give to preliminary attitudinal changes before action.

CHAPTER 6   *The Major Psychotherapy*
Professions

IN DISCUSSING the four major forms of psychotherapy, we mentioned the three major practicing professions—clinical psychologists, psychiatric social workers, and psychiatrists. Professionals in these groups receive the bulk of their most advanced training in how to help people in trouble. Yet none of the three as a group practices psychotherapy exclusively or even mainly. Psychiatrists as a group alone can use physical (medical) means such as prescribing drugs and shock treatment, and generally do diagnostic, evaluative, and consulting work more than they do psychotherapy. Most psychiatric social workers collect personal data, evaluate eligibility for public benefits, and supervise, more than they practice counseling or therapy. Psychologists do more teaching, testing, and research than treatment. Still, each of the other tasks that most of these professionals perform is intended to contribute toward more effective therapy.

These are not the only professional groups to whom troubled people take their personal problems. In fact, they are not even the most commonly used ones. They are, however, the major professions trained, committed, and socially designated to treat psychological problems. The professionals to whom most people go with their problems, at least initially, are physicians (other than psychiatrists), ministers, and lawyers.

Whether these three latter professions should become involved in treating personal problems is an issue of great concern to them. Some take a dim view of the value of the mental-health professions, and believe that their own "common sense" approaches do more good than the "highfalutin" but "impractical" approaches of mental-health professionals. Others are willing to try to help their clients in modest ways, and to refer them to psychotherapists if the trouble does not quickly diminish. Still others are afraid to become involved with emotionally upset persons and quickly refer them elsewhere.

Our view is that, acting humbly and tentatively, the minister, lawyer, teacher, physician—or friend—can make many limited but practical suggestions which may work to resolve a temporary problem, and that, in any case, no harm can result from a modest effort. The encouragement of religious practices, of an extra effort to do congenial things with others, of experimenting with solutions to a specific problem, of a temporary breaking off from an activity or taking a vacation, can provide the push sometimes needed to get a depressed, or anxious, or bitter person to resume his accustomed life momentum.

It is easier to get to see and talk with a physician, lawyer, or minister whom one already knows and trusts than to start with a professional psychotherapist. Yet simultaneously you, as well as these professionals, must be prepared to judge when you are getting nowhere, and when you should receive more professionalized psychotherapy. Many problems can be solved only by intensive, specialized attention that ministers, lawyers, physicians, or teachers do not have the time or training to provide.

Finally, there are other professional persons who practice psychological methods of helping troubled persons, but who tend neither to call what they do psychotherapy nor to see themselves as peripheral helpers. They are relatively few, yet they are an integral part of treatment resources. Among them are marriage and family counselors, personnel counselors, school counselors, group leaders, and vocational counselors. All are in viable professions with their own organizations, training courses, journals, meetings, and research.

Each of these latter groups is trying to isolate a limited kind of personal problem in which to specialize. Most human problems, however, overlap, worsen, or improve together; they also change according to the same methods. Does it make sense for you to see several different practitioners simultaneously, one for problems in raising a rebellious child, one for headaches, one for sexual trouble with a spouse, and another for job unhappiness? If you initially choose one problem, should you reveal others to your counselor and expect him to help with them? Is the body of specific information and method in each of these areas sufficient to justify a specialized profession?

Our tentative conclusion is that psychological problems can be subdivided and treated within a limited area if they are acute in that area; that the results of learning *how* to solve a problem, as well as the solution itself, are likely to radiate to other problem areas; and that solving any problem, even if small, can only be useful in solving other problems. If a deeply depressing sense of inferiority is attributed to working at a menial job, far below your ability, instead of to sexual impotence, it seems as likely that getting a better job may improve sexual potency as that working on the sexual problem will improve job adjustment. It also seems likely that the solution to either problem may improve the inferiority feelings.

Of course, any professional person working with any human problem should be as knowledgeable about human psychology and psychotherapy as possible. He should be aware of his own skills and limitations, and be well prepared to make referrals to other professions. He should know more about his field of practice than you do; yet you must be prepared for the possibility that he may not, or that he may be biased or immodest. You will always finally have to judge his limitations and your needs for yourself.

Any of the professional groups which will now be discussed may practice any form of psychotherapy. While many psychoanalysts are psychiatrists, there may be even more psychologists and social workers practicing psychoanalytic methods. Group therapists follow no one form of therapy. Ministers and pastoral counselors similarly may follow any theory or mixture of concepts. So you must decide on and judge the type of therapy independently from the name of the profession. And, as we have repeated many times, nothing should be as important in your choice of a therapist as your informed opinion of the particular man who does the therapy.

Training in psychotherapy is probably the weakest area in the training of the three major mental-health professions (as well as of the others who help). Until quite recently, many accredited schools of medicine, social work, and psychology have offered little or no training in intensive psychotherapy. Practically none now train students in all of the four major forms of therapy. Each profession has tended to give most training time and emphasis to collecting information about patients and diagnosing and handling them administratively rather than to the direct and ultimate goal of teaching clients how to solve their problems.

So most psychotherapists, according to their respective professions, learn at school mainly how to diagnose, how to test, how to take a case history, how to make a referral, how to hospitalize, how to interview, how to process. If you examine the curricula of the university programs in any of these professions, you will find relatively little on "how to change human behavior." Nor is the internship or "practicum" much better defined on this subject. Most discussion and supervision of psychotherapy goes on and on with how patients got this way and what their problems "truly" are, according to this theory and that. Meanwhile, the student trying to learn psychotherapy, who is the subject of such seminars, meetings, and supervision, usually wonders when he will be told how to help the patient efficiently. But finally he too will start to talk about causes, and his early eagerness to find efficient solutions will often dim.

Nevertheless, each profession tries to pre-empt a certain area of the enterprise to itself alone. No laws whatsoever effectively support any limits on psychotherapy, yet physicians will often claim that the practice of psychotherapy is a medical specialty which only they should be allowed to practice. They have never been able legally to enforce such a view. In limited form, however, some health-insurance plans, organization regulations, or referral-agency policies limit treatment to physicians (even though they may be subject to antitrust prosecution in so doing).

Psychiatrists had traditionally practiced the bulk of psychotherapy. While social workers and psychologists have had equal reason to challenge this situation, social workers have often seemed more closely aligned with psychiatrists in their traditional views than with psychologists on the newer concepts about psychotherapy. They have seemed more willing than psychologists to play the game with medical rules; psychologists have tended more to challenge a medical view of psychotherapy.

A broadened view of treatment is currently taking hold in the United States, although enlightened psychiatrists have always held it. Freud wanted to train school teachers to practice psychoanalysis; Carl Binger, former president of the American Psychiatric Association, has suggested an entirely new psychotherapy profession; Franz Alexander, past president of the American Psychoanalytic Association, enlarged greatly the concept of what constituted psychotherapy. John Gardner, recently Secretary of Health, Education and Welfare, whose Department directs all the national institutes of health (including "mental health"), is a psychologist. Social workers, as heads of state welfare departments, supervise physicians and mental-health services. Clinic heads under the federally subsidized community mental-health program may be social workers, psychiatrists, or psychologists.

The demarcation lines among the mental-health professions are becoming increasingly blurred. What remain of differences among them are mainly certain concrete training and skills with hospitalization and drugs, psychological tests, or community care and referral. But the effort to change human behavior, to solve personal problems, is still open to anyone who can demonstrate the skill and meet minimum standards in whatever profession is socially permitted to try to help troubled people.

PSYCHIATRISTS

Most psychiatrists are eclectic. Only a small minority of them are psychoanalysts, and the majority do not spend most of their time practicing psychotherapy. All psychiatrists are physicians, having completed medical training before specializing in psychiatry, although practically none practice medicine once they become psychiatrists. Most of them have probably never practiced medicine outside of their early training.

A psychiatrist need not have completed specialized training beyond the ordinary medical degree to practice psychotherapy. His sole degree usually is the M.D., based upon graduation from a medical school and an internship. He has no degree which reflects training in handling human psychological problems. If he has passed specialized national-board examinations in psychiatry, and thus is designated a diplomate in psychiatry, he has taken (except for "grandfathers" who went into practice before standards were established) several years of special education and training in psychotherapy comparable to what a diplomate in clinical psychology has taken. If, however, he is not "boarded," you have no assurance that a psychiatrist has had any such special training nor, indeed, that he has had the basic courses in human behavior that a graduate of a nationally accredited school of social work or clinical psychology program has usually had.

Most psychiatrists going into practice today complete part or all of a medical school–directed program of training in psychiatry. But most psychiatrists practicing in most American communities probably have not. They call themselves psychiatrists with no approval necessary from a public accrediting body, and while they may by virtue of personal qualities and experience be excellent therapists, there is no indication from the title "physician" of what their training has been in human psychological behavior, since their only degree is in medicine. Physicians who have not been specially trained in psychiatry probably have little or no training in psychotherapy, although they have often had relatively brief periods of clerkship and internship in handling mentally disturbed persons. They have little or no experience in helping persons solve their most pressing personal problems through psychological means. They are primarily taught how to handle patients administratively with drugs and hospitalization, how to take case histories and make diagnoses, how to prescribe medicine, and how to give psychological first aid.

Training in psychotherapy is at best primitive for all the professions under discussion. It is particularly difficult for physicians training to be psychotherapists because, in some important aspects, the training and habits of the physician are obstacles to the practice of psychotherapy.

There are around twenty thousand psychiatrists in the United States today. Of these, according to a 1956 article in the *American Journal of Psychiatry*, about two-thirds practice mainly like physicians, with such devices as medicine, black bags, home and hospital visits; only about one-third practice primarily as office psychotherapists. Now this majority may appeal to you as your choice for treatment, but since this book is about psychotherapy and how you can best use it, you are forewarned that when medication and hospitalization are viewed and used as the mainstays of treatment, you are not likely to receive psychotherapeutic help with direct solutions of your problems through learning new ways of handling yourself.

There is generally a kind of incompatibility between dependency upon drugs and an emphasis upon a personal effort to solve your problems; between being handed a "cure" and taking responsibility for making changes in your behavior; between seeking temporary relief from discomfort and finding long-term solutions to your problems. This kind of incompatibility plagues all psychotherapists, even when they do not use drugs, but try instead to provide temporary relief and comfort through soothing words, support, reassurance, and encouragement. The problem unique to psychiatrists is that they can prescribe drugs, and when so readily available a method is at hand to comfort people, it is difficult to resist using and depending upon it.

The young psychiatrist, particularly, fresh from his medical training and not fortified by a personally tested theory or experience with psychological methods, seems likely to prescribe tranquilizers quickly in the attempt to relieve anxiety and to give his patient *something*—and then, afterward, to worry about talking to him and trying to help him to handle his problems with the world. But once a patient is given tranquilizers, he is easily diverted from the idea of changing his self-defeating ways of living toward the idea of taking medication in various combinations and doses to ease his anxiety. The psychiatrist can also be diverted in this way, so that psychotherapy as such may never become the intense, overriding effort it needs to be to accomplish its purpose.

When you see a psychiatrist for therapy, you need to know particularly what his attitude is toward psychotherapy in comparison with medical methods of treatment, especially with psychotropic drugs, but also toward hospitalization, shock treatment, physical rest, and other kinds of medication such as hormones, vitamins, and thyroid extract. If you want to use a psychotherapist who will help you to change your ways of living, you will find many available and should avoid becoming involved with a psychiatrist who is likely to do something else.

This is a true example of what can happen otherwise: Richard Stone was in psychotherapy for a year. He had been an honor student and athlete at college, and had begun work and marriage with immediate success. He was, however, erratic as a lawyer, overextended himself at work and financially, and lost his wife and two jobs. He was acting as a file clerk for his father at the onset of therapy, but gradually with counseling resumed legal work and began going out again with his second wife. He developed symptoms of stomach ulcers, however, as he began facing up to his father's arbitrary orders to him and his need to learn how to handle his father. While his psychotherapist was on vacation, he went to his physician for treatment of his stomach pain and ended up at the hospital for ulcer surgery. After surgery, his physician referred him to a psychiatrist who immediately gave him intensive electric-shock treatment because he was middle-aged and depressed (the conventional signs to that type of psychiatrist of the desirability of shock treatment).

Mr. Stone's original therapist was appalled upon his return to discover that his own psychotherapy could be so completely ignored. Yet he should not have been surprised; he knew that different therapists *do* treat the same symptoms differently and that many psychiatrists are likely to treat middle-aged depressed patients in just this way.

You—and professional helpers—cannot find out in advance whether shock treatment, drugs, or any other form of therapy are most likely to help you. You can, however, choose the kind of therapy and therapist making the most sense to you. You should do this before you begin treatment and thus exercise your free choice in the matter.

There is no easy way to determine whether a psychiatrist is committed to practicing psychotherapy exclusively or even mainly. The phone book lists psychiatrists under "physicians and surgeons," but does not indicate an accrediting organization or designation that tells you whether they have had training in psychotherapy, unless one lists himself as a "Diplomate, American Board of Psychiatry and Neurology." You would then know that he has had extensive specialized training (unless he is old and accredited as a "grandfather"), though not whether that is his main interest or practice.

Hospital-oriented and medication-minded psychiatrists have dominated their profession in the past, although there has been some shifting toward psychotherapy. Medical kinds of treatment are easier to provide and are more lucrative. The psychiatrist can in this way see patients for a ten-minute conversation in the hospital and then tell a nurse to follow through with this or that treatment by way of drugs, diet, rest, or occupational therapy; or he might do the same in his office. He may thus see three to six patients in an hour, charging each ten dollars or so a visit, and boost his annual income to a height denied to the psychotherapist who sees one patient an hour and usually charges no more than $25.00 or $30.00 a session.

Health-insurance plans contribute to this kind of hospitalization–drug treatment. It is usually easier for the therapist to collect from insurance companies and employers for hospital and drug care than for office psychotherapy. Thus, unless health-insurance plans become more enlightened, or the public much better educated and demanding, even the psychotherapy-minded psychiatrist will be under increasing pressure to treat patients in a way that will make it easier to be reimbursed by insurance, rather than according to what he may think is the best kind of therapy. And patients will be under pressure to seek out psychiatrists who will treat them in a way that insurance will cover.

Probably few psychiatrists would say that they do not practice psychotherapy, even in a daily ten-minute hospital visit, or a monthly half-hour office session during which they adjust a medication schedule. Because you are asked by the psychiatrist how you are feeling, and you list your complaints and are told to go out more often or take up a hobby, or you describe a stomach-ache and are told to relax or take a vacation—you are not necessarily being exposed to psychotherapy. Somehow, to have scientific meaning and validity—to make sense as a professional activity—psychotherapy must mean more than what two casual friends might say to each other in fifteen minutes over cocktails. Yet this is what often is called "psychotherapy," especially when associated with community hospital care or brief office calls. You should know this and your alternatives ahead of time, and decide for yourself what to do about it.

There is another issue which is assuming less importance as federal and state programs increase. Psychiatrists sometimes own or invest in private sanitariums, rest homes, and small hospitals where they care for their patients with greater profit than is otherwise possible, in somewhat the same way that some physicians (including psychiatrists) have investments in pharmacies to which they refer their patients. The danger of abuse and of a conflict of interest seems so patent in such cases that public safeguards seem to be justified. Since the profession itself has not guarded its ethics vigorously in this regard, surely laws should require that psychiatrists not have a financial interest in hospitals, homes, or pharmacies to which they refer patients.

SOCIAL WORKERS

Fewer psychiatric social workers by far work primarily with psychotherapy than do psychiatrists and clinical psychologists. Yet because there are about five times more social workers (105,000–115,000) than psychiatrists or psychologists, even the small number of psychiatric social workers doing psychotherapy probably contributes a significant proportion of the psychotherapy available in the United States today.

Only about 20 per cent of the persons employed full time as social workers in the United States today meet the minimum standards of accreditation generally set by the major professional organizations. The minimum standard for professional membership is a master's degree—two years of training beyond the bachelor's degree, including a year of social-work internship—from an accredited school of social work plus a year or more of supervised experience. No state laws license the practice of this profession, but there is national certification by the Academy of Social Work, and strong local, state, and national (National Association of Social Work) organizations that try to enhance professional standards.

A small minority of social workers (most social workers determine the need for financial and other public assistance) practice in the field of mental health; they number perhaps around five thousand. Usually called psychiatric social workers, they constitute one of five divisions of the national organization, and it is mostly from among them that the psychotherapists in this profession come. Very few practice privately on a full-time basis, although many (perhaps two thousand) do so part time. Most social workers are reluctant to call themselves psychotherapists, apparently because they are afraid of seeming presumptuous, and also because their label of "case workers" has a unique and honorable history.

A recent ad for the field proclaimed, "Social workers are everywhere," and indeed this is true to a surprising extent. Social workers generally fill the key posts in community social planning and public facilities for personal problems, and they also fill most of the mental-health positions in community clinics and related activities. They lag only in the private practice of psychotherapy and in their willingness, through their major professional organizations, to state clearly that they are trained in and practice what others call psychotherapy.

For years many have said that the casework they did was different from psychotherapy because it did not treat with the "unconscious." Yet it is practically impossible to talk to a patient, or "client" as social workers tend to call him, without discussing material or behavior of which he may be unaware (another way to designate the "unconscious"). It is a tenet of the most recent behavior-change therapy that effective psychotherapy can be done with little or no attention to the "unconscious."

Social workers are the most reluctant of the groups in the field to admit that they practice psychotherapy, even when heavily engaged in trying to help their clientele to solve personal problems. They tend also to be the most passive about applying a theoretical approach, and the most hesitant to recommend or block action based upon a theory. At the same time, they are the most active in making referrals to community facilities that might help their clients to solve daily problems such as finding jobs, socializing, solving financial problems, getting help with managing a house, and obtaining birth-control information.

This, then, would be the forte of the social worker, which you can take advantage of: practical information or referral, particularly with regard to inexpensive or free community facilities, for help with specific problems. While there are many exceptions, the social worker is not as likely as other therapists to apply a consistent theory of psychotherapy for the purpose of changing behavior comprehensively. The most pervasive theoretical influence in social work has probably been that of psychoanalysis. A very few social workers become psychoanalytic therapists, but mostly the analytic influence shows up as a way of interpreting in case notes what the social workers think are the client's problems and their origins. What he does about them is an entirely different matter, usually involving referral, tentative interpretations, and practical advice.

Because they are the main agents of referral and approval for public benefits, social workers do most of the critical work in mental health despite their reluctance to practice psychotherapy. They are not as assertive about their role, nor do they seek to exclude those of lesser or different training as much as do psychologists and psychiatrists. There are no state laws accrediting social workers and excluding others from doing similar work.

Yet large-scale social enterprises are developing to reach the needs of far more people with problems in our communities than individual psychotherapy can touch today. Here the social worker, as a therapeutic agent, should shine. The largest groups of personally troubled people are the so-called unemployables, the withdrawn, the bums, the alcoholics, the delinquents. Individual psychotherapists see few members of these groups. Such troubled persons tend to be disinterested in ("unmotivated for") therapy, too poor to pay, or too dull to attract therapists. Yet they constitute the important problem groups numerically, far more than those whom therapists see today.

Thus, the major groups of personally disrupted persons will likely become the focus of social workers acting as therapists, because social workers are most likely to be committed to working with these people. The theories and techniques of psychotherapy have mainly come from psychology and psychiatry, and social-work therapists tend to imitate these other professions regarding therapy. But the new, larger-scale, more effective methods that are needed for the largest problem groups may well be generated or at least affected by social workers applying the research findings of psychologists and others about human behavior change.

For you, meanwhile, social workers can provide practical advice and referral and, perhaps, if you press them, whatever other therapeutic help you need. You are likely to have to press them more than the other groups if you want intensive psychotherapy from them.

In the larger cities, social workers in private practice can be found listed in the yellow pages of the phone book. Their accreditation is likely to be listed along with their name, whether it is their national certification or their degree (usually M.S.W.). This says nothing whatsoever about their background in psychotherapy, however. That is an individual matter you will have to investigate further.

PSYCHOLOGISTS

A psychologist is not necessarily competent at psychotherapy. Accredited psychologists have usually trained far more extensively in principles of human behavior than have the general run of psychiatrists or social workers, but they may have had no experience whatsoever with psychotherapy.

There are approximately two dozen specialty divisions, based upon interest or practice, within the American Psychological Association, and only a small minority of its approximately twenty-four thousand members primarily practices psychotherapy—perhaps around four thousand out of the approximately eight thousand in full-time clinical work. The specialty that includes most of the therapists is clinical psychology, but perhaps only one-third of the clinical psychologists practice psychotherapy primarily. The others mainly teach, administer tests, and do research. Clinical psychology is the most rapidly growing of the three professions. The Counseling Psychology Division of the American Psychological Association also includes some psychotherapists, but most counseling psychologists who do not belong to the Clinical Division tend to consider that they specialize primarily in vocational, rehabilitational, or educational problems rather than with personal or emotional difficulties.

The major accrediting agency for specialized clinical competence is the American Board of Examiners in Professional Psychology, which has certified approximately 1,500 clinical psychologists. All but the "grandfathers" (older practitioners who were blanketed in when the Board was established) must hold the doctorate degree, have five years of post-doctoral experience, and pass national written and oral exams. In the training and examination of "boarded" clinical psychologists, evidence is required of proficiency in psychotherapy. This Board is the only one that attempts to make examinations for therapeutic competence. The psychiatric Board tests only for diagnostic skill and knowledge. But the psychology Board asks the psychologist-applicant to present verbatim protocols of his therapy sessions, and to recommend a therapeutic plan for a patient seen during the examination process. The conflict this has aroused in the profession and the relatively few practitioners accredited by the Board emphasize the highly uncertain and idiosyncratic nature of psychotherapy today.

There are two major degrees in clinical psychology. One is the master's degree, which generally requires two years of specialized training beyond the bachelor's degree. However, the experience of degree holders is often erratic or nonexistent, the training program is not well standardized nationally, and the degree is generally considered to qualify its holder for diagnostic (testing) work primarily, under the supervision of the holder of a doctorate degree.

The doctor's degree is increasingly considered the minimum requirement for the independent practice of clinical psychology, including psychotherapy. Universities are nationally accredited to train in clinical psychology; it usually takes five to six years beyond the four-year college degree to complete the work; and the equivalent of two full-time years of supervised experience is generally required.

A majority of states have laws governing the practices of psychologists; only six states lack accreditation either by law or professional regulation. State regulations have no effect upon psychotherapy, however, any more than do medical-practice regulations. You will find protection in them only from quacks and off-beat amateurs who may call themselves psychologists. They may also rule out many amateur counselors—*not* from doing whatever good they can, but rather from calling themselves psychologists or providing such concretely definable technical services as testing for intelligence.

Variety in therapeutic practices is probably greater among psychologists than among other professional groups. Psychologists in large proportions practice each of the forms of therapy. Their most distinctive type, however, is behavior-change treatment. This approach stems directly from learning theory, which has been largely the psychologist's domain. Psychologists have been the major researchers in the human problem-solving area, and it seems natural that they should be the leaders in applying the research clinically.

Theory-making, too, has been a major domain of psychologists, and they have been leading contributors to psychoanalytic and nondirective and existential views. Indeed, clinical psychologists often have seemed to be more interested in theory, research, and testing than in therapy. Their desire to study and classify human behavior often seems boundless, and many are thus diverted from trying to help the individuals with problems who come to them for help. The psychologists seem at the other extreme from most social workers, who seem boundless in their desire to help people, without commensurate interest in improving their relatively primitive tools through better theory and research.

The major influence of psychologists is exercised through college teaching. Alone among the mental-health professionals, psychologists teach a broad range of undergraduate courses in a wide variety of preprofessional and liberal-arts programs. Almost every college student encounters a psychologist as a teacher of the basic elements of human behavior, development, personality, learning, or mental hygiene. Such courses are also reaching increasingly into high schools, and could provide the groundwork for the kind of consumer education which is the purpose of this book.

However, such psychology courses are seldom integrated with guidelines on how to judge need for help, where to look for it, or how to evaluate its usefulness. Psychotherapy somehow has usually been treated with reverence or anxiety or as an unfit subject for discussion in general-psychology classes. Psychologists could play a far more important role here than they do in carrying through with the implications and applications of the material they teach to personal problem-solving.

Just as you are most likely to find social workers in social agencies, and psychiatrists in medical settings, so you are most likely to find psychologists in educational settings, particularly in colleges. Such a setting suggests both some of the strength (theory and research) and weakness (service attitude) of the profession. Yet here again, the individual therapist is far more important than the setting, and hopefully you will be able to make a choice on the basis of more precise knowledge of the man than of a setting—or profession, theory, or degree.

Most *clinical* psychologists work in institutions of various sorts, clinics, hospitals, and schools. The private practitioners you might want to consult will be listed in the phone book, often under a heading indicating state certification or national board accreditation. These attest to little about therapeutic competence, however, and indicate mainly training and experience in psychology or clinical psychology. In none of the professions discussed above is there any public accreditation of competence at psychotherapy alone.

CHAPTER 7 *Related Professions*

THE MAJOR psychotherapy professions may have largely reserved to themselves the title "psychotherapist," but they have not preempted the work of helping people to solve their problems.

If you want a professional service specifically called "psychotherapy," or if you want to analyze and gain insight into general problems of your upbringing, depression, alienation, or feelings about your place in the world, you should probably seek out a "psychotherapist" in one of the three major professions. If, however, you are primarily interested in getting advice on a concrete problem, such as job choice or adaptation, marriage adjustment, sex, religious belief, or child rearing, then you can appropriately look for a counselor specializing in one of these specific areas. Whether your concrete problem is best attacked as deep and pervasive within your personality, or is better handled in its specific form, is a matter for your own final judgment. Psychotherapists themselves split along these lines. Some work on general personality troubles, others concentrate on concrete difficulties from within their special areas. Counselors vary greatly in their relative focus upon general and concrete problems.

You will have to decide for yourself whether to choose a therapist from one of the three major professions or one from a more specialized area. It is probably not as crucial that your counselor come from this profession or that. If he is competent, he will know when he can best handle a problem and when he should refer you to others. Again we are saying that, within reasonable limits of background, the man and not his profession is the crucial consideration; and also that it is reasonable to try first to solve your problems efficiently in their simplest and most specific forms before deciding that they require some more general, more abstract, and more time-consuming consideration.

There are many professional groups devoted to helping people solve their personal problems. We have chosen to discuss here those which seem to have the clearest form and most professionalized qualities. Others are springing up and still others will be born. Perhaps the most hopeful are just now being started in the "store-front" mental-health clinics and advisory agencies appearing in poverty areas in our large cties.

VOCATIONAL AND EDUCATIONAL COUNSELORS (COUNSELING PSYCHOLOGISTS)

Vocational and educational counselors have had a steadier existence over the years than the other professions discussed in this chapter. This profession received major impetus during World War I when intelligence tests were first used massively to place men at appropriate levels of work in the military.

Theories and fads about human behavior have not played as major a role with vocational and educational counselors as they have with psychotherapists. Growth and sophistication in the field has stemmed primarily from improved tools to measure interests and abilities and to predict success at school and at work.

During the forties and fifties, counseling psychologists drew closer to psychotherapy as they grew more aware of how personality factors vitally affected their work. Lines have blurred between personality and vocational problems. Vocational problems, like those of sex, marriage, child rearing, religion and values, socializing and education, may provide the specific battleground on which you must unravel your feelings of guilt, depression, inadequacy, inferiority, or whatever. The seriousness of your unsatisfying behavior may be defined by the number of these areas involved or by the intensity of the trouble in any one area.

And why should not vocational dissatisfaction be considered as much a personality or emotional problem as, say, sexual or social disturbance? Your working life takes more of your waking time, is basic to your survival (for food, shelter, medical care), and may well be the main source for your sense of adequacy as a person.

Many vocational and educational counselors may not *want* to become involved with your serious emotional or the so-called more "personal" problems. Yet, like social workers who may be similarly reluctant to become involved, they cannot help trying to treat with such problems in some way if they are to help you solve your vocational or educational difficulties.

If you cannot stand the detail work in an accounting office or the statistics course in a college program, and you go to a vocational or educational counselor for help, the chances are remote that he will discover you have made a clearly inappropriate vocational choice according to your interests and abilities. The chances are much greater that he will find, for example, that you have never learned very well to endure the unpleasant tasks that are part of any job, or that you do not like to work around people (as required at any job), or that you have trouble getting along with superiors or regulations.

Vocational and educational counselors, or counseling psychologists, can help most with tests and direct advice about jobs and schooling when you are fresh in school and are indecisive about what to go into, or are succeeding at work but are vaguely dissatisfied with it. If, however, you are an adult who has an erratic history of employment or has worked unhappily for years, the chances are strong that you will profit more from attention to the ways you get into trouble with others or yourself on your job than you will gain from an assessment of your aptitude for the work.

In any case, a vocational counselor can provide you with useful initial information, and some will be able to help you with your problems of personal adjustment. They will give emphasis to your working life which many psychotherapists may consider unimportant compared with your social and sexual behavior. The weakness of vocational counselors may be that in their effort to apply their primary tools, vocational tests, they might overlook attitudinal and personality problems that make you ineffective or unhappy at any work.

Vocational counselors can be found listed as such in the telephone book yellow pages. They should always have at least a master's degree from a special university program. Increasingly they have doctor's degrees. The most comprehensive university training programs, which include courses in testing and counseling, and internships, are approved by the American Psychological Association.

The major professional organizations are the American Guidance and Personnel Association and the Division on Counseling Psychology of the American Psychological Association. The major accrediting organizations are state agencies—which usually certify counselors only as psychologists, not specifically for vocational counseling—and the American Board of Examiners in Professional Psychology. The latter body requires the highest level of training and experience, the doctorate degree, five years of post-doctoral experience, and passing a national exam—and awards "diplomate" status in "counseling psychology."

There are special subdivisions of counseling psychology which will only be mentioned because they are not relevant to the main purpose of this book. There are rehabilitation counselors who help especially with the handicapped, and are generally trained in programs similar to those for vocational and educational counselors. Their major organization is the National Rehabilitation Association, and they are found mainly in state and community agencies and centers, and in private institutes. Employment in a reputable agency provides some assurances of their competence.

Educational and school counselors will generally be available at any large school. They seldom operate privately to help choose school courses or training programs, except in the form of vocational counselors. Those in good schools have usually been trained in special college programs, but sometimes at smaller public and private schools some teachers with little or no special training are simply called counselors. Professional accreditation is usually through state departments of education, and a master's degree or equivalent training in the field is usually required where standards are set.

Personnel-office employees sometimes function as counselors in private industry and in federal, state, and local civil-service offices. Seldom do they have any extended training in vocational or counseling methods. They are best used to advise you on concrete problems in your particular office. Many private employment agencies offer counseling services and even list themselves in phone books as "vocational counselors." The good ones may be helpful for practical advice on where and how to get a good job, and a very few may employ an accredited vocational counselor or coun-

seling psycho`ogist, or refer you to one. But if they merely
give you tests, and an employment counselor or agent attempts
to guide you into an occupational field you have doubts about,
you had better check his credentials and reputation as a counselor
or psychologist.

In some states, school psychologists are distinguished from
the above groups in their training, accreditation, or duties. Generally they function as diagnostic technicians, testing for and analyzing problems of intelligence and behavior, and advising on sources
of treatment other than themselves.

MARRIAGE COUNSELORS

Marriage and family relationships are probably the most sensitive, intense, complex, and valued in all social behavior, yet only
in recent years have they been singled out for large-scale special
attention. Marriage and family counseling is now growing fast to
meet a widespread, specialized therapeutic need. Counselors seldom
call themselves psychotherapists, yet they overlap so greatly in
their clientele and methods with psychotherapists that it makes
no sense to overlook them when you are considering professional
help.

Marriage counselors (along with family counselors, sometimes
called "marriage and family counselors"), among the related professions, are especially exercising great influence on therapeutic
practices by reason of their numbers and specialty.

Today it seems most sensible that if you have serious problems
involving your wife or husband, you should go first to a marriage
counselor. Their major national organization, the American Association of Marriage Counselors, sets minimum standards for membership which include training in any of a variety of professions.
While most marriage and family counselors appear to be social
workers, anyone with a background in handling human problems
can practice in the field. The training program in this field at the
University of Minnesota, for example, has included sociologists,
educational psychologists, and physicians, as well as social workers.
The title of "marriage counselor" says nothing about the practitioner's background, nor do the telephone listings help except where
they also include a statement about accreditation or professional

degree, as in social work or clinical psychology. California is one of the few states with a law regulating this field; it allows for a wide range of acceptable backgrounds.

There is, however, a growing body of research and of formal university training programs, which offer hope that by looking carefully you can find a number of competent counselors among whom to choose. Social agencies often provide such services unless your income exceeds something approximately in the range of seven to twelve thousand dollars, and they tend to charge for their service on a sliding scale. The larger cities contain many private practitioners.

How can they help you? First of all, this relatively new profession is least bound to conservative theories. Its practices tend to be almost entirely eclectic, and depend a good deal upon providing information. The problems the marriage counselor deals with tend to be well defined. When you go to a psychotherapist for physical complaints of fatigue, or head or stomach pain, or because you are depressed or unhappy, he will have to press you to discover the "real," concrete sources of the troubles in your daily life. You go to the marriage counselor, however, knowing your trouble; you cannot get along with your spouse. And you want, need, and press for help quickly, since you fear separation, divorce, or at least devastating conflict.

The counselor's and your task is clearly defined: progress is easily observable. You must learn directly how to handle your marital problems better. The clear presence of criteria of success, as well as the concrete nature of the problems and guidance, make this an appealing alternative to psychotherapy.

You can, of course, seek psychotherapy instead of marriage counseling for your marital problems. A psychotherapist *may* work the same way as the marriage counselor, but he is more likely to work indirectly. He may discuss at length, for example, your early history, you attitudes toward your mother, or your sexual past rather than come to grips immediately with your marriage conflicts and ways of acting differently to improve the situation.

In addition, the well-trained marriage counselor has a growing body of information that he can give you about typical marital behavior, sexual practices, birth control, and their related matters. He can tell you what frequency of intercourse is typical at various ages, how to obtain competent birth-control information if you are misinformed, and about common communication problems and areas of conflict.

He may, of course, pursue therapy in any one of the other ways described elsewhere. He may also be incompetent. He may believe in and advise divorce readily; some marriage counselors, for example, have many clients proceed to divorce, other counselors have very few divorces among their clientele. It remains your vital task to root out as much information as you can about your marriage counselor, his background, attitudes, methods, and results, just as you should with any other therapist to whom you go for help.

Often you and your spouse will work toward goals together, being seen together during the same interviews, being seen separately by the same or different counselors, or being seen sometimes together and sometimes apart. No one knows what combination is most effective. Our view about changing behavior and solving problems is that well-directed maximum effort is likely to produce maximum results. Applied here, two people trying to change the same situation are more likely to succeed, or to succeed sooner, than if only one is working at it. This assumes that they are working toward the same goals and in rational ways. But even if only one party in the marriage is willing or able to come in, there is no reason why that one person cannot produce change in the marriage by changing his own behavior and learning to handle his spouse differently.

FAMILY COUNSELORS

Less clearly defined as a specialty than marriage counseling, family counseling is sometimes combined with it. Children are drawn into the situation with the parents or are seen separately, with the same or different therapists involved.

While such a treatment complex can produce additional pressures and material for change, the effort can easily bog down in complicated descriptions and interpretations of who does what to whom, when, and why. The therapeutic change effort can thus be overshadowed by the fascinating complexities of describing the interaction among family members.

After all, in human behavior change, whatever the method, the emphasis eventually must rest upon what an individual human being does to make things go differently in his life—or upon what is done with him by someone with the power and control to make him change. Bringing children into family therapy can contribute to change only if the children thereby learn to handle themselves or their parents better, or their parents learn to handle them better. Sometimes guided family interviews help the members to understand one another, but as in individual therapy, understanding does not necessarily lead to more effective behavior. Whether better behavior can best be learned through working with family groups, or with individuals or couples who learn by themselves how to handle their own environments more effectively, is an unresolved issue.

If the therapist can handle the complicated situation and increase simultaneously the efforts of all family members to produce changes, then family counseling may be more efficient than individual counseling. You should never choose family group counseling, however, because you consider it hopeless to change your family situation by yourself. An ingenious and competent therapist can always make suggestions for handling yourself and others differently, judging the results and changing your methods until you do make progress toward your goals.

Deciding that it is not you who needs to change, or that you cannot change the reactions of your spouse or children, is itself a form of self-defeating behavior, and is usually a poor reason to think you must depend upon therapy involving your whole family.

Family counselors usually have the same background as marriage counselors, although if you want to draw your whole family into group counseling, you will have to look hard to find counselors interested in doing so. It is a new though growing practice. The methods are generally eclectic, although you will find analysts trying to transplant their theories into group practices, and therapists committed to other theories doing the same thing.

PASTORAL COUNSELORS

Pastoral counselors usually are ministers turned counselors (therapists) rather than counselors turned ministers. They have often held pulpits, but prefer to devote much of their time to helping their parishioners on a personal basis. Pastoral counseling has the vaguest methods and rationale of any of these related

professions since it overlaps so greatly with one of the most variable of human activities—the practice of religion. Gradually, however, it is becoming professionalized, and with special training
courses, journals, books, and organizations is acquiring the appearance of a profession that transcends any particular religion or sect.

Pastoral counseling has the enormous advantage over the other
therapist groups of maintaining generally a closer, more confidential, and more selfless personal relationship between professional
and client. It is waging its main battle for professional standing
within its own ranks in trying to decide whether to be more closely
tied to religion or to psychotherapy.

Many therapists have tried to ignore or take a stance of neutrality on the subject of values; pastoral counselors are more likely
to confront this problem squarely. They too seem torn, however,
about what to do with the most intense problem in the area of
emotional disturbance—deciding on and practicing a set of values.
In choosing this specialty, they have decided that religion in its
broadest sense is more than the practice of specific rituals and
obedience to church precepts. In their practice, it involves, in
addition, attitudes toward helping one's fellow men, toward choice
of a meaningful occupation, toward hate and love, toward specific
sexual practices, toward the treatment of spouse and children.

It is not within the scope of this book to try to present a clear
role for the pastoral counselor in practicing psychotherapy or for
the psychotherapist in working with values. Some men from each
profession will take on each task; some will try to hold tight to
narrower limits. At best, a competent, humble, objective, democratic-minded pastoral counselor will function in the same way as
the competent, humble, objective, and democratic-minded psychotherapist. He will be capable as a psychologist as well as a minister.
You can probably find out more easily about his attitudes from
public discussions, and about his professional methods and effectiveness from your fellow parishioners, than you can about (other)
psychotherapists.

Yet the ideal person is rare in this profession as in others. You
will more likely get a person of mediocre capability and paro-
chiality of views, and the information you will need to collect, the
judgments to make, and the requests to make of him when you
see him will be about the same as for other therapists already

discussed. The major caution here is to guard against the man of narrow interests and autocratic attitude. Many ministers are used to a position of considerable power and authority when discussing values and personal problems. You should give particular attention, in choosing a pastoral counselor, to your ability to relate to him from a position of equality and to control your own decisions. You should seek one you can consult and withdraw from according to use of your best critical faculties.

CHILD PSYCHOTHERAPISTS

Most child-guidance specialists have, over the years, been psychologists, but psychiatrists have increasingly trained in this specialty, while school visiting teachers and group leaders who do much of the first-aid work in this field tend to be social workers.

For years child psychologists devoted most of their time to analyzing what was wrong with children who misbehaved or withdrew into themselves, that is, whether they had high or low intelligence, schizophrenic tendencies, or brain damage, or whether parental strictness or family disruption was involved. But improving matters always seemed secondary and futile compared with diagnosing the trouble. An enormous amount of time and effort was and still is wasted in analyzing children's problems, which are then seldom effectively treated.

Today an increasing number of specialists are working to change the behavior of troubled children. Psychoanalysts, eclectic psychiatrists, clinical and child psychologists, and group (social) workers particularly work the field. Medical schools, psychology departments, and colleges of education especially train child therapists, although most of the work with children is probably still done by psychologists and psychiatrists who work with adults as well as with children. Very few telephone book listings indicate who are child specialists.

The two main areas of child problems are misbehavior and withdrawal. The former includes hyperactivity, bullying, "sassing," showing off, stealing, lying, and similar disrupting conduct. Withdrawal is much less conspicuous and upsetting to most adults; it is often even considered desirable since such children seldom bother anyone. Yet withdrawal is of greater concern to the child experts than is aggressive misbehavior, since it is harder to communicate with such children who, without attention, may drift into the completely unreal world of psychosis.

Problems and solutions with children are the subjects of special books. They are mentioned here only to provide some background on how you might choose a child therapist. A major difference in the approach to treatment lies between those therapists who prefer to work with children to help them handle their problems, and those who prefer to work with their parents and others with control over children's lives. Many child therapists will work with both parents and children.

Thus, in addition to choosing a child therapist for your children's problems according to the criteria of competence discussed for the major three professions, and according to his specialized background in child work, you should consider his views about the involvement of children and parents in therapy. The decision is similar to that which you will have to make about family versus individual therapy.

The child may be viewed as a relatively self-contained human being who can be shaped during therapy interviews toward better understanding of himself and his parents, toward affection for and appreciation of affection returned by the therapist, toward learning how to express himself more successfully in words and deeds, and toward more disciplined behavior that gets him what he wants.

Some therapists would work in this way with all children, others only with children older than ten or twelve. Most therapists would always also see the parents (or have them seen by some other counselor); a few would not care whether the parents were seen, and would take the child's part against the parents. Some therapists would see only the parents or see the children only occasionally.

The way in which parents are drawn into child therapy seems to depend more upon the attitude of the therapist than upon the problem or situation. The major views are:

A. That the parents have harmed the child and that the child needs good new relationships (with the therapist first) to make him effective. Therefore the therapist gives his time and attention to the child, trying through analytic, nondirective, eclectic, or behavior-change methods to effect improvement. He tries either to ignore the parents or to encourage them to leave the child alone.

B. That the parents are the most hopeful vehicle for changing the child, that they tend to be well intentioned though misdirected and self-defeating, and that with competent guidance from the therapist they can accomplish much more because of their time and power with the child than can the therapist working directly with the child one or two hours a week.

These two views challenge each other at all age levels except in the case of babies, very young children whom the therapist is obviously unable to help directly and where the parents or parent substitutes *must* be depended upon, and with young people over eighteen or so where the parent obviously can and should exercise little control so that the therapy must be done as with an adult.

After you find out the views of various available therapists on these important issues, you as a parent must decide according to your best judgment and resources. Can you, for example, afford the interviews which will probably be more frequent if your child alone is seen for therapy rather than having therapy channeled through you to your child? Do you want the therapist to see your child because you have prematurely given up your own effort to help? Are you afraid to have the therapist see your child alone for fear that he will take him away from you emotionally, or that he will think you are a terrible parent?

The choice should of course be made as rationally as possible, according to whatever method and therapist seems to you most likely to improve your child's condition. Our own preference tends to be for the maximum exercise of parental influence under professional guidance. There is evidence that counseling between parent and therapist produces changes faster and better than interviews between child and therapist, that it contributes to family understanding, is less expensive, and preserves, improves, and utilizes the family, which will have to continue to deal with the child's problems as they arise after therapy is over.

PERIPHERAL PROFESSIONS

The professions to which most people with personal troubles turn for help practice no systematic form of therapy or counseling. The lawyers, physicians, ministers, and teachers whose clients, patients, parishioners, and students ask for advice or support have seldom had special education or training in providing such help intensively.

On the other hand, all of them have had training and experience in how to handle people for special purposes. Obviously the lawyer who is competent in individual lawsuits must know how to handle wisely a man who frequently wants to bring suit with little provocation, or a couple who fight frequently and twice a year want to sue for divorce. The competent physician must learn to do something effective for the woman who complains constantly of head or stomach-aches which have no demonstrable physical basis. The minister who handles his congregation capably must know how to deal with the chronically guilty man and the impulsive misbehaver. And the competent teacher has learned how to constrain the bully and relate to the withdrawn child.

All of these problems can be considered psychological and appropriate foci for psychotherapy. Yet, within limits, most of them must be handled by these nonpsychotherapist professionals. Their clients who come to them for their special legal, medical, educational, and religious services often would be unwilling to seek psychotherapy by name, and can often get cheaper and still effective help from these older and trusted servants.

Yet these professions do not have a systematic way to help solve the most serious personal problems. Professional psychotherapists have often been criticized for treating problems not in their field. One such attack has been exemplified in stories that so and so knew of a patient who was treated for emotional disturbance for two years, and then was discovered to have a brain tumor. Aside from the fact that such instances practically never occur, and that emotional disturbance even with a brain tumor often requires psychotherapy, it is also true that there are thousands of persons in the care of ministers, lawyers, teachers, and physicians, presumably for religious, legal, educational, and medical problems, who more properly need psychotherapy. Misdiagnosis and mistreatment for brain tumor is but a grain of sand compared with the desert of misdiagnoses and mistreatments of paranoid, hypochondriacal, obsessive, and schizophrenic people in terms of legal, medical, religious, and educational problems.

Mr. Samuel Pepper has been suing state and federal governments for fifteen years now, at the cost of tens of thousands of dollars, over a $5,000 piece of land taken from him for a highway right-of-way. Mrs. Cohen has begun divorce proceedings against her husband four times in five years and withdrawn each time. Mrs. Slamberg goes to her physician three or four times a year with different complaints, each time receiving different medicines. She now has eight bottles in her medicine cabinet from each of which she takes at least one pill or teaspoonful each day. Joseph Noven confesses weekly to a pack of "sins" that bore his priest to deafness, while brilliant Jimmy Arno sits by himself, as silently as possible, in the classroom, getting A's in Conduct, but nothing else, while his teacher acts kindly and permissively toward him.

It is by no means certain that the thousands of Peppers, Slambergs, Cohens, Novens, and Arnos would respond better to psychotherapy than to the kind of neglect of their emotional problems they receive. Medicine, lawsuits, confession, and kindness are all sometimes considered to be psychotherapeutic. Yet much of the time such persons are not told that they have a problem in handling the world; their beliefs are reinforced that the world is malfunctioning and that they must suffer or fight the consequences. They may be given no chance to be told and to learn that it is they who are out of whack, and that there is a professional way to make themselves more effective in handling their world.

The wisdom nonprofessional helpers can contribute to your welfare depends almost entirely, then, upon their persons rather than their professions. They can act as valuable friends or relatives might, and further, they can help you to distinguish whether your problem can be dealt with by their specialty or outside of it.

Surely you should press them to tell you whether they think you have mainly a medical, legal, religious, or educational problem—or an emotional or behavioral one. If it is an emotional or behavioral one, you must then decide whether the help they can offer you is worth trying first instead of professional psychotherapy, or whether you should proceed directly to a more specialized kind of aid.

CHAPTER 8

Choosing a Psychotherapist

IT IS important to spend considerable time and care in the choice of the best available therapist. Fortunately, however, this choice is not crucial to obtain benefits from therapy, if you follow guidelines for controlling your own treatment. We will suggest ways to elicit more help from a therapist than he may ordinarily provide, and means of correcting his mistakes, omissions, and limitations.

Not only can you contribute greatly to the nature of your therapy and its success through your own direction, but you can also change therapists. Your first choice should not be considered irrevocable, nor should you continue to invest in a course of help and a relationship you judge a failure because you fear to make a change. When you look for technical help with concrete problems, you can afford to experiment judiciously.

So large an investment should not be made impulsively. There are a number of guidelines to aid your search for a good therapist. You will profit from being systematic, careful, knowledgeable, and open-minded. Seldom do your problems become such an emergency that a few weeks' delay will have serious consequences.

If you do need emergency care because you are physically debilitated by inadequate eating and sleeping, or because you are too depressed to go to work, you can get such help on a temporary basis—committing yourself to first aid only. This will provide the time to choose your therapist at leisure if you want longer-term help. It is quite likely that care and knowledge in the choice of the therapist, and experimentation in working with him or others, can increase greatly the chances of a successful outcome. Most therapists would probably agree that their success rates for a variety of goals differ enormously, and that choosing your therapist with care may be the single most useful way you can help in the entire process.

COST AND PAYMENT PROBLEMS

For most people, the cost of psychotherapy is a major factor in the choice of where and to whom they go for therapy. Private psychotherapy is an extremely costly enterprise, and it cannot promise a worthwhile result. There is near anarchy in conditions governing payment, depending upon local, private, and public resources and erratic insurance company, employer, and group health-plan practices.

The range of charges is also enormous. Most private practitioners charge from $15.00 to $40.00 for an "hour" that runs 45 or 50 minutes. The charges of psychoanalysts in large cities tend to be at the high end; the charges of psychologists, eclectic psychiatrists, and social workers, toward the low end. Some private practitioners will see a few financially poor patients for little or nothing, and at the other extreme some will charge $50.00 or $60.00 an hour or essentially *whatever* a rich person is willing to pay.

Increasingly, health-insurance policies will pay for part of the cost of therapy, but are hedged with such restrictions as a deductible provision requiring the client to pay the first $50.00 or $100.00, coverage of only half the cost of each session up to perhaps $25.00 to $30.00 an hour, and a maximum yearly amount of about $1,000 or $2,000. Some insurance companies will not cover therapy outside of hospitals, thereby forcing some patients into hospitals and disrupting their normal living unnecessarily. Some insurance plans will pay for psychotherapy only by physicians, thereby forcing some patients to see physicians who may have little or no training in psychotherapy. Some plans are controlled by employers who insist upon screening employees to determine if there is a need for therapy. One major American corporation refuses coverage to its employees and their families, who are otherwise covered, unless they appear to be psychotic and will receive strictly medical treatment, preferably in hospitals.

Some restrictions reflect the most powerful form of pressure now being exercised in our society to make sense of treatment, to try to reduce the indeterminate costs of therapy to bases which can be predicted and covered by a reasonable insurance charge. Professionals often object to such restrictions on their freedom to practice, but the professions themselves have not provided adequately for the handling of these practical difficulties.

The problem can only be sketched here; to cover the enormous cost of psychotherapy in reasonable ways will require concrete goals for therapy, efficient methods for reaching them, and effective controls against the extreme length of therapy which often results when treatment is cheap or free.

Most public and private agencies charge something, not necessarily because they need the money, but because they believe it is good for you to pay. Paying is supposed to make the service seem more worthwhile, and also to provide some control against interminability. Charges by agencies or clinics vary perhaps even more than do those in private practice. A few charge nothing, and a few charge as much as local private practitioners. A more general policy, however, is to charge something midway between the two extremes, often with a maximum fee just below local private fees, to set an income maximum above which the person is not eligible, and to apply a sliding-scale fee based upon income. In one Midwestern state, for example, the fee you would be charged per session at public clinics is most likely to be 1 per cent of your Federal income tax. To be eligible for clinic treatment, your maximum income would have to be below eight to ten thousand dollars, depending upon the number of your children and other special financial obligations.

Most private practitioners have a sliding scale of their own ranging from high to higher based upon their assessment of your ability to pay. Thus it will ordinarily be worth your while to mention any circumstances which make it difficult for you to pay. Such circumstances may make a difference of as much as $15.00 an hour, and permit you to see a therapist you would prefer but whose charge would otherwise be beyond your means.

The phrase "beyond your means" is vague. Most people in this country are able to buy a new house or car with some sort of terms and financing, and most of the time the same could be true of psychotherapy. Therapists may ask, "Isn't it as important to be happy with your life, or to be relieved of misery, or to get on the road to achievement?" Of course it is, and if the results of psychotherapy were certain, if they were as tangible and permanent an investment as a house, or as much a source of pleasure as a car, or as rewarding as a child's education, the money would inevitably be well spent, at whatever sacrifice it were raised. But the results are not certain, and it is wise to limit your investment to an amount that will not pinch you for future years.

Many therapists will insist upon payment on a current basis. You might for your own protection also insist on this, and pay only what you can afford out of current income. That way, if you are disappointed with results, you will not be reminded of the fact each time you pay on a loan long after therapy has ended, and you will also preserve some financial freedom to use a new therapist when you wish to. Current payment also places a practical limit upon what otherwise might be interminable therapy, and in the balancing of your needs and wishes, what might be a relatively unjustified luxury.

Often, it is not possible to pay on a completely current basis. The cheapest arrangement in such a case would be to pay when you can afford to do so, assuming the therapist will carry your debt without interest. Many will do so provided you show good faith by making regular payments according to your ability.

Charges for psychotherapy are deductible as a medical expense from your Federal income tax. If your costs are high, you should try to combine payments to reduce your taxes to the maximum extent possible during each year.

Payment problems should help to determine the place and the person you choose. If quality were highly correlated with fee, you would not want to stint. Fortunately the correlation is probably low even if positive. One patient whose friend was paying $35.00 an hour while he was paying "only" $25.00, referred to his friend's therapist as the "Cadillac" of local practitioners mainly because of his charge. Consumer's guides should long ago have disenchanted us with the notion that price and quality go together. Many excellent therapists in private practice are affiliated part time with clinics which offer inexpensive services, or are sensitive to the need to reduce their fees for the poor or for students. Many other competent therapists choose to work full time in inexpensive agencies and clinics because they do not approve of or do not want to function as required in private practice.

CHOOSING THE PLACE

A wide variety of places to seek help is open to you in any big city. Professional resources dwindle rapidly outside of urban population centers, however, until one reaches small towns and rural areas where there are no professional resources at all, but only peripherally related professional persons, most conspicuously ministers and physicians. Although mental-health centers are expanding rapidly to blanket whole states—for example, rural Minnesota is entirely covered by county-based centers—many areas remain uncovered, and even when nominally covered, prospective clients often will not travel to use facilities because they are perhaps ten to fifty miles away.

Most Americans now do live in cities or urban areas where a variety of psychotherapeutic resources are available. In rural areas, an hour or two of weekly travel may be necessary to reach a competent therapist. It is better to spend such time traveling than to take whatever service is locally available without regard to its quality.

Your search for a therapist should begin with an assessment of local prospects, and those within a radius of what is for you a reasonable distance for weekly commuting. Public agencies, semi-private and private organizations, and private practitioners should be noted. Your local family, social-work or welfare agency will probably have such a list; you may also consult your state mental-health department, state or local mental-hygiene, state social-work, psychiatry, and psychology organizations, and libraries.

PUBLIC AGENCIES

A rapidly increasing number of public agencies are being organized to cover states with geographically convenient and inexpensive psychotherapy. Such services usually begin by supplementing private services, extending help to the financially poor and to the geographically deprived. Because psychotherapy is expensive, however, and because agency staffs like to treat middle-class patients, these clinics tend to extend their services so that their clientele eventually overlaps with that of private practitioners.

With Federal aid, most states now have community mental-health centers, and such services will probably cover all states within a decade. Some such clinics are "outpatient" departments of general hospitals; most are independent. The trend is toward creating an outpatient center geographically and psychologically in the midst of the community and away from a physically and psychologically isolated hospital—although some organizations, most conspicuously the Veterans' Administration, remain hospital-oriented.

Such community centers have special merit in their physical availability, in their low cost (some are free, some charge a standard small fee, some bill on a sliding scale according to your income and obligations), in their resources and willingness to handle emergencies, in their experimentation with new methods, in their tendency to be oriented toward short-term results, in their service orientation to major community needs, in their vulnerability and responsiveness to community criticism, and in their exposure to supervision and criticism from professional organizations. While therapist brilliance is not as likely to be rewarded as in private practice, neither is incompetence as likely to be overlooked.

Such centers also provide special services. Psychologists are often available to give intelligence, personality, and vocational tests, social workers to arrange for help in finances, housekeeping, and social activity, and physicians to check on physical complaints. While the private practitioner can call upon such services, he often finds it inconvenient and is less likely to do so.

Public facilities, however, do have serious disadvantages compared with private agencies and practitioners. They usually are training grounds for students in each of the three major professions —psychiatric social work, psychiatry, and clinical psychology— and as a result you are more likely to be assigned to a student than to an experienced practitioner. He may be well supervised, but he is not (yet) likely to be fully competent. If your therapy is long-term, you are not likely to be able to complete it with the same therapist. The student will leave after a year or two; even the staff often has a high turnover rate.

Training and turnover problems create another disadvantage in public clinics: many will treat you as a "clinic case" and consider the therapist somewhat interchangeable. The "clinic," instead of your therapist, may arrange for and cancel appointments, provide special services, insist upon certain procedures, or handle your emergencies. Your therapist is less likely to take full responsibility for your treatment and to maintain contact with you than would a private practitioner.

You will also find it more difficult to change therapists within the clinic than to move from one private therapist to another, since clinic therapists know each other and are usually reluctant to shift old or to accept new responsibilities. As a clinic case, you are, in addition, much more likely to be a research subject. Clinic staff and university professors who also practice psychotherapy privately are much more likely to use you for experimental purposes if you are a free or low-paying clinic patient than if you are a paying private patient. Being a research subject has some advantages as well as disadvantages. You may be subjected to excellent new methods of therapy, but considering the many ill-founded fads in therapy, you are not likely to fall into such good luck. At least you should have a choice. You are not always told you will be a research subject; so it is best, if you take therapy at a public agency, to ask specifically about your inclusion in research, the design of any experiment which includes you, and its implications for your treatment.

One more disadvantage should be mentioned. Despite precautions, agency records are available to file clerks, secretaries, and students. Agencies also vary widely in the degree to which they release records to sister agencies, private practitioners, schools, employers, and insurance companies. While they try to safeguard your privacy and will usually ask for a signed release statement from you for the information someone may request, you cannot expect an organization to be able to be as discreet or confidential as a single individual practitioner can be.

While community centers are increasingly the major public agency for psychotherapy, other public sources are available. In all states, the Veterans' Administration mental-hygiene clinics provide free psychotherapy to war veterans with service-connected emotional disturbances, or disturbances related to service-connected physical disabilities. Most major universities maintain clinics free for their students, and also often, for teaching and training purposes, for local residents.

PRIVATE AGENCIES

A great variety of private organizations provide psychotherapy, some for standard rates, many at especially low rates. Almost all are in large cities. Some are simply business organizations providing a convenient way for private practitioners to use office space, do billing, share office services, and take time off, with no special advantages to you. Others are subsidized by private individuals or foundations to serve a special group such as children, the poor, or a religious congregation. Still others are operated as clinical training centers for students learning to do psychotherapy, particularly psychoanalytic; if their rates are low, it is because students do most of the work. Some are also outpatient departments in private hospitals.

One can make few generalizations about the private organizations; each is usually a special case. You should investigate such resources if you live in a big city; they are the easiest resource to overlook, but occasionally are very rewarding to find. You will need to probe at some length, however, to discover exactly how they measure up to the advantages and disadvantages of public agencies and private practitioners. They can easily share any of the best or worst features of either.

PRIVATE PRACTITIONERS

Most psychotherapists are not in private practice. Not only are most psychologists and social workers who practice psychotherapy employed by public organizations of some type, but a majority of psychiatrists also are. As community, state, and federal social services continue to expand, it seems likely that the private practice of psychotherapy in the United States will shrink, as it has in England, to serve only the well-to-do who are not satisfied with public care. Meanwhile, however, private practitioners flourish in American cities. All three professions are expanding rapidly in part-time as well as full-time private practices, mainly perhaps because of higher income and freedom to work as they wish. They often also teach, do research, attend lectures and meetings, give talks, and visit with professional colleagues.

The private practitioner is likely to establish a closer, more totally responsible relationship with you than the public agency.

He is more likely to be available to see you through to a termination, and is less likely to use you as a research subject. He is better able to protect your privacy.

He tends also to have some serious disadvantages. He usually is, after all, in the business in part to make a good living, and he will charge you enough to sustain him well. You will be expected to pay as currently as possible. This raises special problems which will be discussed in Chapter 9. Usually, however, he firmly believes that it is an advantage to you to pay—that you will value more, and try harder to profit from, your sessions. It is also likely that he will work harder when you expect good value for high fees.

His work is unsupervised, uninspected, unobserved. This secrecy is a major source of other serious problems. He may work insensitively or lazily—in the guise of listening, he may be daydreaming—and there are no colleagues around to criticize him. He may develop peculiar practices or convictions which are never exposed to the scrutiny of peers as they would be at clinic staff meetings. He may even develop dangerous personal habits such as overuse of drugs or liquor which can be much more easily covered up if he is in solitary private practice than in an agency. The community professional organizations and state and federal agencies are much more likely to discover and exercise controls over the incompetence of therapists in public organizations than in private practice, and the lesson for you is that you will have to be more alert to deficiencies in private practitioners and to your need to take action yourself when they are evident.

Well-trained private practitioners are not as often found in small cities, towns, and rural areas. In such localities, private psychotherapy is not likely to be specialized or well supported, and the general physician or internist fills in, or psychologists and social workers may do psychotherapy as a side line. There are many excellent persons practicing on a part-time basis, but you will probably be able to choose more discriminately if you seek the most competent person in a widened commuting area.

JUDGING COMPETENCE

Except perhaps in certain extreme conditions of psychosis and psychopathic personality, and among certain special groups—such as children and the senile—the main factor contributing to successful treatment we believe will turn out to be the competence of the therapist. This is still purely a speculation. Practically no research has yet been done on this variable; what data are available relate successful outcomes primarily to verbal fluency and intelligence of the patient, experience of the therapist, and highly nondirective or highly directive short-terms methods.

The problem of determining therapeutic competence goes to the heart of the overriding problem in therapy, namely, how to determine successful results. Once one can establish criteria for that, he then need only apply them to the products of different therapists who are seeing similar patients to compute success rates which indicate competence.

As a client or prospective consumer of psychotherapy, you are not in position to blaze such a trail to establish the competence of psychotherapists. You will have to do what anyone—professional or nonprofessional—must do to judge, as well as he is able, the skill of professions whose work is almost entirely secret. You will have to use indirect indicators of competence almost entirely, although, with diligence, you may be able to get first-hand reports from one or more ex-patients, tape recordings, movies, verbatim protocols, or summaries of interviews.

You can build up a dossier of these materials on available psychotherapists within a reasonable commuting area to help you make your choice.

PAPER QUALIFICATIONS

Simplest to collect is a list of therapists qualified "on paper," that is, meeting minimal requirements of accrediting agencies. A section at the end of the bibliography gives the sources of such lists, which are usually broken down by locality. You can also get from the biographical directories a professional history indicating length and kind of education and experience.

Sometimes you are told or can infer whether therapists have had personal therapy, if that matters to you. Such experience does not indicate that he has had more severe personal problems than his colleagues, nor that he is better adjusted now than they. It merely means he has had this additional intense experience with therapy as "an insider."

Though there are no studies relating "paper" qualifications to competence, there is a general suspicion that the correlations would be very low but probably positive. Extreme incompetents would be eliminated and a certain fund of conventional professional information assured. Perhaps your therapist should be screened through this coarse sieve, at least unless you can establish his competence in other ways. Theodore Reik and Erich Fromm, for example, have been considered among the most brilliant lights in psychoanalysis in recent years, yet neither qualified for the American Psychoanalytic Association. Many creative leaders among psychologists doing psychotherapy are not diplomates of the American Board of Examiners in Professional Psychology. Of all the guides to competence to be suggested in this section, "paper" qualifications are perhaps the best crude beginning to weed out incompetents, but the least selective for indicating the competents.

REPUTATION IN THE COMMUNITY

A more discriminating step on our scale for judging competence is the practitioner's reputation in the community. Again we use a sieve, but one just a little less coarse perhaps than his paper qualifications. Those therapists of irrational thoughts, erratic deeds, or defective character are likely to be eliminated after several years in the same community. Competence is not likely to be well screened in this way; local reputations are more likely to be based upon personable public appearance and speech than skill in the private interviewing room. Still, over a period of years in the same place, any professional man's skills get bruited about, there is an accumulation of ex-clients spreading the word, and colleagues eventually receive some feedback on their own referrals which contributes to the therapist's reputation in the community.

ACCOUNTS OF HIS WORK

You may be able to listen to or see therapists practicing or describing their work. You should attend any lectures or discussions in which your prospective therapists are involved and read any books or articles they have written. You can ask them for loan copies, or ask students you may know in the field to refer you to such publications, or check in libraries.

There is another semi-public source of information. An increasing number of therapists, particularly those affiliated with universities or involved in research, supervision, or teaching, make tape recordings of some of their sessions, and these might be loaned to you. Or they may have typed transcripts of their interviews. Occasionally movies are available, particularly as part of research projects. Libraries of tape-recorded interviews are available, and while you may not be able to borrow them easily if you are not a professional, it would be to your advantage to get them if you possibly can. The best source of a loan may be a psychotherapist or teacher sympathetic to your interest. He will have only to ensure that the recording made was with the full consent of the patient and therapist.

It is possible that increasing consumer interest in exactly how individual therapists work can eventually spark a systematic effort by most therapists to write down what they do and why. Ideally each therapist's waiting room should be stocked with at least one book, article, or brochure in which he has written out a description of his practices, with concrete illustrations. Such statements would not be necessary when, as in law, engineering, and medicine, there are generally accepted principles of good practice in specific, observable situations. Only anarchy could prevail, however, if in a malpractice suit a psychotherapist were required to defend himself by trying to prove that what he practices is in line with generally accepted professional standards. No concrete standards are known; so the consumer needs at least the protection, if his only recourse is to beware for himself, of a statement by his therapist of how he generally functions.

CLIENT REACTIONS

Ex-clients are an excellent—probably the best—source of information about what is likely to happen to you with a particular therapist. They may be hard to find, but if you can locate them, it will almost certainly be worth while to discuss their experiences with them at length.

It is better to talk with clients who have left or satisfactorily completed therapy than with those still in, and better yet to talk with those who have been terminated for several months at least, since they are likely to gain a realistic perspective on the help they have received when, with time, the glow of the personal relationship has worn off and practical problems have come to the forefront. Nonetheless, even patients currently in therapy can be a rich source of information for you, although their opinions are more likely to be distorted or incomplete.

You will have to interpret their accounts carefully, learning to discount unsubstantiated feelings of enthusiasm or bitterness. No alternative ways open to you to judge therapeutic competence in advance of your own experience are likely to be more useful than this—except for the one to be discussed next.

If you ask the therapist for the names of ex-patients who have agreed to be identified and to engage in such discussions, some will be sympathetic and help you to obtain such information about their work, but most will probably consider you odd and say that they must protect the confidentiality of their work.

REPUTATION AMONG PEERS

A therapist's peers are likely to make the single most perceptive judgment of his competence. While you must be the ultimate measure and judge of your therapist's success with you, the therapist's relative competence technically can best be assessed by those who have observed his work over a period of time with many patients, who know what standards prevail in the profession, who know as well as can be known what the therapist has done and can do to produce specified results.

It is a high compliment within any profession to be referred to as a professional's professional—a lawyer's lawyer, a therapist's therapist—and to be called upon by fellow professionals to treat themselves or their relatives and friends. Often there is considerable discrepancy between public reputation and the internal professional one. The publicly notable may be well past their peak, may have damaging personal habits, may be in serious legal trouble, may have a history of instability, may make a good public appearance but have poor professional skill.

Fellow professionals may be reluctant to make recommendations, but colleagues certainly do not themselves hesitate to act upon such information when they make referrals or utilize the services for themselves or their families.

If you can persuade a therapist you respect to give you the names, in some order, of therapists to whom he would go, you will probably (depending upon *his* own quality) have the best single kind of opinion about their technical skill.

CHOOSING THE MAN

You must finally choose one therapist with whom to begin work. He cannot be a paragon of all therapeutic virtues. You had better decide initially simply to choose as well as you can, within a period of weeks after you decide you need help, and start to collect information about therapists. You can always change as you continue to acquire experience and wisdom about therapy. Above all, the therapist should be chosen for his competence, but there are other practical factors which should enter into your decision. Cost, already discussed, is a major one. Availability is another.

AVAILABILITY

For many reasons, the therapist you have tentatively chosen may not be available when you want his help. This possibility should be checked very early in the selection process.

Some busy therapists have waiting lists, in which case you should ask for an estimate of how long you might have to wait to begin working with him. Others are highly selective about whom they will see and may limit their practice to fellow professionals, students training in therapy, gifted people, or only the mildly disturbed and highly motivated.

A few therapists, particularly those well established at universities, may travel a good deal or take off substantial periods of time for research, writing, guest lecturing, consulting. Before you choose a therapist, you need to learn how often and for how long he will be away.

He may insist that you meet certain conditions before he will agree to work with you. For example, if you have an excessive drinking habit or have homosexual affairs, he might require that you give them up before (and while) he sees you.

His charges (and demand for current payment) may be beyond your means. You should inquire about his fee in advance of seeing him.

SHOPPING

How can you obtain the kind of information outlined above to help you decide on a therapist, before you are directly involved in therapy?

A first line of information can be his secretary, though therapists have relatively little need of office help. Many simply answer their own phones or use telephone-answering services. Next, you can seek information from the therapist by telephone. Some will be co-operative and will try to answer your questions at some length without charge. Others will carefully protect their time and will propose that you come in for an interview, at a fee, if you want to talk even in a preliminary way.

Writing a letter may permit you to organize your thoughts and questions better than would conversation. For a single contact for information, a letter may be ideal, although you could organize yourself equally well with notes for an interview. A letter also gives the therapist an opportunity to study your questions more carefully and to reply more pointedly. Again, some therapists may feel exploited, as if you were trying to obtain free counseling; but we believe that such preliminaries should be an essential part of every therapist's service, that you should not hesitate to ask for such help without charge, and that many therapists will be glad to give it to you.

Finally, interviewing him—and paying his usual fee—may be the only way to get him to provide the information you want. In making an appointment for this reason, you should make clear your purpose so that he does not think that you are already beginning therapy. Very few patients now seek an interview strictly for informational purposes as proposed here. Although you may not in this way be able to determine his success rate nor his likely effectiveness with you, such an interview would still probably be the best way to find out how you will react in therapy to this man as a fellow human being.

You might stretch the informational sessions over several interviews, and you might see several therapists in this way. It is most likely, however, that you will not have money to spare, and that one paid personal interview should be only a last resort when free sources of information fail or when you cannot otherwise decide on a man you place high on your list.

This is not to recommend shopping for what you want to hear. You need to enter into and conduct your search for a therapist with an open mind, curious and flexible, listening for what makes sense to you regardless of its source. You should be clear about what questions you need to have answered in order to choose wisely. And you should try as ingeniously as you can to collect the necessary information. Eventually, within weeks, the search should be ended. Shopping well is not the goal; it only provides the information for making a wise choice.

NEED HE BE A MODEL?

Henry Miller[1] has written: "The great ones do not set up offices, charge fees, give lectures, or write books. Wisdom is silent, and the most effective propaganda for truth is the force of personal example. The great ones attract disciples, lesser figures whose mission it is to preach and teach."

Nevertheless, the man you see for help by the time you get to this point will likely have to be a professional therapist, one who does set up an office, charge fees, and give counsel. Nor will he usually want to have his personal life or his way of living subjected to your scrutiny. He will tend to hide his private life from your view and to hold that it is not relevant to his practice of therapy. Many therapists themselves have problems.

Many advise others in how to conquer the problems they themselves have not mastered. The least one can conclude is that the tools of therapy are still so weak that merely knowing them well and trying to use them does not assure one of success in overcoming his own problems. Therapists seldom even try to reconcile any personal ineffectiveness in accomplishing their own goals with their efforts and expectations of success in helping others to reach theirs. Hardly any are paragons or what they would want you to consider models of the best you can expect from their methods of therapy.

So you cannot usually use them as models for your own behavior. First of all, they are not likely to reveal enough of themselves to you to permit you to make a sound judgment of their value as

[1] *Sexus* (New York: Grove Press, 1965), p. 426.

models. Secondly, there are too many different models you could choose to make it logical to be bound to this one therapist's example. While there are rock-bottom ways in which you might well expect him to be a model—such as control of bad habits like excessive drinking or drug usage—in many ways his preferences in manner of living will, like yours, be relatively distinctive.

You will need, then, to draw a distinction between serious uncontrolled problems from which he suffers, and a special pattern of living which is satisfying to him even if not in accord with your taste. The pattern may involve conventional or unconventional attitudes about religion, politics, social activity, money, or living conditions. If they are not obviously disrupting problems to him, and if he does not make a problem of your differences in attitudes or tastes, you will probably gain from learning to accept such differences and profit from his technical skill nevertheless.

NEED YOU LIKE HIM?

If therapy is viewed and practiced as an intense personal relationship which derives its power from the emotions projected by the patient toward the therapist, then of course you will probably develop love and hate for your therapist, and in general strongly like, trust, and have faith in him as a person. If, however, psychotherapy is viewed and practiced mainly as the technical application of special skills and methods designed to solve problems, to change behavior, to mold successful habits as efficiently as possible, then the personal relationship is secondary. Your liking for your therapist can rank behind your respect for his technical proficiency. You can even say, as you might about a lawyer or surgeon, "I don't really like him very much, but I would not have anyone else defend—or operate upon me. He's the best there is."

If he depends upon the "transference" relationship, that almost magical power which leads you to long to please him and which holds you even when you hate him, he will have to maintain your liking for him; without that, you would probably quit. So he must carefully gauge at all times how strongly he can press you toward change; he will have to pull back or reassure you when he senses strong fear or annoyance in you. Perhaps this kind of rule applies: the less concrete your goals and the less measurable your accomplishments in therapy, the more necessary it is that you like your therapist—as a rewarding force which maintains your efforts to change. As a result of this tendency, the relationship-oriented therapist may very well wittingly or unwittingly develop more pleasing personality characteristics and a tendency to do what pleases you, more so than the behavior-change therapist. The most glowing accounts of their therapist and therapy have come from patients who have felt strong personal relationships in their treatment. By contrast, the therapist who practices as a technician trying to help you solve your problems may seem cold and calculating. But the measure of the success of your therapy lies in the persisting changes in your attitudes and behavior that please you, and that make you more satisfied with the ways you handle your life. This is an issue separate from how much you like your therapist.

CHOOSING WITHIN AN AGENCY

Even if you have decided to go to a public or private agency where you are assigned to a therapist according to agency policies and procedures, it is often still possible for you to pick a particular therapist within the agency.

This possibility for choice is practically never mentioned to you. Almost all applicants at an agency or clinic are herded through a standard intake procedure, at the end of which they are assigned to a therapist according to who has free time, what student needs cases for training purposes, whose "team" happens to get the case, who happens to like this kind of patient. Practically never does an applicant investigate the competence of the different staff therapists and then ask for a particular person. Some clinics would probably bridle at any effort by a patient to interfere with their usual procedures; others will welcome the well-informed applicant, and the therapist he asks for may well be flattered and help arrange for the requested assignment.

In any case, you have little to lose by asking, by name, for a therapist whose qualities you have learned about and respect. Second best, if you have found out nothing about therapists by name, you can ask to be seen by an experienced staff person rather than by a student in training. Obviously if everyone indicated such preferences, the agency would be forced to impose an assignment system. Just as obviously, however, you will currently be in so small a minority if you ask for a particular therapist that it would seldom be an imposition on the clinic to respect your choice.

You can profitably get background information on the clinic therapists as you would on private practitioners, and be prepared upon application to ask for a particular therapist—or at least for someone who is experienced. While agency personnel are usually screened by some employment process as private practitioners are not, they still differ enormously in their skills, and you should always try to get the best help you can.

A SCALE FOR CHOOSING

In choosing a therapist, you should assign the highest priorities to the following considerations. First, his competence. It should be placed above all other factors, and you should make the greatest effort to find out about it when you set out to collect the kind of information discussed earlier. Next must come cost, the omnipresent practical circumstance of money in your life that almost always limits your use of goods and services. And next, the therapist's availability should be taken into account.

All three of these variables are prerequisites to your choice of effective help. After you have chosen a pool of names which satisfies you (and in most places in the United States the "pool"— therapists within commuting distance—will consist of only several names at most), then you can go on to less crucial considerations.

Foremost among the secondary considerations should probably be the therapist's orientation. Does the method he practices make sense to you as the best way to solve your problems? In this section, "competence" has been placed in the "crucial" category, on the assumption that it transcends therapeutic orientation as a major factor in successful treatment.

Next, do you respect and like what you know about the man? Again, your attitudes on this score are not likely to be crucial to successful treatment, but are merely desirable factors to consider if you still have a pool of names of therapists who appear to be about equally competent. Finally, you might be able to afford the luxury of considering the possible nature of your relationship with the therapist outside of therapy. If you might be in touch with him socially or in some other nonprofessional way, or might be considering employment with him, you might prefer not to enter into a therapeutic relationship with him.

Part III

THE PATIENT'S ROLE
IN THERAPY

CHAPTER 9

The Opening Interview(s)

THE CONTENT of this part may annoy some psychotherapists and disappoint you. The therapist may not want you to question him about his person, his methods, or his views. He is after all supposed to be an expert in his field. By coming to him for help you acknowledge the fact, and he presumably knows better than you do how to handle the first interviews—and all the rest—to help you achieve your purpose. You may *want* to lean upon your therapist and put yourself entirely in his hands.

The aim of this chapter is not to encourage you to take charge of the therapy. The purpose is to help you to learn how to expedite its earliest stage, to know what you can contribute to it, to distinguish between your reasonable and unreasonable criticisms, to press your therapist to do the best he can from his own and other resources, to decide early when your legitimate objections to him are too strong to permit you to progress with him, to find out the practical aspects of seeing him and how best you can adapt to them or seek help elsewhere before you invest much time and money, and to discover the limits of his commitments and practices to avoid later disappointment.

Much of this your therapist may overlook, be uninterested in, not want to take time to cover adequately, or disagree with you about as any two people might differ. Your "handling" of the early interviews should have the sole purpose of improving your therapy and the chances of reaching your goals as efficiently as possible.

You may be disappointed with this chapter because you prefer to trust, respect, and entirely depend upon your therapist when you finally have chosen him. It may therefore disturb you as much to question him as it may bother him to be questioned.

The answer to you must be the same as to the therapist: you

are the consumer and should choose wisely as possible. Respect the expert of your choice for his specialized knowledge and skill, and try hard to gain as much as you can from him. Still, your informed participation in and informed control of the process will make it progress more easily. The questions you are to try to get answered, truthfully and fully, cannot hurt the success of therapy. They involve what your therapist probably already knows and merely bring you up more nearly to a position of responsible participation in therapy with him.

PREPARING FOR THE FIRST SESSION

Your most crucial preparation for the first session comes in deciding upon your need for help and from whom to seek it. The specific immediate preparation for coming to the first interview is less vital. It consists of making and getting to the appointment, and organizing your questions.

It may be difficult to make an appointment with a private psychotherapist. Often he has no office staff (he needs a secretary only for billing and occasional dictation), and his phone may not be answered when he is not there or is interviewing, or an answering service will take your message. He may not be able to give you an appointment for several weeks, even if you finally want to get started right away, or perhaps he cannot see you at a time convenient for you.

But you persist, get an appointment time you can keep, survive the tense waiting period until the day arrives, and at last find yourself en route to his office. You may be assailed by excruciating doubts over the wisdom of your decision or embarrassment about showing up, and you may search for an excuse to cancel. Or you may be so eager and grateful for the opportunity to reveal yourself and to hope for change that you abandon all efforts to ask questions and judge this man and his approach critically.

Your best insurance for getting a good start lies in utilizing your intelligence and critical faculty to interact effectively with your therapist from the start. We will propose a number of questions you should be prepared to raise with your therapist. You could record them in a notebook to take to your first interview—a notebook you could perhaps use to prepare for all subsequent sessions.

While some of your questions may turn out to seem premature and while some answers will have to be tentative and incomplete, they should establish the most effective and desirable working relationship between you and your therapist as more adequate answers are forming.

HANDLING THE INTAKE PROCESS

An increasing number of clinics—public, semi-public, and private—are providing psychotherapy through the "team" approach already discussed. Here we will refer simply to the way you can handle the team intake process best for your own purposes—if you choose not to see a private psychotherapist immediately. The most common intake process consists of an interview with a social worker during which you describe your history, problem, and need for treatment; a battery of tests given by a psychologist primarily to assess your intelligence, personality, and difficulties; and an exploratory session with a psychiatrist to determine the history and nature of your symptoms and diagnosis. Then the three meet to discuss whether and how to treat you.

If the place you choose for psychotherapy operates such an intake "team" or simply provides for a first interview by someone not designated to be your therapist, you should know ahead of time what the steps and purpose of the process are. You will invest considerable time (and if the service is private, considerable money as well) in preliminaries to psychotherapy without directly working on your problems. If such preliminaries are primarily for the benefit of the organization—to determine whether it will accept you for therapy, what your diagnosis is, how you would fit into its research plans, what kind of therapist will want to see you— then you should probably not be asked to pay for them. Even if there is some secondary benefit to you, you should at least be told what the purposes of the preliminaries are and how long (and costly) they will be. It is important that you have full knowledge of a clinic's procedures before undergoing therapy there.

If the process seems too uncertain, drawn out, or unlikely to end up with your assignment to a therapist you want to see, you should go elsewhere. Unfortunately, many community clinics have a monopoly on free or inexpensive services, so that if you do not like their method of operation, you have only the costly alternative of going to a private practitioner. Often community-center personnel do private practice on the side and in that capacity do not require you to go through an intake process.

You can sometimes by-pass the intake process at a clinic by insisting upon your need for immediate therapy and to see a therapist directly. Your view will sometimes be respected. Better yet, if you can find out which therapist you prefer to see on a clinic or group-practice staff, you can ask to see him specifically, alone, and immediately. A firm request may carry the day.

You should find out the purpose of the intake process, the kind of decisions based upon it, and the information it is designed to yield. You are entitled to and can profit from knowing the data collected from you about your history, psychological make-up, and problems. You are probably even legally entitled to the results. A parent in New York State recently sued to get psychological test results on his child released to him, and over the psychologist's objections, the court ruled that the material belonged to the subject.

Professionals may object that you are too poorly educated or too irrational about yourself to use properly the information you seek. It is true, of course, that you may distort or misuse it. It requires skill for someone to transmit it accurately to you. But it is of most concern to *you*. In the author's experience with hundreds of patients who have been given the results of their intelligence and personality tests, diagnoses, background evaluations, and even treatment files, no known harm has ever resulted. It is only when the language of reports is highly speculative or hostile that the professional need worry about permitting you to read them. What the professional actually *knows* about the patient from tests and interviews is, after all, usually what the patient tells the professional, put into the perspective of comparisons with other human beings and their problems.

If such information is disclosed to you, you can take any useful data with you if you change therapists, or as you assess your problems outside of therapy. Just as you should know anything that is unusual about your blood pressure, vision, hearing, or strength, to handle yourself wisely, so you should know what objective information there is to discover about your psychological characteristics. You will be operating with them long after your therapist has stopped seeing you.

The clinic often transfers the information about you to another therapist with your permission. Usually this is done without your seeing it. It would seem desirable, however, for you to see what is being transferred, to insist upon your right to such a review if your permission is to have any meaning. You should know what your new therapist is being told. You may want to explain or modify it to provide greater accuracy from your standpoint.

An interesting community problem is involved here for the public mental-health centers: some will screen you out of therapy on the basis of the intake process, saying you are not a fit candidate for their help. You might well object, both as a consumer and as a citizen. Is it not incumbent upon such a public agency to take on those in need, and to tailor services to care for them, rather than deciding not to accept those who do not meet professional notions about cases who can profit from their service? It is a strange community service indeed that would deny an applicant legal, medical, or social services because he is in too much trouble or is poorly motivated to get the help he needs. Yet this happens frequently in mental-health organizations.

If you feel in acute need of help, it is wise to press the clinic or therapist for early attention. Otherwise several weeks may pass between the time you ask for help and your first therapy session. In one large Midwestern clinic, approximately seven weeks elapses before requests are acted upon. This lag is not because of waiting lists; it takes that much time to "process" a case. Private practitioners also may keep you on a waiting list for weeks.

Some therapists believe that such a waiting period is good for you. Trivial or impulsive reasons for seeking help tend to pass harmlessly away, and poorly motivated applicants drop out during the process. Some studies suggest that many people "cure" themselves during such waiting periods just as well as if they were in therapy. Seldom, however, do waiting periods have such purposes. They occur at clinics because several people are involved in the process of evaluating you prior to beginning treatment. They occur with private practitioners apparently among those who see a very few patients for two or more sessions a week for years, and who thus can accept few new patients.

ASKING FOR DIAGNOSIS AND TREATMENT METHOD

The intake process in a clinic or group practice is primarily designed to arrive at a diagnosis of the applicant and his assignment to a certain type of treatment or therapist. This purpose of the process is often duplicated by the therapist operating alone who either gives tests or arrives at similar decisions simply through his first interview(s).

Many therapists, in public or private practice, like to assign a diagnosis to you and decide about a mode of treatment. If yours does so, it should be useful to you to get your therapist's diagnosis and treatment decisions, on the same grounds noted earlier for you to ask for your intake material.

After all, if he is diagnosing you and deciding whether you are a good candidate for his methods, or for long, short, "deep," or twice-a-week or once-a-month therapy, it will help you as a critical consumer to know his decisions and particularly his grounds for them.

The value of making a diagnosis or attempting to apply different treatment methods according to the diagnosis is itself questionable, and this issue has been discussed elsewhere. If this is your therapist's way, however, it may determine his practices with you in ways you cannot understand without knowing his grounds. He will not be working directly as possible with the problems you present, but rather will be modifying his efforts with you according to ideas he holds related to your diagnosis and the approach he thinks works best with such a diagnosis.

If, for example, he diagnoses your problem as a "character disorder," he may not want to see you at all, or may content himself with offering casual advice, because he considers you to be set in your ways and poorly motivated. Thus he might write you off as a prospect for what he considers to be his best therapeutic efforts.

Or he may diagnose you as basically schizophrenic (sometimes called pseudo-neurotic schizophrenia) despite your appearance of being neurotic, and be fearful of pressing you to face your irrational thinking and to change because he thinks your "defenses" would crack and you would break down completely. So he would tread more lightly than otherwise and not try to produce substantial change. In such a case he might even try to strengthen your irrational thinking (defenses). Surely you are entitled to know what he is about in instances when he is not trying his best to change you as he would try to change others—especially when other therapists would not agree with his view and would press ahead with their best, most intense efforts to change your behavior as they would anyone else's.

You are forced, then, to make your own decision. The profession splits on the relevance of diagnosing, on adapting treatment to diagnosis, on changing diagnosis as treatment proceeds. When diagnoses are made, you should know at least that they have low reliability and that professionals seldom agree on them.

UTILIZING A TRIAL PERIOD

In the earlier days of psychoanalysis, the psychoanalyst often insisted upon a trial period before he would decide whether to accept you for his therapy. He considered his work so arduous and limited in applicability that he did not want to plunge into it until he had tested your motivation, endurance, and congeniality for his method.

The trial period might last about a month, and the patient paid for it at the usual rates. It is seldom used any more. With rare exceptions, applicants for analysis no longer get it.

The idea of a trial period remains a good one, however. It is in effect used, even if not called that, whenever a therapist says after one or several interviews that he feels he cannot work with you effectively, or you, after a similar number of interviews, say this to him. A trial period is rarely used in a predetermined systematic way, however, and it is that way which is being proposed to you now.

The trial period that the analysts once used was unilateral: that is, they decided whether to take you on, and it was not for you to decide on them or their method. What counted was to appeal to them as an appropriate kind of patient. You could only decide whether you liked the man or his method, and your dislike would probably have been (and still would be) interpreted as "resistance," consisting of irrational views founded upon your reluctance to face your problems or to change. You are given little credit in this schema for the capacity to judge rationally for yourself.

What we propose here is a more equal, predetermined, systematic use of a trial period during which both your therapist and you will decide whether you can work well together, and that there is probably no better alternative. Whether your therapist will accept such a plan and whether you can use it wisely are serious problems in using it well.

As with many other suggestions in this book, your therapist's personality, particularly his open-mindedness, will determine how interactive and experimental the relationship between you—and the effectiveness of your suggestions—can be. You will have to try to gauge for yourself how well he will receive a tactfully put suggestion implying a judgmental attitude by you, and whether it is worthwhile to risk his antagonism even temporarily. You might be better off discovering such an attitude early and either trying to change your attitude or his, or finding some other therapist who will work with you in a trial period—if you are convinced of the merit of this idea.

You can, of course, avoid discussing the matter with the therapist, and simply defer your decision about committing yourself to therapy until you have experienced a few interviews. Therapy is now often begun in a tentative way, but it is usually because of anxiety about the enterprise rather than to permit a thoughtful tryout of the therapist. You will gain the most, however, if you and your therapist can discuss a trial period openly and fully at the onset, define the purpose to be served, and move toward a more informed decision after perhaps several sessions. If you then decided to go on, or to change therapists, or to give up therapy, you will have a chance to gain considerably from these first few interviews.

What are the purposes to be served? First of all, even though all of your decisions must be tentative and subject to change as you move along, you can decide whether you and your therapist accept a common set of goals for therapy. If you will persist in working toward different ones—he, for example, toward your insight or freer sexual expression; you, for example, toward a better job and more control of sexual behavior—then you may as well part company early. You will be fighting each other unnecessarily. There almost always are other therapists available who will work with you, within broad limits, toward the goals you choose.

You can decide whether there is a sufficient liking or respect between you to sustain the therapeutic effort through rough times. Some therapists will refuse to continue to see you if they sense an antagonism or feel vaguely uncomfortable in your presence, and you might well exercise the same privilege.

Of course, this choice should not be made hastily or superficially. The therapist credits himself with some stability and validity of judgment, and you should assure yourself that this is so as best you can. In any case, if either your therapist or you senses a continuing distaste or antagonism during the trial period which may interfere with the openness, trust, and experimental attitude necessary to make progress, and if this attitude persists in spite of open discussion aiming at dispelling it, then the trial period is as good a time as any to try to find an alternative kind of help which gives promise of working better.

The practices of your therapist may displease you, they may seem very different from what you imagined them to be, and you may decide that you would prefer a different approach. Your knowledge at this point is certain to be very incomplete, and you should not be impelled by impulsive or trivial reasons. But it is quite possible, using all the information you can gather and evaluating and discussing it thoroughly, to decide wisely that you had best not go on this way, that you would do better to seek out a different therapist.

One other major decision may be made as a result of the trial period besides whether to continue with this therapist or to change. You may decide not to go on at all with anyone. At this point, if you have carefully assessed your need for therapy in the first place, such a decision would be poorly founded. You would probably be responding to disappointment about the therapist or therapy rather than correctly assessing your need for help. It would be desirable therefore to try a different therapist or try to correct your (false) expectations of the process.

The tryout period should be initiated and structured to *teach you something.* Its special merit is that you can set realistic goals and concentrate on testing for them during whatever period is involved.

It also permits an easier ending, if you do quit therapy or this particular therapist. If quitting or changing is an alternative considered carefully and mutually from the very beginning, the anxiety often felt on both sides about termination can be diminished.

ASKING PERSONAL QUESTIONS OF YOUR THERAPIST

The most ticklish questions of all that you can raise with your therapist will usually be those concerning his personal background. Questions about his age, marital status, religion, politics, and values may suggest prejudice on your part, even if you are simply curious or trying to be open-minded or thoughtful about your preferences in these areas. He may be offended by them, and you truly may be prejudiced. Why raise them then?

For one thing, wondering about what he is or believes may nag at you, however irrationally, just as wondering about your religion, age, and marital status would nag at him if he did not know them. They may color your attitudes and behavior in ways not otherwise understandable. Similarly, if your therapist becomes cool when you express concern or ignorance about birth control, or when you inveigh against the President and the war, you are entitled to know any strong views he holds that may affect his conduct toward you. You and your therapist might hope that neither of you would function in a prejudiced way, and you may both try hard not to. Still, a strong possibility exists for some prejudices to exist and affect behavior on either side, and this possibility should be squarely faced, discussed, and critically evaluated.

You may believe that your therapist is too old or too young or is of the wrong religion, of the wrong sex, or of the wrong nationality to understand you; but there is no evidence that having the same background leads you and your therapist to more successful results. Nor is there evidence for the converse. Besides, matching for more than one or two such variables is an extremely difficult task to add to the already heavy burden of trying to choose a *competent* therapist who can deal effectively with your problems.

Of course, your prejudices, or at least your notions about who can understand you and your background best, do contribute to your confidence in your therapist and to your decision about whether he can help you. But therapeutic competence, like competence in any other profession, apparently transcends the bounds of religion, sex, politics, nationality, age, and color. Experience and goal-direction are the only major factors that research has related to therapist effectiveness. You would do well, then, to try to discuss openly and bring under rational control whatever biases you may have about your therapist's background.

It is very easy to understand, especially if you are a woman, a Negro, a beatnik, or an indigent man, why you might think that a male, a white man, an old man, or a rich man might not be able to understand and help you as well as a person could who shares a major characteristic with you. But in any case, you will have to put up with a long list of differences between you and any therapist. Most therapists are urban, middle-class, middle-aged white men: many are Jewish, and foreign-born if psychoanalysts; so you won't have much choice anyway.

A competent therapist must be able to understand a wide variety of clients whose backgrounds differ from his. He will also usually be open to discussion with you on any such question and could thoughtfully and honestly preface his answer to you with an explanation something like this:

"It is true I have a background different from you. I am thirty [or sixty], Jewish [or Catholic, Protestant], of German [or Italian] origin, wealthy, married [or divorced], and received a Ph.D. from the University of Illinois in 1946 [or an M.D. from N.Y.U. in 1928].

"You are entitled to know these things about me and to question me further about them or any other information about me at any time you think my background is interfering or might interfere with our handling of the problems before us. On the other hand, even if you are curious and ask, I will not answer certain questions about my private life because it is my privilege to keep it private, and I do not believe it affects my practices. After all, I am not your patient, and my private life, problems, and views are not proper to bring up here unless they might affect your therapy.

"It is true that if I am having a hard time with my wife, it may affect my attitudes toward you and your marital problems.

Still, I must keep them hidden from your view, and you will have to trust me to refer you elsewhere if I think such problems impair our work together. Similarly with my politics. I believe they should remain private, but that will not affect my work with you, regardless of your political activity of any type. I have been able to empathize and work effectively with persons committed to a wide variety of political beliefs. If I feel constrained, I will tell you so and we will do something about it."

A stickier problem concerns your therapist's intelligence and knowledge of the world or of psychology. Can you gain from a therapist who is not as bright or as well-informed about psychology as you are?

First of all, it is difficult to establish your superiority in this matter. Your sense of superiority may be unjustified. It is difficult to gauge intelligence and knowledge in a therapeutic situation; personality variables often overlie and distort their appearance. Just because your therapist is slow-talking or uninformed about a social setting or a theory of psychology does not mean that he is intellectually dull or ignorant about human behavior.

But assuming you are intellectually brilliant, and extremely well read in psychology, or highly sophisticated socially, and that you can establish that he is none of these, then what should you do? If you are not superior to him in these areas, you almost certainly will be in others involving your special skills or knowledge that come up in therapy.

Intelligence, social sophistication, and psychological knowledge probably enter into his ability, but how they do has not yet been determined. You cannot infer his competence to help you from the signs of intelligence and knowledge you may be able to detect.

You may at times be properly annoyed with his slowness of perception, his lack of knowledge or sensitivity, his efforts at oversimplification. You should face up to this problem in your early interviews. If he feels threatened by your bringing up such an issue and becomes defensive or antagonistic toward you—and if your manner in this regard has not been generally offensive to others in your life—you may be gratified to discover this attitude early and to be able to do something about it by hammering out a solution with him or by changing therapists.

It is good to ask these personal questions early in your therapy so that you can learn to use the answers properly, establish a congenial relationship with your therapist, and avoid a feeling of constraint as you go along. They almost always seem most important at the beginning of therapy, before you are well acquainted with your therapist. Anxiety about therapy itself is at its peak when your therapist's competence in handling you has not yet been established. The importance of some of these questions will probably diminish as therapy progresses even if they never are asked; but the advantage of avoiding their possible interference, plus the gain of testing out and establishing an open relationship with your therapist as soon as possible, commend bringing them up as early as they occur to you.

DETERMINING WHAT YOUR THERAPIST WILL TELL YOU

Therapists differ greatly in how much they will tell you of their thoughts about you. At one extreme they speak very little, and then mainly to ask you a question, comment on what you have said, or direct you to talk on a certain subject. When they do occasionally speak a few lines, it is to interpret what you have said, presumably keeping themselves and any advice and opinions out of the discussion as much as possible.

At another extreme are those therapists who speak freely about almost anything you or they are thinking, using their own reactions as a kind of anvil against which you can hammer out more rational ways of thinking and acting. They may tell their patient of their own indiscretions, that they don't like a patient when he acts a certain way, that they are having the same trouble with their wives. The point here is that some therapists will express their thoughts freely while others will not.

Some therapists believe that they should share their thinking with you at all times. This includes not only speaking their thoughts as therapy proceeds, but also letting you see their notes about you. They keep no secrets, and while they cannot give you all their thoughts (if they did so, they would be competing with you to talk), they do not hold anything back just because they fear you could not "take it," because it might harm you, because you might not be ready for it—or for any other of the many reasons other therapists *do* hold back their thoughts from you.

You should know what your therapist's attitude is in this regard so that you will know the kind of relationship you will have with him, how he views you and your problem, how protective he feels toward you, to what extent he wants the therapeutic relationship to be one of equality of information and interpretation even though it cannot be an equality of technical skill.

Certainly you should ask at any time it occurs to you what he is thinking about you and your problem, or why he prefers not to comment at that particular time—and you are entitled to an honest answer. Many patients complain that they go on and on giving information and answering questions, interminably it seems, wondering when they are going to begin getting something back. Sometimes you must ask for your return!

SETTING THE LIMITS OF CONFIDENTIALITY

It is often taken for granted that anything you say to your therapist is confidential. Yet the confidentiality of psychotherapeutic material is subject to many varying interpretations and practices, and you are entitled to know the policy of your therapist. Most states do not have laws protecting the confidentiality of psychotherapy, and even protection through court decision in most states is not assured unless your therapist is willing to go to jail if necessary to protect the information he has. Except for lawyers, many confidential relationships have had to be established by court test rather than by written law.

If a legal problem may be involved in the confidences you give your therapist, you should ask specifically that your therapist tell you what he is willing and able to do in court to protect your information. But in the much more frequent situations where he is in more control of what he reveals about you and to whom, you need to know what questions to put to him and what safeguards to ask him to preserve if you are to have assurance of confidentiality.

Does a secretary, clerk, or colleague, for example, have access to the therapist's files? If he refers you to a physician or a lawyer, a minister or employer, what will he reveal about you? If he refers you to a different therapist, how much will he tell? If your wife, employer, insurance company, parent, relatives, or friends call or write him with a question about you, what will he answer?

One response he might give you is: "No one will see your file except me—and you, if you wish to read what I have put into it; without their consent I cannot show you what others may have sent me. I will answer no questions about you and will give out no information except as you request me to, and then specifically only what you ask to be released. I will always let you know what I have released, whenever possible letting you hear me giving it out, or giving you a copy of the letter or report before I send it. The only exception to these procedures[1] will come in case of an imminent danger to you or others, or a court order over which I have no control."

Few therapists will be as explicit to you as in the above example in their promise of confidentiality, and few will observe confidentiality this rigorously. Clerks, secretaries, colleagues, students, and researchers often have access to the files; bits of information sometimes are given out to callers involved with you; when you do authorize release of information, the statement you sign often is put in general terms and what is released goes beyond what you intended or would want released; information that is kept from you may be released to others, such as parents or physicians.

Confidentiality is almost certain to be even less rigorously observed in a public or semi-public agency, or in a private clinic where many people are involved in the office and have access to the files, than by a private practitioner. In addition, your case may be the subject of discussion in team meetings, staff meetings, case conferences, research sessions, or simply informal discussions over coffee. Often it will be to your advantage to be so discussed, since colleagues may have useful observations to make to your therapist.

However, if you want strict safeguards on the confidentiality of the information you give to your therapist, you had better discuss the matter of specific limits with him. The privilege of confidentiality, when it exists legally, is yours and yours alone with regard to the information (as opposed to your therapist's opinions) about you. It is *not* legally your therapist's option to decide what is to be revealed and what is not to be revealed. If in a showdown you demand that certain information about you be released, he must

---

[1] I have had only one exception in my professional life, in a suicide threat. (Author's note.)

release it despite his misgivings or objections, unless you have been adjudged incompetent to decide such matters for yourself.

All this attention to confidentially might be considered by some therapists to have a whiff of the paranoid about it. After all, very seldom does any harm befall anyone from information being released, and safeguards are observed and are sufficient most of the time.

In addition, a hypersensitivity about being discovered and about protecting personal information, as if it were potentially explosive (when it seldom is), characterizes many disturbed persons. Elsewhere we comment on the irrationality and damaging effect of the effort to maintain secrecy about one's problems and therapy. Most of what you want to keep confidential is not really likely to be as damaging as you think, and sharing it *judiciously* with carefully chosen people is likely to be beneficial. But here again, it is your control of the process that is significant. Your therapist, carefully selected by you, should be respected and trusted; but the process should be mutual, and certainly any abridgement of the strictly confidential relationship you expect of your therapy should be fully discussed with and approved by you.

One further issue may arise regarding confidentiality. You may worry that friends or acquaintances might find out that you are in treatment. If you know that any are visiting the same therapist, you can tell your therapist this and ask for some separation of your appointments. The possibility of being seen at his office by someone you know is so slight that no other safeguard seems justified. A wide variety of small possibilities always exists of being "discovered": a secretary doing the typing who knows you; a clerk handling an insurance claim for the cost of your treatment; a friend seeing you enter the building; an acquaintance in the same group therapy as you. Such chances cannot be avoided, but rarely do you suffer from having it known that you see a therapist, even though it is probably best to be discreet about letting people know.

GETTING AN ESTIMATE OF LENGTH AND RESULTS

"How long will my treatment take?" or "When will I get results or be cured?" are the impatient questions of many patients.

No therapist can answer these questions with precision or even with a good estimate. As we point out elsewhere, the therapist and patient often disagree on goals and on when and what results have been achieved; so his answer at best speaks only for *his* goals rather than yours. In addition, you may quit, for sound or unsound reasons, before he thinks you should. Or, much less often, he may quit with you before you think he should.

The two crucial considerations here, the only ones that you can use to provide a tentative answer, are the specific goal(s) you want to accomplish, and the length of time you are willing to stay in treatment and to get what you can from that (limited) period of time.

You should press your therapist for an answer to these questions about time and results on two grounds: having some kind of answer to them is vital for the coming months since it is the only way you can intelligently plan your time, budget, and such other practical matters as leaving town for a job, taking long trips, or being free of a crippling complaint. Also, his answer will give you crucial information about your (prospective) therapist's way of thinking about and doing therapy.

A corollary to your question of how long therapy will take is that of what will happen if you leave it. In psychoanalytic therapy, for example, you might well be told that you cannot stop at certain times because you will have been "taken apart," and will need to be put back together before you can safely quit. Another therapist might tell you that you can stop at any time in the process, and he believes that you will have gained something since each interview with you is directed to advance you toward your goals.

It is important that you ask your therapist for his opinion of whether you need to finish at a point he approves, and what will happen if you don't. You surely do not want to be committed (even if the commitment is only his debatable opinion) to a process you are told you should not dare to interrupt, unless you have begun it with far more care than you need to give to other forms which take a more experimental attitude toward the process and changing or terminating it.

Some therapists will not adapt their method to a concrete problem you present. If you say to such a man, "I just want you to help me to decide within three months whether to marry this girl

I'm going with [or whether to change jobs]," he may reply, "I don't know just how long therapy will last, but I do deep therapy, and never in less than about two years."

Another therapist may be willing, even pleased, to try to help you solve so specific a problem in three months. For better or worse, he will be willing to advise you on the decision in three months if you have not by then decided yourself.

If your problem is more general—such as describing yourself as unhappy, anxious, and tense much of the time—and you want to get over it and begin to enjoy life more, the therapist may estimate things differently.

The psychoanalyst, however, will give you a kind of course of treatment which will vary in length only from long (perhaps two years) to very long (perhaps five or six years) according to how "well-defended," "deeply disturbed," or "characterologically pathological" he considers you to be.

Other therapists are more likely to tailor their estimates to you in two ways: according to the average time of the patients they see, and according to the nature of the problem you present and their guess as to your desire and ability to work to change.

One highly structuring therapist tells his patients: "After several sessions, I will probably be able to write you a prescription for how to change which, if you could and would do what it says immediately, would make it unnecessary for you to see me anymore. But no one seems to do such things immediately. So a good deal of the therapy that follows will have to consist of helping you do the things we agree are necessary for you to reach your goals. I do not have much control over how quickly you will do them."

Some discussion of this problem is desirable. If, however, you merely go round and round with the same questions without progress or decision, then you may have a more general problem of indecisiveness. *That* rather than the realistic questions about length and results should probably become the focus of your discussion.

The most crucial question of all, of course, is whether you are likely to get good results in return for the time, effort, and perhaps money you will be spending. If you do, you might well feel that any amount of them would be worthwhile. But a definite answer here is impossible.

We have indicated the grounds for pessimism and optimism

about over-all results for all kinds of patients in therapy. For specific problems directly attacked, results will tend to be better. If your therapist keeps statistics on his own results objectively, broken down according to the kinds of problems and his patients' backgrounds, such as age, sex, and marital status, and if he summarizes them for you, so much the better. The more closely he follows his own results, and the finer he breaks down classifications of outcome, the more accurately he can tell you the likelihood of good results for you.

One therapist, for example, can tell a patient who comes to him for help in overcoming smoking that, with middle-aged males who have smoked heavily since adolescence, he has had a two-thirds rate of success in getting such clients to stop and remain stopped for at least several months. Another therapist is able to tell his patients that of those adults, male and female, who come to him suffering from severe anxiety and panic attacks, approximately three-quarters get over or greatly reduce such "spells" after a month or two of weekly or twice-weekly sessions.

The vaguer the goals you have for therapy, the more difficult the prediction of results becomes. If you want to become "mature" or "creative," the prediction of results will be practically impossible. Furthermore, there is probably a strong tendency for both you and your therapist to say that something was gained, especially after a long, tough, tedious process, so as to put the best possible construction upon the end product. If your goals are vague enough, this can easily be done.

DECIDING ON PAYMENT, COST, FREQUENCY, TIME, APPOINTMENTS

If you cannot make cost and payment arrangements, and arrange details of appointments before your first interview, then you should decide these issues during the first session.

You might think that the therapist would take the initiative on these details which may be important to you, but he does not always do so, and you should be prepared to cover each of these items if he does not. He may think that money is of no concern to you, or that you are prepared to come in whenever he has free time, or that you naturally expect to be billed if you miss an appointment for whatever reason. Or he may simply not want to discuss such matters because of embarrassment, oversight, or indifference. He may believe that if you are concerned, you will raise such questions.

You should of course at least know about costs and the availability of continuing interview time you can keep before you make your first appointment. You will be billed for the first session anyway—although some patients think it is free, especially if they or the therapist decide not to continue beyond it.

Costs are usually substantial only with private practitioners. But most private practitioners will adjust cost per session based upon their estimate of your ability to pay. This calls for effort on your part to make a case for a lower-than-usual fee if you think you can. The range of fees is usually substantial, from perhaps $15.00 to $20.00 an hour to students, other poor or heavily obligated people, or fellow professionals; from $25.00 to $40.00 an hour for the comfortably middle class or wealthy. Some therapists will make no concessions, preferring that you go elsewhere if you cannot afford their usual rate, although even they may see you on some basis if you appeal to them as unusually interesting or meritorious.

In any case, if you think you deserve special consideration, you had better gird yourself to ask for it right away. Once you start at a rate you cannot afford, you are both under more pressure to continue, regardless of cost, and your request may be treated as a sign of resistance to the therapist. It will be much more difficult to change the rate after the first session.

Sometimes your circumstances may also change. You are not likely to tell your therapist that increased affluence makes a higher rate justified, but you may have to request a lower rate. You should learn to present to him any case you consider justified. The worst he can do is to disagree with you.

If your therapist is excessively interested in money, that is his problem—and one you should take into consideration in selecting or continuing with him. Naturally, he is aware of the fact that if he gives you a reduced rate, and if he therefore cannot take someone else at a higher rate, he is to that extent reducing his income to accommodate to your need. You may as well be aware of this reality, and then gauge for yourself whether his concern is excessive, whether your financial sacrifice is likely to be rewarded, and whether you have good, less-expensive alternatives.

You should work out whatever payment arrangement is necessary, assessing before your first session what your financial resources are, and what you can afford in your current and anticipated budget. Otherwise you may prematurely run out of money for payments.

A therapist may say to you (or think it even if he does not say it): "If you are really desperate—or well motivated—you can afford my services as well as you can afford a car, or a color TV set, or a vacation." And he may not wince at charging you a third of your annual income for his services during a year. It is then up to you to decide whether you agree with him or have reasonable alternatives.

Here again therapists differ drastically. A few stand pat on one expensive rate, a few are extremely sensitive to charging much and make many concessions. Most will have some set of standards which are adaptable to your financial situation but depend upon your initiative to make arrangements.

The frequency of sessions is also inextricably bound up with costs. There will often be an optimal number of sessions weekly if you disregard cost, and a minimal number to maintain the impact of therapy. Except for psychoanalysts, who usually insist upon two to five interviews a week throughout most of the course of therapy, therapists are generally flexible in this matter. They will differentiate between what they consider to be desirable and what you say you prefer or can afford; and they will be willing to thin out the number of sessions when you think you need fewer than you did initially.

Therapists differ as widely in their practices in this regard as in most others, so your views will deserve as much voice here as for any other factor. For the same problem and intensity of discomfort, one therapist you happen to choose may want to see you every other day, another once a week, and a third every other week or even once a month. A few will insist that you come in at the interval they believe is best; a few will ask *you* to decide how often to come in; most will probably recommend a certain frequency but will compromise according to what you prefer.

The most common frequency is probably once a week. Perhaps twice a week is more common when you are acutely upset, and once every other week will be common when you are able to progress smoothly toward your goals. There is perhaps this common-sense advantage to once a week: a week seems to be the maximum length of time you are likely to work consistently on your problems, to remember what you learned at your previous session, and to be able to endure discomfort and upset while looking forward to your next interview.

There are no firm data, however, indicating the best interval, and you can only ask your therapist for his views, make your decision tentatively, and ask that he be open-minded to whatever changes in interval your experience suggests as you go along. You and your therapist should be seeking an interval for maximum efficiency according to this guideline: the least frequency that seems to advance you as fast as you can move toward your goals. This is not necessarily the greatest frequency you can afford. Several times a week may be wasteful of your time and money; you may not be capable of applying effectively the results of so much therapeutic time.

Most therapy "hours" last fifty minutes. The therapist thus has a ten-minute break to use the bathroom or indulge in other niceties of comfortable living such as eating and drinking and generally to gird himself for his next session. Some therapists, however, cut their "hour" to forty-five minutes and take no break, thus squeezing four sessions into three hours. Others see patients for various periods of time—fifteen minutes, half an hour, or whatever—according to their assessment of client need, their own patience in sitting still, and their financial gain.

It is likely that public clinics and eclectic therapists range most widely among the time alternatives. Public clinics practice flexibly because they often are judged according to how many patients they see. Sometimes their staffs are bored by certain kinds of patients whom they cannot turn away. Such patients are seen as briefly as possible. If they do not need to keep their schedules full to keep up their income, therapists may cut their work by trimming the length of sessions. Eclectic therapists may see patients less than an hour because they practice "first aid," give simple advice or drugs quickly, have little interest in systematic behavior change, and charge three or four patients seen in an hour more in total than they would feel justified in charging one.

Scheduling for a fifty-minute "hour" has no magic. There is no proof of its special merit. It does provide a pace into which therapists and patients often fit comfortably. If you find it too short or too long for your most effective gain, you should say so. It is not likely, however, that many therapists who practice psychotherapy systematically would be willing to change the length of their sessions with you very often. It would be at least inconvenient to their schedules.

One more practical arrangement: You should ask about your therapist's policy on missing or changing appointments. This is a simple informational matter in which you have little or no voice, but you may save yourself from later annoyance or argument if you ask in the first session about his policy if he does not volunteer the information. The therapist will seldom charge you for a missed or cancelled appointment if an emergency is involved, notice cannot be given, or notification is given several days ahead so he can schedule someone else at your regular time. If you could, but do not give him what he considers to be sufficient advance notice of cancellation, he will usually bill you for the missed appointment. The questions to raise with him should concern how much notice he requires and how he defines an emergency. Some therapists, especially at public clinics, do not care much whether you show up. Others are always annoyed when you miss and even expect you to arrange your vacation to coincide with theirs.

In addition, if you miss frequently, for whatever good reasons and advance notice, your therapist may feel inconvenienced because he has reserved a certain hour each week for you, and if most of his patients are seen on a regular schedule, he would be reserving a particular time for you that he could give to someone else.

If he does not tell you directly, you will sense his feelings about such arrangements and behavior on your part. If he does not, you should take the lead in discussing such mundane matters.

SETTING CONDITIONS FOR
CHANGING, CONSULTING, QUITTING

Even when you have chosen your therapist as carefully as you can, and have worked conscientiously to profit from therapy, you may come to believe that your therapy should be changed, evaluated by an outsider, or terminated before reaching your goals. Reasonable ways of reaching a decision in these matters will be discussed in a subsequent chapter. Here we will discuss only the way you might well set the tone in the first interview about such considerations.

Mainly, you need to discover your therapist's views on these matters so that you can decide whether you can work with him flexibly and critically, and so that you will have prepared the way as much as you can for taking such steps.

When he expressed the desire to change therapists, one patient was told that it would be like quitting an antibiotic when he was dying of an infection. It is almost always difficult for a therapist to accept failure, especially when you want to consult someone else. He will often think he has done as well or better than anyone else could do, and it will be hard for him not to blame you for such failure. Any steps you can take to prepare the way for a freer exchange of critical and experimental attitudes toward changing, consulting, or quitting should make such subsequent steps easier.

Ask your therapist in the first interview for his attitude. He may, in response, consider you an uncongenial candidate for his services, in need of analysis of such "resistances" to his services, healthily critical, or whatever. It will always be useful to know ahead of time what his views are. You should solicit feedback from him that will be useful to you in deciding whether you can work well with such a man.

CHAPTER 10

Helping Therapy to Progress

MOST THERAPISTS will tell you that by wanting to change yourself in certain ways and working hard and persistently at it you can expedite your therapy. But they differ enormously in *how* they want you to contribute. Some will counsel you to cooperate in ways diametrically opposed to the suggestions of others.

We will discuss the various ways in which therapists may encourage you to help your therapy along, and try to give you some bases for evaluating these and other suggestions. Your therapist will have to adapt somehow to whatever modes of contributing to your therapy you pursue. He may decide to reject you as a client— or you, him as your therapist—but usually there is substantial accommodation to each other's views and manners; you are each ultimately forced into considerable adaptation to each other, as indeed are any two human beings in any close relationship, no matter how carefully they choose each other.

What your therapist may want of you may vary widely, however. One therapist may, for example, prefer you to be extremely passive and dependent upon him, and be pleased by your constant deference. Another therapist may choose to battle your self-defeating ways.

Fortunately, not only can the two of you adapt to a wide variety of differences in each other with regard to your helping role—if you are both willing to be open-minded and experimental—but you also can profit from any of a wide variety of therapist views. Happily also, the professional market place will usually permit your therapist to give you up with no financial loss if he finds your differences intolerable, and you to change from him if you find your differences persistently blocking instead of contributing to your progress.

WHAT MAKES THERAPY PROGRESS?

Varying views have been advanced about what helps therapy and what is most important for its progress. Some aspects are in the control of the therapist, such as his skill in convincing the patient to take specific action; some are in the control of the patient, such as taking a desirable step outside of therapy. Some are inherent in the method of therapy, for example, the nondirective encouragement of self-expression; some depend upon the background of the patient or therapist, such as the therapist's knowledge of community social activities he can recommend; some derive from the environment, for example, the opportunity the patient may have to establish himself with a family.

Depending upon the approach to therapy, any of a large number of factors may be considered to expedite your therapeutic progress. We can try to gain perspective on them, to cull those that seem to be of most direct importance, using as guidelines the available results of research, and to learn to evaluate which make most sense for you.

In their summary of research data about what makes behavior change in psychotherapy, Stieper and Wiener[1] have indicated these five "power factors": 1) control and direction of the process by the psychotherapist; 2) shaping and focusing of "motivation"; 3) setting concrete goals; 4) using historical material (only) to analyze and solve current problems; 5) maximizing conditions for learning.

These are broad variables which cut across all schools, methods, and theories of psychotherapy. They may be practiced by followers of any approach, and can also be lacking in others. Research, sparse as it is, suggests that they provide the power that makes psychotherapy move—regardless of what the therapist may *believe* makes therapy move. You can sensibly found your judgment upon these factors filtered through your firsthand observations, intelligence, and experience.

Something special must go on in therapy, something different from your daily activity, something that *intervenes* to interrupt and change your usual modes of behavior.

Power Factor 1, the control and direction of psychotherapy by

[1] *Dimensions of Psychotherapy* (Chicago: Aldine Press, 1965).

the therapist, is simply a way of saying that whatever his professional skills may be, the special kind of intervention required to make your behavior change must reside to a great extent in him—else you should not heed or profit from his special services. If he cannot or does not control and direct the therapeutic process, what can he do for you? Perhaps he conceives of his role as one of (merely) unleashing you, or of helping you to search yourself for answers. Yet even in such case, he must show you how to unleash or examine yourself. This is a kind of control and direction in no matter what passive, neutral, or nondirective guise the therapist may function.

The shaping and focusing of motivation, Power Factor 2, is also an active contribution of the therapist, at least the one who does not insist upon reserving his practice to those who come to him eager for his help. For him to see only strongly motivated clients is to see only those least in need of help. To see the less-motivated requires that the therapist teach his patient the advantages of working hard to change his behavior. If you cannot anticipate the gains you can make and do not find satisfaction in contemplating them, you are not likely to work eagerly to profit from therapy, to move toward change. You must be shaped toward sufficient motivation to initiate and sustain tough effort.

Nor can change be random or insignificant if you are to judge your therapy as successful. The setting of concrete goals, Power Factor 3, is necessary for concrete movement to be detected. Otherwise you and your therapist may easily disagree about whether genuine progress is taking place. Setting tangible goals—a better-paying or more stimulating job, a congenial marriage, frequent sexual satisfaction, more satisfying social activity, reduced physical complaints, capacity for relaxation, or whatever—rather than such intangible goals as creativity, social maturity, sexual maturation, or self-understanding will reduce misunderstandings and self-deceptions.

Analysis of your personal history, Power Factor 4, can have value in helping therapy to progress, but only if it is focused upon current problems. It has no power in itself, unless it demonstrates how you have habitually defeated yourself and suggests how you have been neglecting opportunities to advance toward your goals.

Power Factor 5 consists of optimizing the conditions for learning from your therapist what can help you to change. Anything that blocks this process will increase the prospects of failure.

The principles that apply generally to learning apply here also. You change so as to gain rewards and avoid punishment. Thus, coming to see and respond rationally to rewards and punishment in relation to your goals is a vital part of the therapeutic process. Overcoming the fear of a situation, object, or person by doing something effective to handle it or exposing yourself to it under friendly or protected circumstances is an application of the learning principle of "desensitization"; labeling situations and problems accurately and precisely involves the principle of "discrimination learning." There are other such principles which, properly applied to the therapeutic situation, can increase your chances to succeed in making the changes you seek.

There are many other widely practiced techniques in psychotherapy which have no scientifically demonstrable power to make therapy move. By themselves, such methods as the following generally have no demonstrable usefulness in making change occur: understanding yourself; ventilating, or catharsis, which means simply that you talk about things that bother you; analysis of your past, of dreams, of free associations; fascinating interpretations which are presumably insights into obscure connections in, or reasons for, your behavior; transference, which appears as intense faith in or distress with your therapist as if he were your father or mother.

The major value of such techniques lies in the way they advance a particular form of therapy in theory and perhaps your knowledge of yourself, rather than in their demonstrated usefulness in moving you toward concrete goals.

Here we have attempted to isolate what it is in *any* form of therapy that can help you to change your behavior. In the rest of the chapter we will consider what you can do to enhance your movement toward your goals regardless of the kind of therapy or type of therapist you choose.

THE PROFITING ATTITUDE

What attitude will permit you to learn as much as possible from your psychotherapy? Generally it will be the stance of being a good student. In this case it is learning what to change, how to change, and how to sustain the change in yourself.

In today's most advanced teaching methods, the student cannot escape learning if he has the material put before him and if he follows directions. He is forced to learn in order to continue in the process. He fails to learn only if he refuses to turn pages, press buttons, or otherwise do what he is told.

Psychotherapy has not yet been well programmed, however. Materials have not been agreed upon, relationships have not been established between what a person knows (learns) and what he does, and good programs which change complex behavior have not been developed. Nor has the problem of applying a program to particular personal situations been solved.

In trying to learn what your therapy seeks to teach you, you must, unfortunately, contend with a conglomeration of imprecise, often ambiguous, nebulous, sometimes contradictory material.

Of the major variables effective for learning, perhaps the most important is a sense of responsibility, control, and mastery. Your therapist alone can not and will not convey efficiently to you everything you need to know to solve your problems. He will usually do his best, but any therapeutic system is too haphazard and imprecise to be fully dependable. You too must know what you are about so that you can make wise decisions and provide intelligent guidance to make your therapy progress as well as possible. To ensure the most efficient progress, your attitude must be stripped of blind faith or belief in magic. You must assume some control, even if you exercise that control at times by being willing to experiment with ideas and behavior proposed by a therapist you trust and respect.

Previously we suggested that you exercise—and only calculatingly relinquish—control as you would with a lawyer, physician, architect, or accountant. We are also suggesting, however, that you adopt the stance of the good student. This means that you choose, and attend sessions with, your therapist in terms of his being an expert in human problem-solving who will bring his knowledge and skill to bear upon your particular difficulties. Within certain limits dictated by your knowledge of yourself, the field, alternatives open to you, your experience, and your critical faculties, you, like a good student working at anything, should listen carefully, try to understand what he says, and try experimentally at least to do what he suggests. Even if you end up disappointed with the results, you should be able to learn a good deal from him about human behavior, his technique of therapy, or how you look to a trained observer. Even an unsuccessful experience contains important lessons for you about yourself, the field of therapy, and problems in changing your behavior.

To be a good student you need to study efficiently. A prerequisite to learning, in therapy or anything else, is to decide what to learn.

Even if your therapist does not conceive of himself as a teacher (although it is hard to see how he can logically deny the role), nor you as a student, you still can ask him to tell you what you should be learning. Once he indicates this, you can apply the usual good study methods to master the "lessons" between sessions. He may also advise against this on grounds that you may study the wrong things between sessions, or that you can learn properly only when with him in person. Yet this would make sense only if he exercised vigorous control over your behavior during the interviews and directed his efforts with compelling efficiency toward your learning; it is a rare therapist who functions this way.

If he wants you to learn more about yourself and talk about it at your interviews, is it not sensible for you to use such methods as taking notes between sessions so that you can bring up your apparently significant thoughts and actions? If he wants you to pay attention to how you react to certain people or situations, should you not record your observations outside of therapy so you do not forget them at your interview? If he gives you an interpretation that he believes may account for certain self-defeating behavior you engage in, should you not note his comments in a notebook to study, learn, and try to apply outside of therapy? Might it not even be useful for you to tape-record some of your sessions so that you can listen to his comments as often as you need to, to understand and learn from them?

Another way for you to profit to the maximum from your therapy is to adopt a problem-solving attitude toward your troubles, whatever form of therapy you choose. After all, you go into therapy because you suffer from problems which you hope to overcome with your therapist's help. As you would try to solve any other problem, you will need to state as clearly as possible what the problem is, what some possible solutions are, what decisions, efforts, and actions are required of you, and how effectively you are proceeding with solutions. You almost certainly will need to make constant adjustments in all these matters. Solutions or even efforts to work on problems in any area of human activity often generate other problems or new ways of looking at old ones.

One final comment on the profiting attitude: Ultimately you will probably judge your progress by deeds rather than by words or feelings. *When* deeds should replace words of intent or feelings of comfort as your criteria is a matter of widely differing opinion among therapists. Some will expect the entire process to be deed-centered, others will expect changed actions to occur only toward the end of a long, almost exclusively verbal process, others will not be concerned with deeds at any time, and will be satisfied simply with your spoken report that you feel better.

You therefore have a choice to make. Our assumption is that few patients will remain satisfied with only "feeling better," especially if concrete situations in their lives remain askew.

If deeds or daily habits are therefore your major concern, it would be wise to confront them frequently in the course of your therapy. Your therapist may believe that you should wait more patiently for change to occur, but it remains your privilege to be action-centered, to look for ways from the outset to use what you are learning to change the external pattern of your life.

WHAT SHOULD YOU TALK ABOUT?

Frequently you begin therapy with an outpouring of pent-up fears, anger, hopes, worries, secrets, and complaints. But when the flood is spent, you often find a lapse in things to talk about, and there may follow a silence like those that descend on social gatherings when small talk is exhausted.

Your therapist may break the pause with comments or questions which give you direction for further talk. If, however, as often happens, the burden is passed to you, with such a suggestion as that you should talk about "anything you want to," or "whatever comes to your mind," or "what is bothering you now," then you will need to devise your own way of sustaining your end of the conversation with useful material.

What comes first to your mind might be determined by any

number of irrelevant or random considerations—something you had to eat, someone who got angry with you at a party the night before, a dream that woke you early. Your therapist might say that it really doesn't matter exactly what you bring up, that all roads will lead to your most important problems. That may be true, but surely his skill and your resources can be more effectively engaged by finding better than random ways of deciding what to talk about if your therapy is to move as well as it could.

Depending upon his beliefs, your therapist may encourage you directly to talk by asking you specific questions; or indirectly by showing special interest when you talk about your dreams, free associations, self-concepts, philosophy of life, attitudes toward people, feelings such as hatred, anger, love, and pleasure. If he does so, your problem of what to talk about is taken care of at least until you become disenchanted with his views of what is important or with your progress.

The guidelines we have suggested in this book should aid your initial thinking about what your most important current problems are, what solutions to experiment with, what reactions are self-defeating, and what is problem-solving behavior. They should assist your asking your therapist for his thoughts in the same areas, and your trying to hammer out with him new attitudes and behavior.

MUST YOU ALWAYS ANALYZE YOURSELF?

When most oppressed by the tedium of endlessly analyzing your behavior, you may sometimes wonder if you are doomed forever to be controlled, skeptical, and analytical in your thinking, and to abandon spontaneity. After all, "normal" people, who have never wanted or needed psychotherapy, have not needed to deliberate about every impulse before taking action.

Obviously everyone does not have to go through the methods of psychotherapy to attain "normalcy." Most people are trained sufficiently well as children so that they have developed habits that automatically carry them through their lives reasonably well. This occurs not through the self-analytic verbal methods of psychotherapy, but rather through firm direction and action by parents, teachers, youth leaders and other adults, as well as by peers.

Psychotherapy *can* be practiced, with little or no self-analysis, if there is someone in your life who can exercise the kind of direct control of your behavior that most parents can with their children. This is sometimes possible with adults in mental hospitals where they can be controlled as children are. Otherwise, however, it is unlikely that you would willingly expose yourself to the control required to (re-) train you in effective habits. The tenets of democracy in our country preclude doing this to you unwillingly unless you are criminal or psychotic. The best remaining alternative seems to be to expose yourself to the verbal, probing self-analysis used in most psychotherapy. Thus you must curb your spontaneity for awhile, since spontaneity early in therapy will usually be synonymous with continuing your bad habits.

A successful outcome of therapy should be a set of habits which almost automatically will move you to your goals. When this happens, you will have regained spontaneity in terms of good new habits. In other words, only the *process* of changing involves a loss of spontaneity.

GETTING THE MOST FROM YOUR THERAPIST

Your therapist may want to take any of several different roles with you, or regardless of his wishes, you may put him into any of these roles. He may be like a father, a teacher, a controller, an adversary, a beloved one, a magician, a healer, or simply a fellow human.

We have elsewhere discussed how he might thus expedite or impede your progress. Here we would raise the question only of how you can best use him to move your therapy along, regardless of what role he may choose to play or you may attribute to him. You will need specific kinds of help from him. You are more certain to obtain it if you are willing to ask for it, and even if he would be reluctant to admit it, he is likely to work harder to help you if you make reasonable demands of him.

You can prompt him to extend more effort for you by participating actively in, or indeed forcing if necessary, a lively interaction between you. You want him to be alert (when tired he can easily doze off even with his eyes open) and to give you any helpful ideas he has.

You should ask for what you want and press him, within reasonable limits, to give it to you, or to explain why he cannot or chooses not to. You may ask him how *he* would handle a situation that confronts you. You can ask him to give your therapy more direction and shape. You should ask him for his evaluation of your progress in concrete terms. You should freely challenge his observations and advice when you do not agree with them, and ask him to explain his conclusions and suggestions when you do not understand them.

Many therapists will talk little. Sometimes this is because they wish to preserve an ambiguity in your relationship with them so that you will read into their sphinx-like stance whatever problems you have had with people, particularly with parents and others in authority, acting much like a projective test for you. In a study by this writer, several dozen psychologists, social workers, and psychiatrists estimated that in therapy they themselves had received, their nonanalytic therapists talked only around 10 per cent of the time, and that psychoanalysts talked even less—an estimated 1 or 2 per cent of the time.

Unless you ask your therapist to talk, he will probably prefer to remain silent and encourage you to do most of the talking. Nor will his silence necessarily be golden. Sometimes he will be loafing. Or he may be at a loss to interpret what you are saying or to make any useful suggestions from the material you are presenting. Under such conditions, it will be in your best interest at least to press him for more activity.

PRACTICAL SUPPLEMENTS

There are many practical techniques used by various therapists which you may be able to apply profitably even if your therapist does not initiate them. He may not have heard of them, may not have tried them, or may not agree with them. There is no reason, however, why you should not try them if they appeal to you unless your therapist gives you good reasons for not doing so.

Schedules are one such method. Those therapists who suggest them will consider with you what you want to accomplish and what priority you want to give to your goals. They will then ask you to work out an hourly schedule by the day or week, to record how successfully you carry it out, to adjust it according to your experience, and to follow up on it until you have the habit of making it work. If your therapist does not show interest in this technique, you can still do it yourself, helping to structure and put into effect what you learn from the interviews.

Diaries are another example of a method that can help you remember what you are trying to learn in therapy. You can make notes on what you observe of your behavior, and you can write down during or immediately after your session what your therapist has said that appears to be particularly important or useful.

Making and keeping a budget is still another method of organizing and giving direction to your life. While it is primarily focused on financial management, it involves—as do all of the supplemental structuring methods discussed in this section—a much more general consideration of your way of living. To make up an effective budget requires, for example, that you assign values and priorities to what you want in your life. It also requires that you decide upon how you want to work to make money and how hard; that you gain the agreement of family members who are affected; and that you develop the stamina to live by the restraints you set on yourself. If you can make a budget work well, you may have accomplished as much for your interpersonal relations, philosophy of life, long-term planning, and self-respect as you would by learning how to handle sex, children, a job, social relations, or any other important problems in your life.

Some therapists will encourage you to educate yourself in human psychology outside of therapy; some will discourage it; most will perhaps be neutral or lukewarm on the subject. We would advocate that you seek out as much information about psychology, therapy, and yourself as possible by reading, attending lectures, taking courses, and otherwise educating yourself as much as you like and have time for considering other high-priority activities in your life. Unfortunately, most such materials are not likely to be directed to the solution of your particular problems, so you ordinarily will not obtain specific help from them.

At the very least, your therapist should be able to recommend books and lectures that he believes will advance your understanding and implement the kind of therapy he practices. You can hope that he will not believe it necessary for him to have a corner on knowledge about your therapy, and that he will be able to accept and deal with whatever challenges to the process you raise as a result of your pursuit of knowledge outside of therapy. Your therapy can profit from such an interaction.

A similar view can govern your participation in supplementary therapy-like activities, such as study groups or special-problem groups dealing with alcoholism, overweight, or religion. While you may initially try these as alternatives to psychotherapy, they can also be used as supplements, with at least two advantages: You can apply in the group what you learn in your individual therapy, and you can discuss in your private sessions problems you encounter testing yourself out in the group.

Task-setting itself is discussed elsewhere. Regardless of whether your therapist takes the initiative in suggesting things for you to do between sessions, you can set yourself tasks to accomplish according to a schedule that will help to move you toward your goals. You can, for example, decide to try to talk to co-workers whom you have been afraid of, do things with your children whom you have ignored, or apply for a better job that you have been too timid to go after. Your therapist—any therapist—will almost certainly be delighted with such evidence of progress but will seldom directly suggest that you take such steps by a specified imminent target date such as your next interview. If yours does not make such suggestions, you can expedite your progress by setting such tasks and deadlines for yourself.

SHOULD YOU MAKE IMPORTANT CHANGES DURING THERAPY?

Traditionally, the psychoanalysts followed the rule that you were not to make important decisions or changes in your life while you were in therapy. Presumably you were in too much inner turmoil during the process to make decisions wisely; you were likely even to take especially impulsive actions as a reaction to your therapy or therapist. For this reason even today some departments of psychology, social work, and psychiatry prefer not to have students enroll for professional training while they are in therapy, and some therapists will not see patients who tend to "act out" unless they first promise to stop impulsive actions with regard to drinking, drugs, sex, or physical assaults, for example, before beginning therapy.

It may strike you as strange if you should be asked to control your worst problems *before* you can begin therapy, or even to postpone making decisions or changes when they may be your greatest need. Early in therapy, therefore, you should press your therapist for his views on this matter, and specifically ask whether he will work to help you develop the control, decisions, or changes as quickly as possible.

After all, what better time is there for decisions and change than while you are receiving guidance from a skilled counselor? It is true that in some forms of therapy, as discussed previously, you are especially likely to become upset and confused, and that in other forms you are more likely to grow in stability continuously. But in any case, deferring decisions or changes does not mean you suspend all action. Either you continue with your unsuccessful old ways, or you try to develop better new ones. Thus, while you may want to defer a relatively permanent kind of decision such as a drastic job change or divorce, the postponement would not be on the special ground of being in therapy, but rather because, in therapy or not, it is wise to devote time and care to such a decision. The decision-making process should be improved when you can consult with an adviser as in therapy.

You need not, then, accept the view that major elements in your life should be left undisturbed while you are in therapy. You can, with effort, usually get even a reluctant therapist to help you to decide upon and implement change. With few exceptions basic decisions and changes can profitably be developed and tested out while you are in therapy. This will give a drive and practicality to your interviews which is likely to improve the efficiency of your therapy.

HANDLING PRACTICAL PROBLEMS

Certain practical problems in the management of your life are bound to arise during the course of your therapy. These matters may concern car repairs or a trip, whether to ask your boss for a raise, how to get a child to quit wetting the bed, how to make friends in a new setting, where to go for good medical help.

Can or should therapy help directly, or only indirectly, with such problems? Would it be wasting the expensive time of your sessions to try to deal with such matters? Should you ask your therapist for practical help in these matters? Will learning to handle them in therapy help you to solve problems later when therapy is over, or will the therapist's help act merely as a kind of crutch which it will be hard to get along without when therapy must end?

How will you handle such problems if you do *not* discuss them in therapy? You will have to fumble with them somehow, at least mentioning to your therapist what you are encountering and how you are handling matters. He may, for any of several reasons, choose to say little or nothing. He may want to concentrate on what he considers to be more basic problems, in the belief that it does not matter a great deal how you handle daily matters, that they are merely outcroppings which you will automatically handle better when your "deeper" emotional problems are solved. He may not want you to become any more dependent upon him than you already are, may not want to share responsibility for daily mistakes, or may think it is all right or even good for you to fumble through on your own. He may not know how to help you practically in such matters as raising money, rearing children, expanding social contacts, or getting a raise.

His disinterest, his concern about dependency, or his ignorance need not deter you from seeking his help with practical problems, however. By asking him questions directly about such difficulties you can often elicit reactions from him. If you have adopted the attitude recommended throughout this book, you need have no concern about his disinterest, his ignorance, or your possible dependency. You will, after all, be judging for yourself whether his information and counsel sounds helpful and proves useful. By retaining some control of the situation, you will also be reassuring your therapist that you will not be holding him responsible for any failure that follows your application of his suggestions. At the same time, you will be taking the responsibility yourself for injecting these practical problems into your therapy because they are important to you, and because you consider settling them wisely, with your therapist's help, to be as important a function of therapy and value for your money as anything else that can go on there.

TALKING ABOUT YOUR THERAPY WITH OTHERS

Some therapists will advise you not to talk about your therapy outside of the sessions, others will be neutral, and a few will encourage you to discuss it with close friends whom you respect. Which view is likely to accelerate your progress?

Forbidders say that you should protect the privacy of the secrets you discuss, and should accentuate the very special relationship between you and your therapist by talking with no one about it. They may further tell you that it might be harmful for you to discuss your weaknesses or troubles with others, that such information may be used against you, or at least that your judgment is shaky about what you can safely bring up. Further they may suggest that you might use your therapist's interpretations to blame or to try to control others, or to elicit their sympathy; or that you may give others a very spurious picture of your therapy which might in turn upset them or make trouble for you or your therapist.

Dire consequences *can* occur from discussing your problems with others, and you should certainly be discreet in choosing whom you confide in, whether you are in therapy or not. The kind of material you reveal about yourself can be used against you in many ways— an affair you mention to your wife which she later brings up in a divorce action; criticism of a supervisor you make to a co-worker, who reports it to its object, who in turn downgrades you; mention that you are in therapy to a school advisor, who as a result does not recommend you for a position.

The crux of the problem is not, however, that you harm the progress of your therapy by discussing it. True, friends may take a dim view of it, may criticize you or your therapist, or strengthen your doubts about the process. But it is a fragile process indeed that cannot endure scrutiny. Sometimes your tie to psychotherapy *is* fragile and your fears of it strong. But to protect it from all criticism is to raise such spectres of abuse, discussed earlier, that a total barrier of secrecy between your therapist's office and your world outside seems unjustified and even harmful.

You can, on the other hand, gain a great deal by discussing your therapeutic experience with close friends. You can apply in such relationships what you learn in therapy; you can compare the experiences of others in handling problems with your tentative efforts; you can gain knowledge of how their therapy proceeded if they had it; you can discover, as you progress, what changes they see in you; you can cut through the miasma you will sometimes feel yourself in when the therapeutic relationship becomes intense or upsetting.

Of course, you also take the chance that your friends will misinterpret and that you will distort, or that the therapeutic relationship will be somewhat diluted by such discussions with friends. But the potential gains from your efforts would seem to outweigh the possible harm. In any case, if you do decide to accept a hothouse view of your therapy and keep all discussion of it confined to the office in which it takes place, you had better take extra care initially that your therapist is impeccably equipped to carry you through to the conclusion you want, or that he will seek help from objective colleagues if he falters. Otherwise you may be trapped in a closed system in which therapeutic failure is labeled as your fault and the therapist's weaknesses are ignored.

LIVING THROUGH BAD MOODS

You must be prepared to survive bleak moods when your therapy seems completely wasteful, you seem to be on dead center or getting worse, or your therapist seems to be incompetent, disinterested, or even annoyed with you. While we have continually pointed up his fallibility and the desirability of your exercising some control during therapy, you must also be able to recognize and accommodate to the fact of your irrational moods—in therapy or out—and to defer decisions until you recognize that they have passed.

Deciding to quit, interrupt, or drastically change your therapy should not be done impulsively. Many therapists will warn you at the onset of therapy that such wishes will wax and wane with the coming and going of intense emotional conditions, great difficulties, failures. They will want to discuss such moods with you to help you put them in the longer-term perspective of your therapy. If they happen to overlook such a mood, you should take the initiative to bring it up.

One way of judging whether you should attribute your mood to your therapy is to assess how you are behaving outside of therapy. If you are reacting to various people or situations badly, you should consider whether therapy is really responsible for your troubles. If your therapy has made sense to you up to this point, you should especially try to wait it out long enough to determine whether your attitude will shift again.

Furthermore, you should always consider alternative ways of solving the problems that brought you into therapy in the first place. If you have no hopeful ways of attacking your problems other than therapy, and are planning to give up not only on therapy but on

changing yourself at all, you face a bleaker future than that of trying a while longer to make your therapy work better for you.

You should be able to discuss the situation with your therapist
over a period of several sessions. Not only can you interact with
him about your feelings, testing out both of you for objectivity, but
you can also use these sessions to assess your progress, to determine
why you have not achieved your goals, and to find out what may be
reasonable to expect in the future. Such evaluations of progress are
desirable at regular intervals.

ADJUSTING FREQUENCY OF INTERVIEWS

As discussed previously, arranging for the frequency of your
sessions with your therapist is a highly subjective business. No one
knows what frequency produces the best results, therapists differ
greatly in their recommendations, and your time and money also
must be considered.

After you have set a certain interval between interviews, however, it may be desirable to change it according to your reactions
and progress as you go along. Generally you cannot change it often,
at least not if you are seeing a private practitioner, since his time
is usually taken up with regular appointments, and he must fit you
and others into a schedule that uses his hours efficiently. Thus, he
cannot easily schedule you for a session once every other week
unless he has someone to come on alternate weeks; and if he prefers
not to see patients less than once a week, he may have trouble
filling an alternate weekly hour you vacate.

If you maintain a substantial stability in the spacing of your
appointments with him, however, you will ordinarily be able to
change the frequency of your appointments occasionally, with
advance notice.

Sometimes you may want extra appointments because you are
going through a period of great stress or of intense effort to solve an
acute problem. If your concern stems only from the fact of your
discomfort, chances are you should learn to endure it, since it seldom has adverse consequences. A good question to raise before
you step up the frequency of your appointments is whether you can
thereby solve your problems sooner. If so, it would seem wise to
increase them for as long as they enhance your progress.

Mostly, however, you should be able to reduce the frequency of your appointments as your therapy progresses. You should need help less frequently as you learn how to handle your problems better, learn what your therapist is likely to say, learn that you can endure periods of discomfort without harm, learn how to exert effort for longer intervals without the spur of your sessions. In accord with the rule of efficiency that the least therapy necessary to sustain your most intense effort is the most desirable, you should always consider stretching out your interviews as your therapy progresses. It is more economical in terms of time and money, and it contributes to good habits of independence and responsibility.

If your therapist does not take the initiative, you might as well ask him, when your progress is steady, when you are not using frequent interviews fully, and when you feel capable of sustaining effort between less-frequent sessions, about stretching out the time between your interviews. If you do not try to change frequently, you can also probably ask for shorter intervals when the longer ones do not work out well. Flexibility within the necessities of your therapist's scheduling would seem to be highly desirable in this situation where standards are so nebulous. Results in your particular case, instead of theoretical considerations, would thus become the guideline.

OTHER ACCELERATING DEVICES

There are many other ways by which you can accelerate your progress in therapy. Your therapist will probably be able to suggest some he has found useful if you ask him to, although he will probably also counsel patience. A few of the practical devices you can try for yourself will now be mentioned. You can probably invent others that are worth trying.

You can, for example, institute rewards and punishments for yourself for accomplishing or avoiding certain behavior which is part of your goal. For example, you decide that you should complete a course at school (when in the past you have failed), save money (when you have been spending impulsively), spend regular time with your children, join and participate in a social group, or lose twenty pounds. You can pledge to yourself (and, preferably, to someone else also, like your therapist, spouse, or friend, so that you are "on record") that you will not take a vacation that is due or buy a television set or car that you want until you have accomplished your goal.

You can also use your environment to help you do what you want to do. Making a commitment to someone else is an example. Another is to post the schedule you want to keep, so that your family or co-workers can see what you have committed yourself to and how you keep to it. Still another is to announce to others what your intent is, such as attending a certain social meeting on the week end, quitting smoking, or getting to work on time.

Working hard to get the most from your therapy and evaluating it constantly for progress can help, especially if you take responsibility for deriving benefits from it and applying them practically in your life. An attitude of patience also can help, that is, keeping pressure on yourself and your environment to produce those results that can come only after sustained effort and not immediately just because of good intentions or momentary effort.

Above all, you can expect that an open-minded, experimental, evaluative attitude toward therapy, yourself, and your environment will expedite your progress.

CHANGING THERAPISTS

The possibility of changing your therapist as a way of expediting your progress should not be overlooked. Most clients at any one time have had previous therapy, usually from someone else. Even so, changing is so hard for both the patient and the therapist to face that it often is done after first terminating and without the therapist's knowledge.

We would propose that changing be considered sooner and more realistically. It does frequently happen anyway now, but in a manner that benefits both patient and therapist less than it should. They should be able to discuss and agree upon it more readily, so that it is neither an impulsive nor a traumatic decision. The patient should be able to continue smoothly with someone else, and gain from having made the change. The therapist should be able to give up his patient without feeling challenged or annoyed, and be able comfortably to take him back later if the patient wishes it.

You may, of course, change therapists for a variety of reasons in addition to poor progress, such as his or your moving, his sickness, death, or retirement, your dissatisfaction with him or his with you, your improving or declining ability to pay. In such cases, you will need to decide, as you did originally, whether you (still) have problems needing professional aid, and then go through the same process of finding a new therapist as originally.

A useful variation of making a total break with your therapist would be first to enter a trial period with another therapist. You might find that he is less useful than your original therapist, or that it now appears that you, not the therapist, were the major source of your poor progress.

The view of therapy—as of many other life experiences—as a ground for experimentation can be a useful one. Why should you not be able to move about among therapists and in the process gain wisdom about yourself, therapy, and therapists?

There should be reasonable limits upon such experimentation. It is extravagantly expensive of your time, energy, and money to keep changing, and having to repeat a recitation of your background, views, and problems each time. You may be changing to avoid the harsh reality of your problems and deficiencies. You may be trying to escape from becoming "too involved" with anyone, having him "see through you," or feeling trapped into having to take unpalatable or painful steps to solve your problems.

Yet if you operate with objectivity and wisdom, you can gain greatly by moving from ineffective therapy to a more hopeful regimen, by abandoning a less-competent therapist for a better one (for you), even by using the gains you might have made from one series of therapy interviews to judge the desirability of sessions with someone different. Often, for good reasons, change is the rule in therapy. Your problem here is to ensure as well as you can the wisdom of your reasons.

For good or bad reasons, you may not want to discuss the change with your therapist, and your new therapist may or may not ask that you or he be able to consult with or at least notify your previous therapist. If you or your therapist has moved, or your prior therapy has been interrupted for more than a month or two, your new therapist will often not care whether the change is discussed with or mentioned to the prior therapist. Otherwise, he may want the prior therapist informed, as much to preserve his professional reputation for not taking patients away from his colleagues as to ensure that you are not merely a shopper, a nut, a bad financial risk, or otherwise a troublemaker.

As the consumer and purchaser of the service, you are, however, entitled to shop for what satisfies you most. You should be able to profit from any objections or reservations your old or new therapist may express about your changing. Yet the final decision must be yours. And wise experimentation, with consequent losses as well as gains, can be a valuable principle in therapy which is seldom fully exploited.

CHAPTER 11 *Judging Results*

JUDGING RESULTS continuously can contribute greatly to the success of therapy. Yet clients are likely to let evaluation of progress rest loosely upon how they feel. They consider it seriously only when faced with some practical crisis such as running out of money, having to leave town, or feeling quite bored or depressed.

The very process of judging results can enhance your progress. You will be more alert about setting goals, about testing yourself against tasks, about eliciting the reactions of others, and in general about keeping up the pressure on yourself and your therapist to work rapidly for the changes you desire.

DEFINING PROGRESS

To judge results, you must first decide what will constitute progress. Just as measuring a car's movement requires motionless markers, so the evaluative process must be measured against a relatively stationary background. Moving markers can be used, but only if their motion is predetermined. Psychotherapeutic progress must have fairly stable goals against which progress is measured, otherwise you are likely to be constantly improvising your aims and rationalizing about your therapy. Your goals will almost certainly change somewhat during the course of your therapy, but usually as a result of your elaborating upon or making more specific those you had at the start.

Suppose, for example, you have begun therapy with the complaint of severe anxiety or depression. No matter what you discover about the specific causes of your anxiety and depression, and however you go about solving such problems, your original goal of getting over the initial bad feelings does not change. It only comes to be stated in the more concrete terms of what habits and attitudes you must change in order to get over the depression or anxiety.

Similarly, if your problem is one of sexual impotence with your wife, your may discover in the process of therapy that your crucial attitude toward your wife, your mother, and all women is fear of dominance, and that you need to learn how to become more assertive to overcome your unwitting elicitation of aggressive behavior in women. This shift does not change your goal of overcoming sexual impotence; it merely gives expression to the attitudes that may result in impotence. The original goal remains the same.

In this perspective, originally stated goals are usually legitimate and persistent—even while becoming elaborated, concretized, and perhaps expanded to include additional (and sometimes secondary) problems.

Setting initial goals, then, is vital if you are to be able to evaluate your results. While your goal can simply be to overcome whatever it was that brought you into therapy, it can quickly be elaborated and concretized to suggest a specific method of attack. That is, if you come in with a physical complaint such as headaches which have no physical basis, or a general feeling such as panic, anxiety, or depression, the goal for psychological treatment will have to be put in additional terms concerning how you act. Otherwise, the only direct attack that can be made on your physical complaints or bad feelings could be some physical treatment such as rest or drugs.

As discussed earlier, the kind of therapist and therapy you have chosen will to some extent determine how your goal is stated. The analytic therapist will tend to be most interested in helping you gain insight and understanding; the nondirective or existential therapist, in your achieving a satisfying "self-concept." The eclectic and behavior-change therapists are more likely to accept as goals your own simple statements of your purpose without imposing theoretical views of their own.

In this welter of confusion about your goals for yourself and your therapist's goals for you lies one of the more discouraging features of therapy today: Often there will be a sharp discrepancy between your goals and his, but this fact may come out only gradually as therapy is evaluated and in the way it ends. You should work to make goals clear and specific as soon as you can, so that areas of misunderstanding or disagreement are soon faced. It is tragically wasteful to put off the problem for long on the assumption of the therapist that you are being balky, hostile, or irrational, and on yours that he will be able to straighten you out eventually on proper goals. Otherwise, you are likely to rationalize about your disgreement at the end, or end up severely disappointed at a continuing *and* final discrepancy between you and him about your goals.

WHEN TO JUDGE RESULTS

Judging results can be a frame of mind throughout therapy. It involves a pressing desire to obtain results as soon and as steadily as possible. Yet this desire must be balanced against the fact that changing deep-set attitudes and habits requires patience, and that immediate results sometimes cannot be obtained. This is not to say, however, that you should not always strive to obtain them rapidly. Even while you exert maximum effort, you must be prepared to fail or to progress slowly as you keep trying. It is the momentum of constant effort that is important. It is only when you are lulled into thinking that simply attending therapy sessions long enough will change you—that in therapy, time by itself is an important variable—that you may be misled. Time in therapy has no demonstrable relationship with results.

You can usefully judge results from the beginning of your therapy, provided that your expectations are not that you must gain immediate results, but only that you will *try* to obtain them. Many therapists consider therapy that seems to produce results in one or a few sessions to be superficial and even spurious. They describe this as making a "flight into health," perhaps from fear of therapy. Yet other therapists—and you yourself—may be satisfied with such results. Only a few therapists will work toward or be satisfied with such quick success, so that if it seems to happen to you, you should be prepared with some solid background for judging it for yourself. This kind of occurrence makes it all the more important that your goals be set immediately and that the results be judged from the beginning. Even if you continue beyond such an early success—perhaps coming in just occasionally—you can add to the original goal the additional one of maintaining your results or go on to consider other problems.

Some therapists also do "time-limited" therapy. They start out with a specific limitation on the number of interviews they will take to work with you toward your goals. This approach builds on the judging process and makes the drive for results imperative. The goals are set to be achieved in a relatively few sessions, such as three, six, or twelve, and diminish your need to inject the evaluation concept into the process yourself. The therapist and the method do it for you.

You can also add a more formal procedure to the evaluative process. You can ask your therapist to help to judge results regularly, say every month or every three months. In this way, if you tend to be overdriven or unduly impatient, you may overcome some immediate pressures while preserving effective evaluation. It would be a rare therapist who could not be enlisted in the effort to judge results in three months or who would consider such a period too short to produce any progress.

One final gain from judging results from the beginning and continuously: You will in this way be sensitizing yourself to signs of progress and no progress so that you can pick up and profit from indicators that may otherwise be overlooked. Even at the end of therapy, many patients find few touchstones against which to evaluate progress, and often are pleasantly surprised when a friend remarks on changes that he has observed. A co-worker of one patient who did not know the patient was in therapy exclaimed to him, "God, Bill, what's going on with you, you've changed so much recently?" "How? What have you noticed?" the patient asked, in unfeigned ignorance. By taking a constantly evaluative attitude, you are more likely to detect whether you are making progress, should try harder, or program differently.

YOUR RESPONSIBILITY AND YOUR THERAPIST'S

Your therapist will want to produce results for you and, outside of yourself, will be your major source of help and evaluation. He has a dual role in the evaluation process: to observe and interpret the results his therapy is producing as they appear in your expressed attitudes and feelings; and to judge, transmit, and use with you what he observes more objectively in your external behavior.

To use him optimally you should express freely to him your own observations about your attitudes, feelings, and behavior, and also pay careful attention to (or ask for if necessary) what he observes about you.

You can easily distort the objective appearance of your attitudes, feelings, and behavior or display contradictory ones. You may say that you are getting worse even though objective signs indicate that you are doing better. You may feel extremely anxious because you are beginning to act more assertive but are not yet comfortable about it. You may feel and say that you feel loving toward your husband, even while you are making extremely critical or bitter statements about him. You may say that you hate your supervisor or wife for being domineering when she appears from your description, and to others, as a weak, passive person who is merely perhaps less passive than you. Your therapist can point out such discrepancies and confront you with a reality you may have overlooked or distorted. Ideally he can add an objectivity to your views.

He can also observe and point out to you changes in your behavior with him which may be symptomatic of the kind of changes you are showing elsewhere. If experienced, he has also seen in clients much discomfort and many distorted views which are transitory, as they move to better perceptions and solutions. He can encourage you to be patient when you feel hopeless; if he believes you are on the right track he can point out specifically how and when further effort and patience will probably yield results. He can also point out when you slip into bad old ways and how they defeat you. In all this, you need not have blind faith in his judgment even if it is more objective than yours, but instead should listen attentively for his opinions about results. You should try to elicit his judgments and the reasons for them, and otherwise use him as a major source of feedback on your accomplishments in therapy.

There remain, however, ways in which you must make your own judgments about results. First of all, you are your therapist's major, and usually only, source of information about your feelings and behavior outside of therapy. In gauging results outside of your sessions, then, you control what you report and therefore what he has to work with. Your expressed satisfaction with what you accomplish must also be his major guide to the appropriateness of your goals and progress toward them.

After your therapist has contributed as much objectivity, patience, and guidance to the process as he can, the judgment of progress must finally rest with you; and he will presumably have to learn from and adapt to you, when you and he disagree, if you are to continue effectively. From his standpoint, you may have undue faith in results he thinks are transitory; he may consider that you have accepted trivial results as crucial; he may believe that you are quitting prematurely because of disappointment about stalemates that would be temporary, or that you are satisfied with less than he would be. He may be right, but he may also be wrong and he can do no more than deliver his opinion. You may not want the kind of life he believes you should lead. He is only a fellow human with values, learning, philosophy, and goals somewhat unique to him which color his work with you.

If you choose to work as a hospital orderly when he thinks you could and should be a physician, if you prefer to stay married to a tough and bitter woman rather than to seek a warm and loving one, if you decide to lead an asexual life instead of taking advantage of opportunities for close friendships that could include sexual activity, he must stand back and watch you retain control of your life despite his different wishes for you. If he is open-minded, he will learn from such experiences that the human being is capable of more varieties of satisfaction and ways of living in harmony with his world than he might so far have considered. And he will be a better therapist in the future for having worked with you. You may also discover with time that you were wrong and he was right, but it is also your prerogative to postpone such discoveries until your additional experience permits you to arrive at them yourself. Even in such instances, your own ways and time of changing may be better in the long run than accepting and using his views without conviction.

YOU AND YOUR THERAPIST

Several methods are available to you for judging results. We have already discussed how you and your therapist will be the major sources of judgment and can use each other well. For yourself, you will have subjective views—the feelings and attitudes you sense and express from within without measuring them strictly against your external performance in your world. You can also utilize more objective views as you measure yourself against people, objects, and activities around you and try to gain a clear picture of your interaction with them.

Your therapist, too, will function both subjectively and objectively (but hopefully more the latter); he tries gradually to turn himself into a behavioral scientist as he gains knowledge, and his profession into a behavior science as a body of research accumulates. Meanwhile, he will be judging results both through his observations of what is happening, and through placing them in the perspective of his ever-increasing experience.

PROFESSIONAL CONSULTATION

There are other and more objective sources of evidence about your progress than the two of you in the therapist's office. One source which blends the process of therapy with the view of an outsider is available through professional consultation.

Professional consultations are extremely rare in the private practice of psychotherapy. Young therapists may, on their own and without the knowledge of the patient, consult with teachers or with their *own* therapist (if they are in training or receiving personal therapy themselves). In public agencies and hospitals, junior therapists often voluntarily or as a requirement consult with supervisors, or present their cases at meetings for criticism.

The patient seldom has a voice in such consultations as do occur. Yet, as we stress throughout this book, it is the patient who should have most reason to initiate, participate in, and profit from consultation.

The problem is frequently faced in medicine, where patients seek expert views to supplement those of their physician. They also change doctors freely when dissatisfied with treatment. You are especially handicapped in trying to decide where to obtain expert consultation in psychotherapy. In psychotherapy there are no advanced technique or referral centers such as the Mayo Clinic or the major heart, cancer, and surgery centers that exist in medicine. Nor are any psychotherapists known to have outstanding success rates comparable to those of leading surgeons or lawyers. The psychotherapy experts are noted for their stimulating thinking and verbal competence rather than for research-established therapeutic success.

Suppose you decide to try to obtain another expert opinion of your progress and advice about what to do about it. The guidelines for finding a capable consultant must be the same as those used in choosing your therapist in the first place—except that you should have gained some added wisdom from experience with your current therapy.

The major obstacle to obtaining such a consultation—assuming you are objective in deciding upon its desirability and your therapist is interested in it—will be the feelings of your therapist and your comfort in handling them.

It is seldom easy to suggest to a professional man that you would like to add another expert opinion to his, for professionals in all fields vary in reacting to such a suggestion. In the field of psychotherapy they are especially sensitive. While acknowledging their clients' right to free choice, change, and consultation, many physicians, lawyers, and psychotherapists will take it hard, viewing the idea as a challenge to their judgment and skill. They will ask themselves—and perhaps you—"Don't you think I'm good enough?" "Are you dissatisfied with my methods?" "What makes you think anyone else can do better?" Even very capable and successful professionals may criticize, subtly or otherwise, the experts you propose to consult; they may imply that you would waste your money; they may even attack your uncertainty about your treatment as perverse or irrational.

Yet the wiser and humbler professional man will not be upset by your suggestion. He may view it as a whim or an extravagance, but at best he will consider it a useful opportunity for the two of you to see how someone else will react to your problems and his treatment of them. He may as a consequence lose you as a patient, and your loss would probably bother him. Yet he cannot always succeed, and he can learn from others, even if you are misconceiving his methods and accomplishments with you.

You can hope that your desire for a consultation may be fully discussed with your therapist, and that he will respect your wish (if it is not an unreasonable impulse from which he can dissuade you), that he might even suggest consultants to you, that he will pass on his information and opinions to the consultant you choose if you want him to, and finally, that he and you will discuss fully the results of your consultation and make congenial decisions together about it and your future therapy.

Ideally, such would be the process. Yet it can easily get stalled on any step. You may be afraid to propose it to your therapist, and he may be annoyed or defensive if you do. If you are fearful, or if he is upset, you can even gain from discovering and handling such attitudes since they will probably interfere with other important subjects which should be discussed between you. If, for example, you are also too fearful to tell him you have begun drinking (again) on the sly, or that you are not taking a two-week vacation trip because he seemed upset that last time you did it, you are neglecting kinds of problems that should not be evaded in or out of therapy.

He may recommend consultants who are his friends or who he knows to agree with his views; he may be reluctant to pass his material on to them (even though, if you ask him to, he is probably legally required to do so if it is factual rather than speculative); he may prefer not to discuss the consultant's findings with you. If he balks, you must take up the reins and move as wisely as you can on your own behalf.

In obtaining a consultation you take a chance that your therapist, who had seemed to like you and to want sincerely to help you, might seem to turn against you. He may actually be annoyed, or you may only imagine he is. In either case you might feel you had lost a good relationship. Such difficulties, however, must be handled to permit you to move toward realistic and more fully gratifying relationships with anyone, including your therapist. Founded on a childlike innocence and desire always to please each other, the therapeutic relationship becomes a daydream, a curtain between you and effective ways to cope with your concrete world.

Finally, a note about asking your therapist himself to obtain a consultation about you: While you might consider it more politic to ask that he consult with someone, rather than doing so yourself, you would probably find him responding essentially with, "I would already have done so if I thought I should." It is *your* judgment, not his, that is involved. You, not he, are acting uncertain, and you therefore must initiate and perhaps follow through on the consultation. Your therapist is not likely to have his heart in it, or else he would have been the initiator.

FRIENDS, RELATIVES, AND OTHERS

Anyone who knows you, observes you, or interacts with you, and whose judgment you respect, is a possible source of useful evaluation of your therapy. Friends, relatives, co-workers, ministers, fellow club members, many persons can provide a touchstone against which you can test yourself and obtain reactions that will help you to judge your results.

You need not confide your problems to them to gain help from them. You can try out new modes of behavior and watch how they react to them. You can ask how they like your first effort at public speaking or talking on a motion. For the first time you might discuss with your husband directly your apprehensions about how he is ignoring your son, or with your wife, her seeming indifference to your job, and profit from their reactions.

Whenever you interact with others, you will obtain feedback of some sort that you can put to good use in judging your progress. The person need not know that you are using him to help judge results of your therapy. His actions or words in response to your changing behavior may speak louder of your progress than direct discussion about your therapy.

Of course, you can also consult with him directly about changes he may have observed in you and, in observing social courtesies, simply has chosen not to mention. He may think that you are being curt socially or preoccupied, he may notice that you are more relaxed and comfortable to be with, he may believe that you are showing more interest in others, more efficiency in your work, or more callousness or arrogance in dealing with others. If you trust and respect him—a few such persons, if you are fortunate, may exist in your life—you may confide in him about your therapy and derive considerable benefit from gaining his opinions about changes in you.

TEST RESULTS

Occasionally a therapist or agency will repeat during therapy a test or tests given when you begin therapy. Particularly in the area of personality measures, interesting changes may be reflected. Psychological tests are not, however, a good source of measurement of behavior, attitude, or personality changes. They are not nearly as good as intelligence, interest, and achievement tests are in their areas. They merely can suggest, very crudely, some ways in which your standing relative to a large group of people with backgrounds somewhat resembling yours may have changed during your therapy.

For example, you may appear on the test to have moved toward increased or decreased feelings of depression, toward more, or less, bizarre thinking, toward greater or lessened suspiciousness. While such results should be telling you nothing that has not been or at least could not be inferred from the discussions in your therapy sessions, they may occasionally point up areas of change that have been overlooked.

Some tests, most conspicuously the Minnesota Multiphasic Personality Inventory, are so simple and inexpensive to give, score, and interpret that it seems a pity not to have them available initially and at regular intervals, say every three or six months during the course of your therapy, until proven useless. Even if they only occasionally furnish useful leads, they may be worthwhile.

CURRENT ACHIEVEMENTS

Best of all from the standpoint of future significance in your life is the method of evaluating results that emphasizes concrete achievements. By achievements we do not necessarily mean material gains, competitive improvement, self-aggrandizement, or power—although if these are your goals, then accomplishing them is a legitimate measure of your progress.

Achievement can also mean learning to live your life in an equable way with a person or persons you like without needing to strive for things. Even if you turn inward to a life primarily of quiet contemplation and are satisfied with that as the major outcome of your therapy, you have in our sense here achieved a concrete goal—in the way your life will appear, the form it will take objectively. It can be described strictly from outside of you by a stranger observing how you act.

We emphasize, then, achieving specific goals in living and measuring your progress by how successfully you have been able to live in any such ways you may set for yourself. The more specific the goals and ways, the more readily you can measure your progress.

HOW MUCH TO EXPECT (AND HOW SOON)

At the beginning of this chapter we discussed how you can begin measuring your progress from the very first interview and continuously thereafter. We discussed how each session can be conducted to move you along as fast as possible toward your goals even if it does not produce gains each time. Even with those therapists who caution you to be patient, not to expect progress each session, to anticipate setbacks and even disruption and regression en route to your goals—even such therapists can provide a structure for measuring your progress at each session. At least they can try to explain why you have plateaus or setbacks when they occur so that you can judge for yourself whether and how you could have done better.

You may be told, for example, that you are feeling extremely depressed or anxious during a week or two because you are reexperiencing the anguish of being a child helpless in the clutches of an exploitative or seductive parent. Your therapist may want you to go through such a period, may think it is necessary before you can establish realistic, satisfying relationships with your spouse or superiors today. You can profit from being told that such an upset, in your therapist's view, represents progress toward a goal he has in mind. Another therapist will not care to have you go through such misery, will not consider it necessary to establish good relationships in the present. He will be trying to help you more directly in the current situation and not require you to "relive" the anguish of the past.

In addition to the ways in which the therapist, the method of therapy, and your efforts will determine your progress, your original condition and your goals will also contribute to it.

We have already described how certain kinds of patients tend to respond better to conventional forms of psychotherapy, and are therefore labeled "good" patients. Such clients tend to be the least disturbed. There is this paradox, however: The most extremely disrupted also can make the greatest gains because they have the farthest to go. If you come in practically incapacitated—lying in bed all day, totally exhausted and unable to work, so fearful that you can talk to no one, or almost unable to eat or sleep—you can show dramatic gains simply by getting out of bed, talking, or eating and sleeping adequately. On the other hand, if you are already doing these elementary things and are seeking help only because of vague feelings of dissatisfaction or depression, only more modest and less dramatic gains are possible.

For a psychotic person, simply to get out of a mental hospital, on heavy doses of drugs that greatly reduce his potential powers, is a major achievement, even if he is then merely at or below a point at which many nonhospitalized persons begin their therapy.

It is a major theme of this book that you should choose your therapist with wisdom, and then work as hard as you can to achieve realistic goals, and that you can thereby get more from it than you otherwise would. But your expectations can also be nebulous, idealistic, romantic, or magical. You may hope for a grand, shiny new life. Therapists often contribute to such excessive expectations by talking and writing vaguely of "basic change," "freeing the creative spirit," "achieving full maturity." Occasionally a client will consider that he or she has become a totally new person, will feel "liberated," will speak of a miracle performed. Sometimes to friends, the change will appear in no sense so dramatic, and to them he will seem euphoric about very small gains. Very rarely will the change both be felt and appear dramatic.

For an overwhelming number of patients, changes will be modest at best, whatever the form of therapy chosen. To begin by expecting dramatic improvement in your behavior is to court severe disappointment sooner or later, Besides, such false expectations may lead you to avoid more realistic though modest goals, and the sustained, tough effort required to accomplish even them. If your frame of mind is simply to attend sessions, to talk freely, and then to wait for big things to happen to you, you are likely to reduce your chances for *any* gains.

Within broad limits, however, you can set goals which in discussion with your therapist can determine realistically what to expect from therapy. Therapists will of course differ in their optimism—and competence—about moving you toward goals. While they may in a vague way seem to encourage grand aims, they will often try to shrink your goals when you make them concrete. If you are over forty, some may consider the pursuit of further education and radical occupational change to be unrealistic; others will encourage and work toward such goals—if they are within your measured aptitudes—almost regardless of your age. Therapists differ similarly about sexual satisfaction, some writing off your problems as hopeless if you are over forty or fifty, others willing to work with you to gain satisfaction at any age.

Much of what you can expect will have to be determined finally by you and what you are willing to work toward. You will have to accept realistic limits imposed by your physical and psychological resources. Beyond those, however, you can set modest goals or fairly large ones, and you can expect to make progress toward them if you work hard and in small but concrete steps.

OBSTACLES TO PROGRESS

Because the definitions and measures of progress are so diverse, trying to describe obstacles to progress becomes even more torturous. Yet you will frequently encounter factors that you can recognize as slowing up or blocking progress, and you will progress better when they are removed.

One such obstacle may be fear of change. Many people are afraid of exposure to any force that may make them change, as if it were to be done against their will, or without their awareness, so that they might end up as someone they would not recognize, as if they would lose their "self." There is the same fear about hypnosis, brainwashing, and high-pressure salesmanship.

If you gain the control and direction of your therapy suggested throughout this book, any realistic fears of changing or being influenced in ways of which you are not aware should be dissipated. Therapy seldom operates very powerfully to produce change (when it does develop such tools, then fears of being changed "against your will" would be justified and extremely important for society to act upon). Fears of being changed in ways you might not approve of are probably best handled by making your own goals explicit, by asking your therapist to explain what he is doing and why, and by exercising your privilege of disagreeing with him and rejecting his suggestions when they do not agree with your purpose or judgment.

The fear of changing maintained beyond the above limits and without the lines of control indicated above, is obviously a serious obstacle to achieving your goals and should be attacked as soon as possible. It is frequent early in therapy and tends to dissipate in the face of the realities of what happens in treatment. But to ignore it may extend therapy greatly.

You may also choose to deny to yourself and others that you are making progress when you really are by signs that others can observe. The perversity of the human mind knows few limits. That you should choose to deny progress when, by objective measures, you are moving toward your goals has various ingenious explanations. You may not want to admit that you needed and are profiting from professional help. You may be annoyed with the therapist and not want to give him the satisfaction of indicating his value. You may be afraid that if you indicate progress he will terminate your treatment. The more specific you make your goals, however, the more difficult it will be for you to deny realistic progress. It is one thing to say that you feel no better or that you are no more relaxed in your social behavior; it is another to say that you are not furthering your education when you are actually taking courses successfully, or that you are not more active socially when you have begun to take your wife out and to go to parties.

Another obstacle to progress may lie in the pursuit of different goals by you and your therapist. In that case, either of you may believe that you are not making progress when the other believes you are, and the efforts of the party believing that no progress is being made may be diverted from the path of change. You should, of course, strive hard to make your goals both clear and mutual; but if they are not, then at least you should either change yours or his, or insist that your therapist assist you toward yours.

You and your therapist may become personal adversaries, and of course this will impede progress. We distinguish this from an adversary situation where the therapist stands against your self-defeating behavior and tries to block it, while also trying to get you to try new ways. He would thus represent the hopeful, striving side of you. Here we refer to a personalized enmity, however, which sometimes develops in therapy—you toward his person, or he toward your person. If you cannot rid yourself of such an attitude and get back on the main track of your problems within a session or two, and if such enmity is not characteristic of your behavior outside of therapy, then a serious obstacle to progress exists that should not be tolerated for long.

Another kind of obstacle may lie in your environment. You may be living with or inextricably intertwined socially with in-laws who dominate your spouse. You may persist in working in a school or agency where you cannot be promoted to a position that will challenge you. You may continue to live in a small town which stifles you or in a big city where you have trouble breaking a depressing social pattern. The major factor that seems to determine the adjustment of patients after hospitalization for emotional conditions or drug addiction is whether they return to an environment more favorable than before.

Although your environment may thus operate as an obstacle, it is also subject to some control and choice by you, and is in this regard a proper focus for therapy. You can try to change your environment in reasonable ways, performing a kind of bootstrap operation whereby an enforced change in environment might be tried to produce change in your behavior, or you can go about changing your environment or your choice of environment as the goal of your therapy. In any case, if you have substantial environmental stress, it will act as an obstacle to progress unless it is faced and handled effectively. It can easily stifle your individual efforts otherwise.

An appearance of no progress may also occur if you do not attempt to apply new knowledge and attitudes picked up in therapy to your life outside of therapy. Unless you try to apply the gains from your interviews in your daily life, you do not know for sure what progress you have made. What may seem to be no progress may turn out to be substantial change when you put yourself to the test. You may think that you have drifted along in therapy without result, and then when you finally attend a social event, discover that you are for the first time relaxed and can enjoy yourself.

In summary, then, the process of judging results is continuous and is determined by the type of therapy, your therapist, and you.

Your choice of goals must guide your evaluation of results and be an integral part of the process. Above all, your wise exercise of judgment should determine and guide continuously the course of your therapy.

CHAPTER 12

Terminating

LIKE THE judgment of progress, the process of terminating psycho-therapy begins with the first interview. You state your goals, shape them to be realistic, and quit when they are achieved. You may elaborate and modify them as you go along, but seldom so much that they lose all consistency or stability. Otherwise, therapy would never end.

If you begin because you are extremely anxious or depressed, you should logically quit therapy when your anxiety and depression have diminished sufficiently and over a long enough time to make you confident about your future ability to control them and to function well. You may also decide during therapy to get married, change jobs, or quit smoking, although such problems might not relate to your original reason for seeking help. Your original goal would seldom change, although it might be necessary to handle other problems in order to get over your initial complaints, or it might be desirable to attack other problems in order to take full advantage of your professional help.

The clarity and ease with which you terminate will be a function of how your therapy is planned and conducted. The more ambiguous your goals, the more difficult it will be to terminate. The stronger the personal relationship between you and your therapist and the greater the emphasis on emotion rather than reason, the harder it will be for you to break off. If your therapy is centered on the feelings of the two persons involved rather than on your daily problems, it will be tougher to end.

Conversely, therapy is easiest to end when it is well focused on concrete problems in your life. It can then be single-minded and purposely efficient.

Sometimes it takes weeks, even months for patients to break off comfortably. Perhaps there is no special virtue in being able to quit easily; perhaps the more significant and "deep" therapy is, the harder it should be to terminate. Yet terminating can pose so many intense and difficult problems that it seems unreasonable not to try to reduce its complications. Among these problems are uncertainty about goals and how to reach them, breaking off with your therapist, fear of living without help, and concern about whether you can handle your daily problems. If they *can* be avoided during the therapy at no expense to the effectiveness of the help, then you would not need to deal with them when your therapy is ending. By applying certain viewpoints in combination with your judgment and your experience, you may be able to terminate more quickly and comfortably. That is the purpose of this chapter.

Finally, for termination to occur efficiently, there should be discussion early in your therapy of exactly how to decide whether end treatment. Certainly you need not wait for your therapist to tell you when you should quit, for he may expect you to tell him when you no longer feel the need for his help. There might well be frequent references by both of you as to when it would be logical for you to quit. Both of you should mention it whenever either thinks it appropriate.

TERMINATION

In public clinics, therapy is often broken off because the therapist leaves the organization. There is considerable turnover in such clinics because many of the therapists—psychiatrists, social workers, and psychologists—are in training and finish their stint at the agency after a year or two. The regular staff often has a high turnover because pay or working conditions are inferior to those in private practice or universities. Some places terminate as many of a departing therapist's patients as possible. This is administratively convenient, but irrational from the standpoint of effective therapy unless treatment is planned to end in this way. At least, however, this is a way of ending therapy that might otherwise go on interminably, in the absence of clear goals and efficient methods of reaching them. Fortuitous terminations also occur when the patient or therapist moves away, or becomes seriously ill, or when the client has a sudden financial setback.

The lesson to be learned is that therapy can be forced to end in an unplanned way without untoward consequences. One controlled study of arbitrary termination[1] indicated, for example, that even long-term treatment could be ended abruptly without any bad consequences. It is much better, however, to plan for the end of treatment so that the last few sessions before an enforced termination can be used efficiently.

ACCEPTING "CHRONICITY"

Many therapists operate on the assumption that some of their patients are "chronic," that they will never be able to function satisfactorily in society on their own, that they need "supportive" or "maintenance" treatment all of their lives just to keep clear of hospitals, serious trouble, or total incapacity. These therapists sometimes analogize between the mental patient's need for protection and support and the diabetic's need for insulin. Some patients have been so treated for most of their lives.

No physical basis for "chronicity" can be demonstrated despite an occasional promising research lead from glandular, brain, blood, or cellular studies. Sometimes a therapist makes this decision on the assumption that if he cannot achieve a successful termination, no one else can. More often, patients have been exposed to several therapists and methods before chronicity is assumed. Even so, it need not follow that "chronicity" would call for interminable treatment. It is likely that, with or without treatment, the patient could go on with his life, operating at a poor level of achievement and adaptation, but at least causing little trouble.

Is it sometimes necessary for a patient to receive psychotherapy all of his life to save him from getting worse? Although this question lends itself to straightforward research, crucial studies have not been done. Available data do suggest that interminable therapy is not justified, that there tends to be improvement in function whether therapy is provided or not, and that adverse consequences do not accompany withdrawal of long-term treatment.

The need for permanent treatment is, then, a weak concept at best, and it is useful continually to test whether the patient can get along without help, whether he can change some situation or move into a new environment which will help him significantly, and

[1] D. N. Wiener, "The Effect of Arbitrary Termination on Return to Psychotherapy," *J. of Clinical Psychology* (July, 1959).

whether a new therapist or mode of therapy might achieve better results.

Sam, for example, had first been taken to a therapist at the age of seven; he is now forty-two and still sees a therapist. He has seen six by now, including one at a residential home for disturbed children and one at a private hospital. He is still single, unemployed, and resigned to living as a drifter—relieved greatly by the fact that his parents have guaranteed him a middle-class income. There is no clear evidence in his way of living that therapy has helped him. He has never been exposed to a tough-minded behavior-change regimen, although he has had the other major therapies. He leads a largely undisciplined, goalless life, but at least until he has had a course of highly structured therapy, he need not be viewed as hopelessly chronic.

SOME GROUNDS FOR TERMINATING

INEFFICIENT RATE OF IMPROVEMENT

The most common ground for the decision to terminate is likely to involve reaching a point at which continuing gains are too small to justify the continuing expenditure of time and money on therapy. We have described the usual graph of therapeutic gains as "asymptotic," that is, showing a curve that tends with each additional interview to provide a lesser gain, but a gain that never quite reaches zero although the curve extends infinitely.

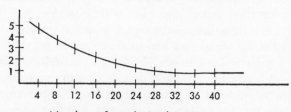

Amount of gain from therapy (hypothetical)

Number of weeks in therapy
(or amount of time and money spent)

Except, perhaps, for psychoanalysis, which may not try to produce early gains, your greatest gains are usually made early in therapy. If therapy has been successful at all, you can probably go on making some amount of gain indefinitely. This is likely to occur at a constantly slower rate, however, since as you solve major problems, there are gradually fewer problems to solve, and thus there is less room for improvement.

Besides, you can go on making gains in personal satisfaction and achievement for the rest of your life—in therapy or out. You reach a point, however, where it just does not seem worthwhile to go on with expenditure of time, energy, and usually money for small therapeutic gains, when you could be using the time, energy, and money in more productive ways.

When you have developed good habits for solving problems in your life, you grow and make gains continually, regardless of whether you are in treatment. Once on the right path, and able to correct for veering off it, you no longer need therapy to progress toward your goals. Furthermore, you can always return to therapy if major problems arise that you cannot solve. You should continue to make gains after you terminate and you should test out your ability to do so as soon as possible after major interferences are overcome and you are able to see your problems clearly, and to experiment with hopeful solutions.

PROBLEMS SOLVED

The most obvious, but rather uncommon, ground for quitting therapy would be because your original problems are completely solved and no other major ones have arisen. This seldom happens. Almost all solutions are only approximations, seldom producing results that completely eliminate the original problem. If, however, you have come in only because of panic attacks and they have been eliminated, or because your wife and you were not having effective sexual relations and you have learned to do so, or because you were lonely and you are developing a satisfying social life, solving the problem should be sufficient. You need not go on with therapy merely because the solution occurred quickly, or you don't understand why it happened, or you are afraid it will not last. You can always go back if the happy result does not last or some other problem develops, but going on provides no assurance of any better or longer-lasting solution.

GIVING UP

You may want to terminate because you think your therapy is going nowhere, or you despair of achieving more than a partial solution. We have discussed in the last chapter some of the many measures you can take to improve the results of your therapy instead of giving up.

Supposing that you believe you have exhausted all alternatives, however. Sometimes it may be desirable to cut any further losses of time and money by quitting. Before you terminate you should try to discover why you have not progressed. While there are almost always some new measures that can be taken or a change of therapist that can be made, practical matters may make the alternatives impossible. Perhaps no other therapist is available in the community, or you have run out of money, or must move out of town.

The termination seldom need be irrevocable anyway. You can expect to make changes and gains in your life even without therapy, and giving up should always be considered as tentative. You do not commit yourself to give up the hope of changing or of obtaining effective help when you quit. You merely give up—temporarily —on your present therapy.

WHO MAKES THE DECISION?

Ideally the decision to terminate would be made by you and your therapist agreeing on the point at which your goals have essentially been reached, and at which more sessions would be wasteful compared with other uses for your time, energy, and money. Seldom does such a clear and congenial event occur. Often even concrete goals are not clearly agreed upon, much less the point at which they have been achieved. The decision to terminate seems usually to be determined by such secondary considerations as one of the two parties moving away, or by the patient's fatigue with the process.

Next best to the mutually agreed upon termination would perhaps be the therapist's decision that therapy can be concluded. Such a decision probably occurs less frequently than a mutually agreed upon termination. The therapist is the expert on behavior change, however, and presumably can best assess the results and the prognosis. He is not certain in his technical knowledge and predictions, however, for his profession is founded on a still-primitive science. He has no great confidence in his own judgment about termination, and because he does not, he will often depend upon his client to say when it is time to quit.

Often he can tell when terminating is obviously premature— when his client wants to quit not because his problems are under control but because he is too quickly discouraged, too fearful about talking, or too anxious to change. The therapist is much less assured about when the approximation of a solution has been achieved, when the patient has the necessary attitudes and habits to handle future problems. So he often waits for the patient to tell him that he feels confident of his powers, and that he has made sufficient progress to quit therapy. He may depend upon his patient to speak up about feeling no further need for help.

Finally, then, you the patient will often need to make the decision, when you may not realize that you have this major role.

You should speak freely on the subject; then you are most likely to elicit your therapist's views. Mainly, however, it will often have to be your decision, and most likely on grounds other than having solved your problems completely. You should know and operate on the fact that hardly any therapy ends in that ideal way. Most often you will have to make the decision after achieving only an approximation to a solution; after gaining a sense only of being on the right path, which will produce continuing gains after therapy ends; after encountering accidental circumstances such as an opportunity to move or a change in financial circumstances; or after concluding that further possible gains are not commensurate with the time, energy, and money you would have to expend on continued therapy.

HANDLING DISAGREEMENT

How can you handle disagreement when it is not merely a matter of one of you taking the initiative while the other remains passive, but where you actually disagree directly on when you should terminate?

Your therapist may believe that you do not have your problems under control and that you are quitting for reasons not directly related to having accomplished realistic goals. You should consider carefully what evidence he presents to substantiate his views. You may wish to continue longer than he wants you to because you enjoy the sessions and are not pinched for time or money. You may believe that seeing him is always good for you, and may never want the therapy to end.

Disagreements about when to terminate can be a desirable testing experience that will permit you to measure your judgment of achievement and prognosis against your therapist's. This can occur either when he thinks you are not ready and you think you are, or when you think you still need him and he thinks not.

As long as even the termination is considered an experimental testing situation from which irrevocable harm cannot result, you can gain from making the decision to terminate. You can always return.

RELATIONSHIP PROBLEMS IN ENDING

It is always a problem to terminate a close friendship, and the one between you and your therapist is likely to be one of the more intense of your life. Even when he tries to keep it on coolly professional, technical grounds (not all try to; the analysts, for example, often try to keep it intensely personal and encourage you to view them as parent figures), your therapist is bound to seem like a very close friend, ally, and sympathetic authority, breaking with whom would be bittersweet at best.

If he has encouraged you to take an objective attitude toward himself, you will have a far easier time in terminating than if he encouraged or ignored your fantasying about him, your imagining and wishing that he were your true and lasting friend as others close to you may be. Even if you do become good friends during the sessions, you know that the relationship must be transitory and that you would not have become friends except for the professional relationship. Facing, discussing, and acting upon the realities of your relationship from the beginning seems to be the best way to avoid trouble at the end.

If you are an engaging person to him, the therapist may act as if this were a friendship like others in his life, and he also may find it difficult to break. Attractive patients who respond to their therapist with appreciation and friendship are among the therapist's most prized relationships, and they brighten his often dull life. He may truly be reluctant to see you leave.

Yet most therapy must terminate, and most therapists and

patients, facing the realities of their relationship, do terminate it. Sometimes, but seldom, they remain social friends. On rare occasions they even marry.

Our point here is that it is best to face the true nature of your relationship from the beginning so that it is not confused with or conducted like an ordinary friendship. When it is not carried on in a professional way, the difficulties involved in terminating may create a major crisis and may take many hours to settle. Such is often the case in psychoanalysis where "analyzing out" the transference relationship between therapist and patient often becomes one of the most difficult and time-consuming problems in treatment.

You may fear giving offense to your therapist when you propose terminating. If this is a problem to you, it is irrational either on your part or on his. If you only imagine that he will be offended, you should discuss it with him until you are convinced that he is not offended and that this is the kind of unreasonable concern about other's opinions that probably gets you into trouble in other situations. If you discover that he really is upset about your quitting, then he has a problem which you should not need to share. If he is competent, he will at most simply point out to you why he thinks you should continue, then wish you well on your own, with the invitation to return when and if you sense the need for further help.

You may also be anxious about being out on your own after receiving help continuously for whatever time. Even when your therapist has encouraged an attitude of independence, you can easily get used to seeing him and be concerned about having no one close to consult. Such attitudes appear inevitable, but the range of intensity is enormous. Some clients are eager to test themselves out independently, others are obviously frightened about losing support. The therapist's attitude and method is probably a substantial factor in this variability.

The major purpose of your therapy, however, is to help you to become effectively independent. If it does not proceed efficiently toward this goal, then your fears are likely to be enhanced. If it does proceed efficiently toward this goal from the very beginning, such fears are less likely to develop or to remain when termination is discussed. The best insurance, then, against the development of dependency and the fear of independence is a confrontation with the problem early in therapy and whenever you sense it thereafter. If you wait until late in therapy to face it, you have probably wasted considerable time working on less-vital problems and let yourself in for suddenly intensified and extended therapy when you thought you were ready to quit.

What is a reasonable view of the personal relationship between you and your therapist when it seems time to terminate? When therapy is successful, it is something like this: You and he give up a friendship, having achieved your goals. It is like that of the parent watching benignly as his matured child goes out on his own, trained to cope with the world and well equipped with attitudes and habits to achieve according to his resources and to be pleased with his way of life. It is also like that of an effective teacher whose student moves on at the end of a school year. The job is done, the reason for the dependent relationship is gone.

TAPERING OFF

The most effective way to break a habit usually is to quit all at once rather than to taper off. For example, this general principle of learning applies to smoking and drinking. If you view consulting with a therapist as a habit, a clean break is probably best.

Other considerations do enter in, however. You may want to test yourself in lengthened but still relatively short stretches of no help, so that if old problems crop up which you still do not handle well, you can quickly enlist the help of your therapist. You may also want temporarily to use his help with new problems as they arise, although you will have to be able to grapple alone with them eventually. Your anxiety about being on your own may also be relieved by stretching out the sessions for a while, lengthening the periods of absence until the sessions have little impact and your reliance on them fades away by itself.

To work effectively, however, the purpose and length of the tapering-off process should always be clear so that you do not come to depend upon infrequent interviews as you did upon more frequent ones. Termination as soon as possible should be the goal constantly kept in mind, and the purpose of tapering off as a means to this end held foremost.

TEMPORARY TERMINATION OR PERMANENT?

Psychotherapy is often greatly extended by the unrealistic, even pernicious view that it should end when—and not until—you are practically free of problems or symptoms, and are ensured against their recurrence. Sometimes this view is explicit, more often it is only implicit and therapy goes on and on as if this were to be its outcome.

Such an attitude, whether yours or your therapist's, is unrealistic because therapy seldom ends in that way, and there is no evidence that going on and on produces anything closer to such a result than briefer, more direct methods. Thus, therapy may go on much longer than it otherwise would and ends in disappointment anyway because of this false expectation; the realities about results finally do force themselves on your mind, but later rather than sooner.

In the sense that you expect therapy to rid you of all constraints and to convert you into a highly creative man or woman, you are likely to be disappointed. If you face this fact early, you are more likely to terminate sooner than if you keep hoping for more than therapy ordinarily produces. More important, you will not need to view your course of therapy as final, or that change should be complete and permanent.

A more realistic view of therapy can help you substantially to overcome your problems and develop habits and attitudes that will help you to handle your life more successfully. You will continue to have problems, however, and may at times need further professional help. When, for a period of weeks, you are stymied by obstacles or a sense of helplessness, when you are overwhelmed by misery, depression, or anxiety, you can return to therapy without feeling that your previous help had failed.

When you breach the concept of completeness and finality about your therapy, you can quit sooner, with less concern for the future. You need have no concern about the permanence of the results, nor about feeling like a failure if you ever should return. Your life and problems are everchanging, and you cannot anticipate what you will want or need in the future. Nor need you do so, as far as therapy is concerned.

The anxiety, therefore, about whether you are "really" finished, whether you should break off now, whether you might be quitting prematurely before you have squeezed out all possible gains, is misplaced if you do not view your course of therapy as final. You do not have to decide about its permanence. This can remain an open question for your lifetime. When you need help, you can get it. Therapy does not have to be viewed as a long-term, emotionally complicated matter. You can view it simply as technical help with problems of living which you cannot solve with the nonprofessional resources available to you.

STRUCTURING THE FINAL INTERVIEW(S)

The final interview or interviews can be an especially useful source of help when you have terminated. Your therapist can review and stress with you what you have accomplished and learned. You and he can discuss guidelines to help you to determine when you are slipping into bad habits and slackening in your progress, and when you should seek more help. And you can discuss what your relationship has been and what it would be if you ever want additional services from him.

The final interview need not be substantially different in tone or content from the others. It should perhaps not introduce new material, but merely be a culmination and summing up of what has happened since the first session, with a special orientation to the future.

It can be particularly useful for you during the closing session to review those ways you have learned of working effectively on your problems. Most important for your future is that you stay on the right path to obtain solutions, rather than that you encounter or generate no serious problems. You will want to stay on such a road all of your life.

WHEN TO GO BACK

A rationale for returning to therapy has been outlined in the above two sections of this chapter. It involves a concept of your life—and of therapy—as fluid, requiring that you grapple with problems continually with a flexible, experimental frame of mind that never gives up the effort to find solutions, if not on your own, then with technical, professional help. In this sense therapy need never be considered final, and it is more likely than not that you can use professional help profitably again sometime in your life. It is unreasonable not to seek it at such times, and to consider yourself a failure in previous therapy makes no more sense than using the services of a lawyer, engineer, or physician repeatedly indicates failure of other consultations from them.

Having had therapy once you are, in fact, probably in a better position to find and use it successfully than if you have never had it before. It need not be as long the second or third time, especially if you see your original therapist, but it need not be as long even if you see a new man. Having had a successful experience, you should be able to strip what you need to bare essentials, to concentrate more directly on your problems and why you are stuck on them and what you need to do to get unstuck. Because of your experience, you should be able to exercise usefully more control and direction in the sessions.

Certainly you can specify that you do not want to go through an intensive analysis of your past and that you do want to solve a particular problem as quickly as possible.

Of course, if your earlier therapy has not been successful, if you left it for reasons other than accomplishment of your goals, then you must approach it more as you would a first course. But you should have learned something from the earlier course, anyway, from the way that it terminated, and from what has happened to you since. It would seem wise to begin additional courses of therapy with a review of these factors.

Part IV

DRUGS AND PHYSICAL PROBLEMS

CHAPTER 13

Medical Problems and
Psychotherapy

It is practically impossible to avoid dealing with physical or medical problems or complaints during the course of your psychotherapy. Not only are they a common aspect of daily living, but the line between physical and psychological troubles, between physical and psychological causes, between physical and psychological treatment, is extremely difficult to draw.

Internists, those physicians specializing in internal disorders, estimate that two-thirds or more of their patients have emotional problems. General practitioners also have a high proportion of emotionally upset patients. Traditionally, physicians have treated most of the psychologically troubled both because physical complaints are often the introduction to or an acceptable mask for psychological difficulties, and because the nature of the complaints forces them to develop some of the skills needed for psychological care. That is, much medical treatment, to succeed, must become quite similar to psychological therapy.

Most physicians, however, unless they also are psychiatrists, have grave limitations as psychotherapists. Some may be intelligent, kind, and wise men, well seasoned in handling human problems, in which case they may be as competent as any other similarly gifted professional or nonprofessional man. But few physicians— or any other professional men—are automatically good psychotherapists. You are more likely to find skilled psychotherapists among those selected and trained specifically for that specialized profession.

Most physicians—like most lawyers, ministers, teachers, and other professional men—practice a vocation at least somewhat different from that of psychotherapists who specialize in methods of accomplishing changes in attitudes and behavior. Physicians

215

are trained primarily to use physical methods or brief bursts of advice to solve their patients' problems. They usually ignore the longer-term, systematic, concentrated approach often needed to achieve lasting human behavior change—including the analysis of complex problems, patient experimentation with methods of change, and vigorous follow-up.

Some physicians, when they recognize the inadequacy of their methods, will refer their troubled patients to psychotherapists, particularly when the patients show psychotic symptoms. Others will keep their patients in a diluted kind of physical or psychological treatment for years, trying this drug and that, this dosage and that, this bit of advice and that. The only firm prediction you can make is that if you are bizarre, obnoxious, or acutely distressed for weeks, your physician is likely to refer you elsewhere for treatment. But if you are only moderately upset psychologically, you cannot count on your physician to refer you to psychotherapy. As a matter of fact, many physicians consider themselves as equal to or better than psychotherapists in caring for most psychological conditions.

Curious things happen, however, when private practice is not involved. When large clinic complexes are considered, such as those of the Veterans' Administration, the medical clinics are often eager to refer all psychological complainants to the mental-hygiene clinic. A study at the Kaiser Permanete Clinic in Los Angeles indicated that psychological treatment reduces medical bills overall, but the average private practitioner cannot afford to work on the basis of much separation of psychological and physical treatment.

With insurance plans covering a rapidly increasing number of workers in the United States, company policies are becoming increasingly influential in determining the kind of care you receive. Some insurance companies and employers are notably chary about paying for psychotherapy, assuming it will open a Pandora's box of costly and endless treatment. But when they insist upon paying for only physical care, they invite physical complaints and endless physical care instead of psychological care—and may provide it in a way that would make psychotherapy cheaper in the long run.

It would seem to be logical and convenient if the same professional man could treat both mind and body, and this is the theory behind the profession of psychiatry. Yet physicians of other specialties—or not specializing—often insist upon the same privilege, and the Veterans' Administration and many state agencies will pay fees to general physicians to treat "mental illness." Furthermore, even psychiatrists eschew the combination: It is a rare one who will do any kind of physical examination or treatment, and who will not insist, as would the social worker or psychologist, that his patient with a physical complaint should go to a "proper" physician for a checkup.

Whether it takes a physician (psychiatrist) to recognize a physical problem is a moot issue. It does seem logical that, if you suffer from a serious physical problem, you should choose a psychiatrist for your psychotherapist, if a good one is available, since he should have better awareness of physical changes in you and better access to good medical care than would a nonmedical psychotherapist. Otherwise, however, the ways of recognizing, evaluating, seeking treatment for, and living with medical problems, as discussed in this chapter, can be adequately applied by you and by anyone you may choose to see for psychological help.

Some wise men have believed that human emotional distress will eventually be "reduced" to neurology or to physiology. Freud thought that neurological treatment some day would substitute for psychotherapy, while Norbert Wiener has said that "psychology is like a tapeworm that keeps losing its segments to physiology."

But as B. F. Skinner would answer, behavior is a thing in itself, which can be studied and shaped quite independently of its antecedents or more molecular "causes." Specialists in behavior change are available to you now to help you reach your goals, while neurological and physiological methods currently are neither as logical nor as certain to help you gain your ends of better daily living.

Physical problems can be divided into four categories: the first are those related directly to simple, obvious bad habits such as overeating, smoking, using drugs, overdrinking. While most physical complaints might in a sense be related to poor living habits (e.g., stomach ulcers to eating and working habits, some cancers to eating and breathing circumstances, heart disease to poor work and social habits), this group is the most concretely so.

The second category of physical complaints are those having relatively well-defined, observable physical syndromes, such as heart disease caused by restricted heart valves, and arthritis diagnosed from swelling and calcium deposits at joints. Ways of living always affect and can cause such disease, but at least the diseases in this group can be seen and treated by medical means, while the psychological process is often obscure.

The third category consists of the psychosomatic disorders whose distinguishing characteristic is usually readily observable as both a physical process and a psychological one. Thus you can literally see stress generating acid into the stomach, which leads to ulcers; the skin breaking out in response to fear; and severe headaches and tachycardia developing in reaction to severe anxiety.

The fourth group is primarily psychological with only overtones and labels of a physical condition. Thus while aches and pains, fatigue, faintness, and sinking feelings can occur from clearly physical causes, these complaints far more commonly have no physical basis, and once physical grounds are ruled out, they can often be effectively treated only by psychological means.

HANDLING HABIT PROBLEMS

Although obesity, heavy smoking and drinking, and abuse in drug usage are often considered and treated as medical problems, they can also be viewed as habit problems subject to the same methods of analysis and control as learning how to study, how to read fast, how to make friends, or how to succeed in sexual relations. That is, unless these habit problems are a result of physical malfunction, which they seldom are (overweight, for example, from glandular malfunction), they are subject to the same rules of learning and change that any other habits are, and are not likely to be overcome simply by administration of medicine or casual advice.

Sometimes, of course, the impact of getting "bad news" from your physician is enough to tilt you toward control—particularly if he can point to resulting disease of your heart, lungs, stomach, or liver. Sometimes, too, the fact that you are seeing your physician for weekly visits provides supervised follow-up similar to that of psychotherapy. And drugs to "control" weight (by stimulating you to more activity), or to ease the withdrawal from smoking or drinking (by mildly sedating you), may tip you toward control just enough to help you to succeed.

But such instances do not get at the most difficult situations of control. They require more thorough analysis of the circumstances of the habit, more intense effort toward change, and more careful follow-up than the physician ordinarily can provide.

Psychotherapy approaches these habit problems either indirectly or directly. With the indirect approach, the therapist would assume that the habit is a symptom of some (other) emotional disturbance and that it will disappear or diminish when such "deeper" problems of attitude and feeling are relieved. Thus overeating might be considered to represent a craving for love and dependency which one could better satisfy through actively seeking affection or discovering and accepting it. Psychoanalysts, nondirectivists, and some eclectics practice an indirect approach.

In the direct approach, the therapist would work to change the habit through such means as blocking the possibility of its occurrence, providing substitute satisfactions, applying rewards for its control and penalties for relapses.

While the use of drugs in the treatment process might seem to convert psychotherapy into a medical procedure, many physicians are glad to co-operate with a nonmedical therapist in such situations. Many psychotherapists, however, are highly skeptical of using drugs at all, especially to try to control such habits, on the grounds that the person who overuses eating, drinking, smoking, or other drugs in the first place is likely to become overly dependent on any drug used in treatment.

If you have a physical problem directly related to a bad habit, if no physical cause of the condition can be detected, and if the simple methods of your physician do not show results in several weeks, then it is time to consider psychotherapy. The direct behavior-modification approach would be the best first try at psychotherapy, since it specifically focuses on habit change, requires the least investment of time and money, and has demonstrated some success in this area.

HANDLING PHYSICAL DISEASE AND HANDICAP

There are, obviously, physical diseases which not even the most imaginative and dedicated psychotherapist would claim as his domain. Heart disease, cancer, arthritis, and diabetes, for example, are physical pathologies which can be observed even if their causes are not thoroughly known nor independent of one's habits. In fact, personality studies suggest that certain types of persons are more prone to specified diseases, and that certain ways of handling your life can at least aggravate if not cause the disease. Even cancerous tumors have tentatively been differentiated from noncancerous on the basis of personality tests of the patients.

The "proofs" of personality factors in physical disease so far are universally poor, but they cannot quickly be dismissed; you function as a unit whose physical and emotional resources and behavior are inextricably intertwined. The disease or disability are also likely to lead to changes in attitude and behavior reactions to your physical problems.

The principles of good mental health, maturity, self-respect, or effective problem-solving—whatever one calls the goal of psychotherapy—all can enhance physical health, convalescense, adaptation to handicap, or adjustment to dying. In the presence of severe physical disease, your ability to handle your life well is under special strain, and psychotherapy seems even more likely than usual to be desirable.

There is a peculiar line of exception, however. Many people seem to do better emotionally in the face of demonstrable physical disease or incapacity than when there is nothing "real" (physical) confronting them. How often every experienced psychotherapist has heard patients say something like "I'd be so relieved to find out something is really the matter with me—even if it's my heart or ulcers! I just can't believe it's nothing! At least I'd know what to do."

This effect resembles that described in countries under enemy pressure. In England during World War II bombing raids, when the whole population was mobilized for duty, mental health seemed better than usual. Furthermore, soldiers who could fire back at the enemy had emotional trouble less often than those who could not strike back.

It is as if, for many people, a physical disease is a tangible "enemy" that can be attacked with particular weapons, whereas a "mental illness," "anxiety" or "emotional disturbance" are spectres of enemies that cannot be seen, understood, and fought directly.

This feature, plus that of social approval, often makes physical disease a more acceptable kind of disorder than psychological troubles. If you drive yourself beyond reason to the point of breakdown, you are likely to prefer a diagnosis of high blood pressure or duodenal ulcers to that of severe feelings of inadequacy or anxiety reaction.

Physicians often co-operate to give you an acceptable physical diagnosis, however strained, rather than a psychological one. If your heart disease or diabetes is precipitated or aggravated by severe stress in living, logically it could best be diagnosed and treated by changing the stress after a reasonable kind of first aid is administered for the physical symptoms. This is often attempted by "doctor's orders" that you take it easy in this way and that. But the most sensible and often necessary way is to learn how to manage what you must do or choose to do in your life, and that is a tougher matter than simply reducing your activities or taking vacations or rests.

In any case, if you apply the criteria discussed in Chapter 3 and decide you need psychotherapy while you also suffer from a physical disease or disability, you should seek it from the most competent psychotherapist you can find. You should inform your physician and ask that he keep your psychotherapist informed of any changes in your physical condition. Your psychotherapist may want to tread gently until he knows the extent to which psychological help may temporarily upset you and aggravate your physical condition. He should be able to recognize and handle such a possibility in co-operation with your physician, while also maintaining a cutting edge to his therapy so that it works toward substantial changes in your self-damaging behavior.

There is a persistent story about a mythical therapist who treated a patient as if he had emotional troubles—until the patient died from a brain tumor. Neither this author nor any of his colleagues has ever known first hand of such a case, although there undoubtedly have been a very few. Misdiagnosis occurs frequently throughout the fields of medicine and psychology, and it is also likely that people are misdiagnosed as having neurological pathology when they are psychologically troubled, and that the consequent treatment with drugs over a span of years has adversely affected their ways of living.

The consequences of treating a person for a physical disorder when he really has none would seem to be as unfortunate as treating him psychologically when he turns out to have a physical disorder. After all, if a person has a brain tumor, he will still probably need psychological help for worries, depression or anxiety. The mistreatment of a psychological condition as if it were physical usually involves the use of drugs or restrictions on behavior which impair the full use of his powers. Is it worse to live as a cripple unnecessarily than not to take precautions when they are justified?

This is *not* to say that the best diagnostic resources of medicine should not always be employed. It *is* to say that many brain tumors or other brain pathologies are undiagnosable until they show themselves in gross ways, and further, that thousands of Americans are being treated physically, mainly with sedatives, as if they had neurological disorders when the signs for such diagnoses are highly unreliable. Many children, particularly those who actively misbehave, are hyperactive, and have suspicious brain waves on electroencephalograms are given sedatives for many years, although the behavior on which the diagnosis is based (along with equivocal brain-wave findings) is a common result of poor training and discipline and is correctable through improved training methods.

There is a vast disarray in the mind-body field. The range for your choice of services is therefore great. Guided by as much information and wisdom as you can muster, you will have to make some crucial decisions about which treatment to seek.

Two cases may illustrate some of the problems: Mr. and Mrs. Jonas were a middle-aged couple, married for 25 years, who lived in their own home in the suburb of a large Midwestern city. He was a moderately successful lawyer; she was a school teacher who was considering a return to teaching.

Edward Jonas had been considered a hypochondriac for many years, having "doctored" and taken a wide variety of medications for aches and pains primarily in his stomach, head, chest, and intestines. In recent years he had developed high blood pressure, and his treatment had come to focus on that mainly, but by no means exclusively, before his last admittance to the hospital.

His wife Marion during this time publicly had led a vigorous, healthy life, raising her children, maintaining by herself a large, attractive home, and participating in civic activities. Her family knew her as somewhat different, however, because five nights out of seven she used to go to bed at eight o'clock and stay there until seven in the morning. She hated to make decisions and needed to be pushed into essential ones by her husband and children. She suffered torments of uncertainty and guilt when faced with conflict or responsibility and constantly took baking soda and other drugstore remedies for stomach upset.

One September night, shortly after their "baby"—their last child—left for college, Marion Jonas awoke in agony from stomach pain, sure she was dying of a heart attack. Her husband called her doctor, a fussy old man who had to give her repeated injections of a sedative before finally calming her. He said afterward he had never seen a more intensely pained patient, for she was bordering on shock. He rushed her to the hospital, put her on intensive care, and began a series of tests to confirm his initial diagnosis of a coronary thrombosis.

During the attack and for the eight subsequent weeks of hospitalization, all signs but one were negative. As it turned out, the doctor had a hard time confirming his original diagnosis. Electrocardiograms, blood pressure, pulse, and all other tests except a relatively new one which usually indicates muscle damage (the "transaminase test") were negative, and except for frequent gas, she had no clinical symptoms. Although immediately upon hospitalization her description centered the attack in her stomach, and although she was greatly relieved when she expelled a massive amount of gas, her physician convinced her that she had had a heart attack and she thereafter described her symptoms as being in her chest. (While the stomach and gas complaints are common in proved coronaries, they are far more common without coronaries.) She was kept on total bed rest during her entire eight weeks of hospitalization, given tranquilizers, sedatives, and blood thinner continuously, and had severe restrictions on visitors.

During the third week of his wife's hospitalization, Edward Jonas felt too exhausted to go on with his routine. He was having chest pains and stomach trouble, and was constantly edgy. He went to his doctor, who hospitalized him near his wife, for a "good rest" with no restrictions on his activity in the hospital. He received no special care or medications beyond his usual ones, and his physician checked on him for about five minutes on each of two visits a week.

Nothing at all happened to Marion Jonas during her eight weeks of hospitalization except that she learned to live as an invalid. She had an enormous readjustment to make when she got home. Physically she was so weak that even a walk to the bathroom was exhausting. For six months she avoided walking up stairs and inclined streets, doing her housework, going out socially, even preparing her meals, and a year later she was still afraid to extend herself even to the point her extremely protective physician advised. He simply had no idea how the trauma of the attack and his concern about it had exacerbated her previously well-controlled anxiety when she was functioning vigorously, and how he had let loose all her thinly veiled fears about herself.

Meanwhile, after three weeks in the hospital, Edward Jonas had the first of three coronary attacks. Ever since being hospitalized, he finally confided to his sister, he had been terribly frightened of dying and lay awake most of every night thinking that if he let himself relax and sleep he would not wake up. He deteriorated perceptibly in the hospital and was, after his coronary, put on bed care, but he had two more coronaries and died from the third.

Edward Jonas died and Marion Jonas was invalided from coronary attacks. In the former case, physical disease (diagnosed through autopsy) was certainly present, and in the latter case less certainly. But Edward might have had death deferred or at least have been made more comfortable, and Marion might have avoided invalidism, if psychotherapy had been utilized, quite aside from the obvious possibility that psychotherapy in either case earlier might even have interrupted the development of the physical condition.

HANDLING PSYCHOSOMATIC PROCESSES

Your physician is likely to treat your psychosomatic complaints as if they were purely physical by using drugs, dietary injunctions, and advice to "take it easy." Only rarely will he refer you for psychotherapy—unless his means fail or you are grossly upset. His attitude will often be that it is sufficient, or even more efficient, to treat you medically than psychologically, especially since psychological therapy is often so indirect and results are so uncertain. Also, patients may become annoyed or angry with their physician when he advises psychotherapy. They often think they do not need it, and they do not want to be treated by anyone else.

Thus, the physician has some good reasons for his reluctance to refer his psychosomatic patients to a psychotherapist. Besides, many psychotherapists consider such patients poor prospects for their services because of the very fact that they do focus on physical complaints instead of upon psychological problems. Thus they do not seem properly "motivated" for psychological help.

If, however, your physical symptoms are clearly psychosomatic, that is, have pretty directly observable psychological bases, then you would be wise to try psychological therapy to try to arrest or reverse the course of the physical symptoms instead merely of palliating or controlling them chemically or by rest. Some physicians will be encouraged to make such referral if your attitude is enlightened on the issue, but even if he does not (and he may not like psychotherapy or therapists), you can decide for yourself on a tryout.

You should try to gain the physician's co-operation. He should follow the course of your psychotherapy to observe its effects upon your physical condition. The physician can be a good judge of the effectiveness of psychotherapy which is undertaken primarily to get you over your physical symptoms.

You should ask any psychotherapist you are considering to tell you his specific attitudes toward helping you to overcome your psychosomatic condition and how he proposes to go about the process. He may not want to treat a person with your symptoms. He may say that your physical symptoms might tend to disappear during the course of therapy but that he will give them no special direct attention, or he may be willing to discuss them immediately and work directly to help you to overcome them.

In the latter case of direct attention, you should note the exact times and circumstances when your stomach, breathing, skin, head, colon, heartbeat, or other areas of trouble "act up." You would then discuss such circumstances and try to develop different behavior at such times.

If Marion Jonas, for example, had entered the hospital for tests because her stomach was acting up and ulcers were suspected, or because the heart condition was suspected of being psychosomatic, she and a psychotherapist might have come to consider several possibilities. Among these would have been whether her last child's leaving home was confronting her with the disturbing fact that she was getting old, or that she would now have to find a different primary purpose in life, or that she was faced with living alone with her husband.

These, among other possibilities, could be considered as potential sources of serious trouble to her. The process of psychotherapy would be to determine which prospect(s) might frighten her to the point of developing physical symptoms and then to help her to develop more successful ways of handling the condition. Psychotherapy would be tried on an experimental basis, just as a new drug might be tried for a physical pathology.

HANDLING DUBIOUS PHYSICAL COMPLAINTS

The vaguest physical complaints—those attributable to no specific physical organ or system—are so clearly psychological most of the time that it is only by stretching the medical role to its limits that they can be treated medically at all. Thus, once the physician rules out any clear physical cause for fatigue, faintness, weakness, or pain, he can only use the vaguest and most general kinds of treatment such as aspirin, vitamin pills, rest, vacation, tranquilizers, sedatives. He may be justified in the sense that brief periods of using any of these devices may be sufficient to carry you through an especially trying period, or because you will not accept a psychological diagnosis or referral to a psychotherapist.

Since these complaints are so vague and depend so completely upon the report of the complainant, the decision to seek therapy lies even more strongly with you alone—based upon the intensity of your symptoms, but even more upon the extent to which they disrupt your life and prevent you from achieving your goals.

Many people endure all their lives symptoms such as have been described in this chapter without becoming substantially worse or better. Those discussed in this section, however, seem least likely to be progressively worrisome or disrupting. It is not as difficult as for the other categories described to adapt to these complaints. But when they do become extremely upsetting and self-defeating, and when simple, ordinary methods of control fail, then you may gain a great deal by seeking out psychotherapy to try to overcome them.

To cite another case, Miss Land had suffered from fatigue all her life. It had never, however, interfered with a vigorous life of social work, friendships, bowling and skiing, and travel, and she never stopped to worry or do anything about it. When she reached forty, however, she began to be concerned about it. She started to take vitamin pills.

After a year, and for the first time in her life, she went to a physician for a general physical exam. He found no pathology, but advised her to take after-lunch naps and gave her a stimulant to take daily. The stimulant helped her to keep going, she said, but gradually she grew depressed as well as fatigued, reaching a point where she thought she simply could no longer force herself to go on. Finally, her physician suggested that she see a psychologist for therapy and she did. Her therapist, using her fatigue and depression as a continuous measure of whether the therapy was on the right track, concentrated on her concern about aging and loneliness as the paths to improving her attitudes, and actions to keep her life vital.

Stomach pains, headaches, fatigue, feelings of weakness and faintness are perhaps the most common of human complaints. (They also happen to be the most common side effects of tranquilizers and other drugs.) Whether human beings can ever be free of them is a moot question. For yourself, you can take the practical view of doing something about them when they interfere significantly with your life as you want to live it. Then, in the ascending scale of complexity and costliness, you can try treatment—your own devices, first aid from your physician, psychotherapy—to overcome such disruptive symptoms.

WHAT TO ASK OF YOUR PHYSICIAN

When you have physical as well as psychological problems, and you are not being treated in a broad clinical setting where you can expect co-ordination between physical and psychological services, you may have to take some direction of the course of your treatment. In order to do so wisely, there are a number of questions to raise with the physician who is treating your physical condition.

If you have psychological symptoms, you should ask early what his attitude is toward them and the treatment of them. If he seems unresponsive to your psychological problems, to trying to help you with them in concrete ways, or to making a referral to a psychotherapist, you might consider changing physicians.

You should ask him about his attitude toward rehabilitation as compared with protective care. Physicians vary on a scale that might be labeled extreme rehabilitative measures at one end and extreme protective measures at the other. With the same patient who has had a mild coronary attack, for example, the physician at one end may have him doing mild exercise after a few days of bed rest and encourage practically full activity after a month or two, while at the other extreme another physician may keep the same patient on total bed rest (prohibiting him to use even an electric razor or going to the bathroom) for two months and on highly restricted activity for months more or even permanently.

You should always keep your physician informed of your concerns about your physical condition and ask him to take them into account in treatment.

You should always ask the name and purpose of any drugs he prescribes so that you can tell your psychotherapist about them. Otherwise, the psychotherapist may suggest drugs whose effects would be contradictory to your physician's, dangerous in combination with others, or are an added dosage of the same kind of drug.

You should know your physician's attitude toward giving you the facts of your illness. Otherwise you may, for example, worry needlessly that he is withholding bad news from you. Unless such issues are clarified, your psychotherapist will not know whether you are distorting reality when you worry about your condition.

Above all, if you are being treated for physical and psychological conditions simultaneously, you should ask that your physician and your psychotherapist keep in touch with each other. When you have serious psychological problems along with physical problems, you cannot expect to be treated by the same therapist for both. You should, however, expect that your two therapists will talk with each other before you begin with either one, and occasionally thereafter. But you will have to do what you can to ensure that, for neither of them may take such initiative.

One psychotherapist insists upon conducting such conversations with the physician in the presence of the patient; this has the merit of helping to ensure that full and consistent information is being transmitted and being accurately interpreted by the three parties involved.

Incidentally, referrals are not all one way, from physician to psychotherapist. Though it happens less often, they may also be from psychotherapist to physician. After all, you can develop physical problems during the course of psychotherapy, and you should expect your therapist to ask you to get proper care for them, to help with a referral, and to inform the physician, with your permission, of the nature of your psychotherapy.

CHAPTER 14 *Using Drugs to Aid Psychotherapy*

THE AMERICAN NATION is an enormous user of drugs. The problems involved are complex, lying as they do at the very heart of the American ethos. Our culture itself could perhaps be described in terms of our attitudes and practices regarding drug use.

Some Americans are direly apprehensive about ingesting any foreign substance that may cause them to "lose control," "change their nature," or "feel different"—in other words, to behave as if at the mercy of outside forces. Others eagerly swallow or sip pills or potions that promise a taste of nirvana or at least a momentary surcease from misery. There is, of course, also a middle group which professes one or the other of these views at various times, more or less realistically according to life situations.

The most widely consumed drugs—alcohol and aspirin—are generally regarded as the least harmful. Yet it is simply by current national consensus and policy that they are so considered, for at one time the national government designated alcohol harmful to the point of prohibiting its use. Meprobamate has 80 million American users, and other tranquilizers are also abundantly taken. Mood elevators (anti-depressants) and stimulants, too, are widely used.

Nevertheless, our national policy would seem to reflect a Puritan ethos. Those drugs (aspirin, alcohol, and stimulants) that presumably enhance or seem to sustain aggression or hard work are promoted rather than being legally restricted, whereas those (tranquilizers, sedatives, marijuana, and LSD) that tranquilize and enhance daydreaming, lethargy, and passivity are controlled or banned. Of course, these are not the only reasons for legal controls, but since these latter drugs are not as strictly regulated in some other major countries, and have not demoralized their populations, one may question the unique severity and partiality of our policy.

It is often argued that tranquilizers, sedatives, LSD, and marijuana produce psychological dependence, dangerous side effects, or asocial behavior. The number of persons suffering from such dependence, side effects, or asocial trouble in the United States is, however, infinitesimal compared with those suffering similar effects from alcohol, aspirin, and stimulants, perhaps in the ratio of thousands to one. The toll from alcohol abuses to the individual and society are well publicized; aspirin and stimulant dependence and side effects hardly come to the public attention. And certainly neither engages such concern or control as is applied to the tranquilizers. Most people in the United States do not even know that in many countries tranquilizers, sedatives, and marijuana, whose use in the United States requires prescriptions or is banned, can be bought freely without prescription and without any perceptible disadvantage to these societies.

This is not a plea for freer drug usage. This book concerns effective ways to solve your problems, and drugs are very seldom such a way. If they were used *only* to the extent that they helped solve problems, their use would have to be enthusiastically endorsed. Their widespread use to avoid suffering from —*and therefore doing something to solve*—problems argues more powerfully against them.

We would simply point up the irrationality of drug control in our country to show how most tranquilizing or behavior-reducing drugs can only be prescribed by a physician who directs and controls their use according to *his* ideas, and within a distinctive national policy, instead of according to goals you have arrived at after extensive guidance on your problems. Although the most potent tranquilizers require medical prescription in the United States, they are probably more widely used here than in Canada or France, where the consumer can buy them directly without prescription. It is how the drugs are misused—*as if they helped to solve problems, when they only perhaps help to change mood*—by the physician's direction and the consumer's desire that concerns us here, not the physical dangers in their use.

Our purpose is to provide some knowledge of drugs and their uses that will permit you to judge wisely whether they likely will help or are helping you to reach your goals in psychotherapy.

A definitive theory of drug usage has not yet been written and is long overdue. We cannot write one here, but will attempt to broaden your views about the use of drugs by focusing on their crucial problems: Is the use of drugs always antithetical to attacking your problems? Should drugs be used without understanding their purpose? What price must you pay for using any drugs? Why do drugs often not work? Is there a rational way to use them to help solve your problems?

THE PLACE OF DRUGS IN PSYCHOTHERAPY

How does the use of drugs fit in with the effort to solve your problems through psychotherapy? There are two extreme positions. One holds that—or at least operates as if—drugs by themselves solve or at least control problems in living. Thus aspirin, alcohol, tranquilizers, and stimulants are usually prescribed or consumed to help you keep going in the way you are already going. "There's nothing wrong with you that, a) a couple of aspirins, b) a good stiff drink, c) a tranquilizer, d) a couple of cups of coffee, or e) a pep pill won't fix up," is an attitude equally common, it seems, with the public and the medical profession. The trouble is, as one therapist recently told the mother of five children, "Alcohol never improved your ability to handle your children—it only improved your ability to endure them."

If drugs help you to sustain yourself through a difficult time with a minimum of extra effort or change, well and good. But if this approach does not work, according to the criteria given in Chapter 3, then you had better realize that examining and changing your ways of living may be vital, and that the use of drugs will only postpone the day of reckoning.

Even fairly sophisticated medical approaches to drug usage fail in this way. Physicians can keep you experimenting for years with various kinds of drugs, dosages, and combinations—as if that were the best way to try to overcome your anxiety, depression, tension, or unhappiness. Perhaps because of availability, physicians themselves are the heaviest per-capita users of drugs, including narcotics, of any professional group, and their wives and nurses also rank high. You may well take notice of their belief, as illustrated by their own usage, in this way of handling one's life problems.

The other extreme view is that drugs are at best an unmitigated nuisance and at worst a complete barrier to effective psychotherapy.

Psychiatrists, the only psychotherapist group which has the option of using drugs or psychotherapy, split sharply on the issue. According to a survey of psychiatrists, about two-thirds of them tend to prescribe drugs, while about one-third depend almost exclusively upon psychotherapy. The most dedicated practitioners in three of the four psychotherapeutic approaches described in Chapter 5 tend to avoid the use of drugs; only the eclectic group frequently prescribes them.

Psychologists and social workers cannot directly prescribe drugs, but their attitudes toward them probably differ somewhat similarly to psychiatrists. Those who think drugs are useful or necessary can easily get a prescription written for their patient by a co-operative physician. Many physicians assume that the nonmedical therapist is sure to know his own patient's needs and likely reactions relative to psychotropic drugs far better from several interviews with the patient than the physician can discover in one short session.

The very prescription of drugs may damage the application of your ingenuity, courage, and ability to solve your problems. "My doctor, the angel," was a line in a poem written by a patient grateful for the attention and care of his doctor. This doctor had medicated the patient heavily to keep him quiet and relaxed; the patient thoroughly enjoyed the rest and forgot his troubles for a week. Yet as soon as he got out of bed and went home, his problems intensified and oppressed him. (When neurotic cats were allowed to retreat from a punishing shock source they showed no disturbance. But when they were forced to be near it, their symptoms returned.) What a temptation, however, for a doctor to act as an "angel," however briefly and in the long run ineffectually, by prescribing drugs to make you temporarily feel better!

Yet being a helpless or dependent patient, asking for or leaning primarily on drugs (or any other power outside yourself) seems to reduce your chances of getting over a problem, physical or mental. Research indicates that those patients in tuberculosis and mental hospitals who were rated as best behaved, who did exactly what their therapists wanted them to, tended to stay in hospitals the longest and to do least well outside. Consider that—for awhile— a tranquilizer, a depressant (alcohol), a stimulant (No-Doz, coffee, Dexadrine), or a sedative (barbiturate), any and all may help a hard-driving salesman to control ulcers, fatigue, irritability, or anxiety. But for how long? If his goals for himself are extremely unrealistic, he will probably develop symptoms that will break through the drug control. Then, finally, he will have to learn to set realistic sales goals, reduce hours, seek another employer or occupation, enlarge his scope of activity to include affection and recreation—to do *something* different—if he is to maintain control of his life and symptoms.

And why should he not have learned that in the first place, instead of masking the problem with a drug? Because he may not have wanted to change? Or because his physician may have implied that a drug would solve his problem? Or because he thought that the world was bound to make him and his generation hard driving or upset? Or because he thought he was an especially sensitive person whose fate, because of his basic nature, was to have ulcers, tension, or chronic fatigue? Such reasons are common.

Drugs need be viewed neither as the pre-eminent way to keep problems under control nor as pap which merely postpones a day of reckoning. *If* drugs can be prescribed in a way that facilitates solving the problems of living, if they are used only as they do this, and if their value is assessed in these terms alone, then they can be used rationally and effectively. They—like any other potential aids that may be utilized for human learning and change, such as reading, lectures, rewards, games, models—can then be evaluated as contributors to the problem-solving process, and as neither a hindrance to nor substitute for it.

Unfortunately, no such rational view prevails today. Psychoanalysts and nondirective therapists will seldom even consider using drugs in their procedures; if their patients want drugs, the therapists either put them off or send them elsewhere for treatment. The eclectics tend to use drugs generally, trying out most new ones as they come along, experimenting as if they would some day—or some year—find a magic elixir for each particular patient. There are many patients whose drug-taking trials cover ten and fifteen years and a dozen or two different medications. No drug has worked well for long, and it is rare for a disturbed person to find lasting relief with a limited prescription of the same drug. Yet thousands are treated as if they had a disease like diabetes for which they need only a medication like insulin to supply their body's deficiency.

Most psychotherapists perhaps would agree upon the value of

drugs in cases of incapacitating anxiety, in making an otherwise inaccessible patient amenable to advice or therapy. Yet even this is hedged by therapists according to their various persuasions. Some believe that all anxiety is bad and try to suppress it with medication. Others believe that some or even a great deal of anxiety is desirable in order to make you uncomfortable or desperate enough to change poor ways of living. Another widely accepted use of drugs is for emergency purposes, where such help may more promptly than any other method temporarily stave off loss of a job, complete retreat from life, compulsive self-destructiveness, or similar immediately damaging actions.

For the largest group of the most severely disrupted patients, the schizophrenics, heavy use of medication permits them to be released from hospitals. Of course, they also go back frequently, and there is no good evidence that they have learned to handle their problems adequately in their homes; but at least they can be moved out of the hospital, sometimes after many years there. Merely to get patients out of hospitals is a very limited view of the effectiveness of drugs, although it is financially attractive. It may well be, for example, that the patients and society would be better off if they were placed in highly organized, self-sustaining special communities. Or a vast expansion of behavior-modification methods of treatment instead of drugs might not merely get them out but may make them productive and self-sustaining in or out.

In any case, the use of drugs for serious emotional problems is today determined more by the attitudes of therapists, patients, and society toward their use, than by research evidence about their merits. It is relatively easy to determine that psychologically for most insects, fish, and animals tranquilizers tranquilize, sedatives sedate, and stimulants stimulate. What is *not* established at all is how such psychological effects will display themselves in emotionally disturbed human users. We will discuss later in this chapter the dramatic peculiarities that do appear when drugs are used by a disturbed human being who can, through his brain, actually alter the customary physiological effect of the drug. Here we would emphasize simply that the effects are highly varied and greatly influenced by the therapist, patient, and social attitudes and beliefs.

In a study[1] directed by the author several years ago, half of the patients in a group of long-time users of tranquilizers were abruptly withdrawn from all medication. None relapsed and some even improved, but after the study was over, almost all were returned to the drug. When the therapists were asked why, most could give no reason. It was the author's interpretation that these therapists could think of no alternative to use of the drug. Other therapists *do* use alternatives.

TYPES AND EFFECTS OF PSYCHOTROPIC DRUGS

The use of drugs generally in emotional disturbance is too big a topic to be covered adequately here. Some physicians and biochemists (along with Aldous Huxley) believe that some day through drugs one may be able to control and adjust his feelings as he wishes, without harm or undesirable side effects. Some act as if that day had already arrived. Here will be considered mainly the major psychotropic drugs which may affect psychotherapy, and how their use can best be integrated with the view that the most effective ways of handling your daily problems are psychological rather than medical.

"Psychotropic" refers for our purposes to those drugs which are intended to be used professionally to produce mainly a therapeutic psychological effect by changing your "moods." Thus antibiotics and hormones are not included, although they may produce secondary psychological effects—the one, for example, by reducing fevered fantasies; the other by increasing sexual interest. Nor are narcotics or marijuana included, since their main usage in the United States is not for professional psychotherapeutic purposes.

LSD has an ambiguous status since it is hard to say whether its experimental-therapeutic uses or its use for "kicks" is more common. The same is true about alcohol: although it is seldom directly prescribed by a physician, it is often suggested or encouraged in moderation as a relaxant or mood improver. And aspirin is one of the safest, surest psychological comforters, although it is more usually prescribed presumably for physical discomfort than for purely psychological purposes.

[1] Effects of Withdrawal of Tranquilizers," *Archives of General Psychiatry*, IX (1963), 513–519.

The hard-core, least ambiguous psychotropic drugs will be our subject, even though the *principles* discussed apply equally to such other drugs as aspirin, alcohol, cortisone, marijuana, narcotics, LSD, hormones, and antibiotics.

Three major categories among which psychotropic drugs may for convenience be divided are: *calming, stimulating*, and *disordering*. The calming drugs would include tranquilizers, sedatives, and, when prescribed therapeutically, alcohol. Until the middle of our century, the calming drugs used professionally were almost entirely the sedatives—barbiturates and chloral hydrate. They are still widely used, particularly for sleeping, although certain synthetic drugs such as Doriden and Noludar are now also used. They are seldom prescribed any more for daytime use, however, because of the drowsiness they produce and the rather serious physiological dependency and build-up effects over a period of time. For daytime usage, the tranquilizers have practically swept the field.

The tranquilizers can be divided into two categories: major and minor. The major tranquilizers are thought to act upon the central nervous system in some way which deadens or alleviates feelings of tension and worry without, under controlled dosage, impairing seriously such motor activity as walking and driving or ability to think. Among the most popular such tranquilizers are Thorazine, Mellaril, Stelazine, Trilafon, Taractan, and Prolixin.

The minor tranquilizers are thought to act upon the peripheral rather than central nervous system, and to produce a sense of relaxation without affecting the brain. The most popular carry the trade names of Miltown, Equanil, Librium, Valium, Serax, and Vistaril.

Although the tranquilizers undoubtedly can basically relax animals, including humans, when given in massive dosages, they do not, in the moderate doses commonly prescribed outside of hospitals, usually produce tranquil patients, at least for very long. Hospitalized patients have little to lose if they are drowsy or cannot think or act sharply as a result of drugs in heavy enough doses to control their troubled moods. Nonhospital patients, however, can have trouble at work, driving, or studying under such a drug regimen.

Prescribed stimulating drugs have been until this decade practically limited to amphetamines (for example, Dexamyl, Benzedrine,

Dexedrine), with the recent addition of Ritalin. The public depends far more on caffeine (coffee, tea) and nonprescription "pep pills," but these drugs are seldom prescribed (although caffeine, in military experiments, proved to be as effective a stimulant for practical purposes as there is). The amphetamines, however, often produce considerable edginess and other unpleasant feelings, and can build up in the body impairing the user's judgment.

Recently a new type of drug has been developed which is called "antidepressant." The physiological and psychological effects of this kind of drug are even foggier than those of most other psychotropic medicines. It is unclear whether they are effective, whether they are stimulants, and whether they are tranquilizers. They are *called* "mood elevators." They carry such trade names as Parnate, Elavil, Tofranil, and Marplan.

Finally, there are the "disordering" drugs which, with the exception of LSD used experimentally, are seldom prescribed for therapeutic purposes. Any of the drugs previously mentioned can, in heavy doses, in combination with other drugs, or enhanced by patient sensitivity produce disordered effects. But the *major* effects of such drugs as LSD, peyote, marijuana, and narcotics are "disordering." There is no firm evidence that any drug in this category, including LSD, has or is likely to have any practical usefulness in helping you to solve your problems. They do apparently help to produce fantasies and benign attitudes toward one's self, others, nature, and the world, as well as more active illusions. If they are not disruptive, they may be harmful in the sense that they take you away from your problems or lead you to see all objects in life— friend and foe, helpful and dangerous—through a rosy film.

MAGICAL EFFECTS IN DRUG USE

If drugs affected disturbed human beings only as they do the other animals, if human beings would report in words only the same results that experimenters can observe when such persons are not talking, or in other animals, or if humans would act and talk as if their problems were gone when they are physically sedated or stimulated, then perhaps drugs could be generally used sensibly.

But human beings distort the data in all of these areas. When people are given sedatives which they are told are stimulants, they report stimulating effects—even though they are observably slower in their actions. They may show or report no tranquilizing effect from tranquilizers which should have a physiologically calming effect if only the patient did not worry about taking the drug. They may report discomfort from taking a stimulant that must, physiologically, help to dissipate their complaints of lethargy—because when they gain alertness and energy they may not know what to do with it.

There is also an opposite effect. Relief may come from the first swallow of a pill that cannot physically have an effect for half an hour—or just from having a pill in a pocket to take if necessary. This "placebo" effect of feeling better is gained simply from being given something by a respected person; it can be anything, even a completely inactive powder or sugar pill to swallow. In a study which the author conducted[2] using meprobamate for one group and a similar looking sugar pill for the other, neither therapists nor patients could tell any differences in patient reactions to the two kinds of pills—although the patients on the sugar pills took more of them.

The therapist's enthusiasm also affects the results pills will have on patients. The more enthusiastic the therapist is in describing the possible results from a drug, the better the patient's response to it tends to be.[3] And if you have read and are impressed with a laudatory article about a new miracle pill, your physician can expect a temporarily favorable result.

What, then, is the matter with these magical effects from drugs? Why is it not enough for your physician simply to give you an undecipherable prescription form (many patients never do know what they are taking and what effect it is supposed to have physiologically) saying, "Here's something that will make you feel better?" Why should you not just let it go at feeling better, without having to know why?

The reason lies in our crucial principle that *you* should choose, judge, and use the resources of psychotherapy according to the way they help you to solve your problems in living. The magical use of drugs cannot realistically help you to solve your problems; that is

[2] "A Controlled Study in the Use of Meprobamate," *Journal of Clinical and Experimental Psychopathology* (Oct.–Dec., 1958), 323–329.

[3] Unpublished study by D. R. Stieper (St. Paul: VA Mental Hygiene Clinic).

an enterprise that requires the fullest use of your intellect and your other physical and psychological capacities. So far as is known, every psychotropic drug impairs to some extent the maximum potential use of your capacities. Of course, *if* your anxiety is reduced by sedation, you may be able to use your resources better than you could with severe anxiety—but not as well as by overcoming anxiety *without* the price you inevitably pay for taking sedation. Similarly, if your lethargy is overcome by a stimulant or antidepressant, you may become more efficient, though not as efficient as you could be if you overcame your lethargy without a drug.

THE PRICE YOU PAY FOR DRUG USAGE

No effect of drug use is more widely discussed and misunderstood than is dependency upon drugs. Drug addiction in the dramatic form of serious physical symptoms upon withdrawal is a major problem only with narcotics. While a few dramatic cases of physical dependency have been reported with almost all drugs, it seems likely that the vast majority of patients *who are at least not on heavy doses* can be withdrawn from any drug abruptly, and with psychological help alone not suffer serious physical consequences. For example, a group of patients who had been on a wide variety of tranquilizers for over two years were abruptly and completely withdrawn without a single important withdrawal reaction.[4]

So, when dependency on drugs is considered (with the exception of narcotics), one should refer to psychological, not physical, dependency—a desire to stay on the drug or a fear of cutting it off, not a physiological need for it to stave off dire physical consequences from withdrawal.

The dependency that does exist in many patients is not likely to be upon a particular drug or effect, but rather upon the *idea* of drugs. It could as well be on a wide variety of devices including hypnosis and vitamin pills—almost anything, in fact, that promises to do something to you to help solve your problems or make you feel better. It is this dependency upon a force outside of yourself that would seem to characterize the "dependent" drug user. He is taking the drug as an alternative to trying to solve his problems by using his own resources instead of using it only as an aid ancillary to his own primary effort.

[4] D. N. Wiener, "Effects of Withdrawal of Tranquilizers."

There are temporary or hopeless conditions of life where the alleviation of misery through the use of drugs appears justified: terminal cancer, death of a loved one, abrupt loss of job with no prospect of getting another, complete failure of a crucial project, or acute physical symptoms.

Except for such situations, however, the price you pay for usage should be weighed against possible side effects. It has been estimated that 10 to 15 per cent of all patients in New York City hospitals are there because of the side effects of medicines. Liver and blood are particularly sensitive to disturbance from psychotropic drugs. Users of most psychotropic drugs should probably have tests of liver and blood at least every three months. And the interactive ("synergistic") effect of psychotropic drugs with other drugs that may be used should also be of concern. This is particularly true for persons who drink or who work around industrial poisons and insecticides.

There are other psychological side effects. Can a tranquilizer be depended upon simply to calm, pleasantly, without depressing? Some patients on tranquilizers commit suicide. Of course, they may be of the type who committed suicide before tranquilizers were used. But any sedating drug seems capable of increasing feelings of depression. And some patients on sedatives get "hopped up." Is it because, being calmed, they don't know what to do with their energy?

Overdosing is a common problem. Some patients take sleeping pills to go to sleep, pep pills to wake up, tranquilizers to calm down and antidepressants to keep going—all in the course of a day. The effects of these pills tend to overlap and build up, and the body's economy is thrown out of kilter. Many patients end up literally not knowing themselves anymore. They are an amalgam of imposed chemical effects; their bodies are no longer under their psychological control.

Under such circumstances, drug effects and their adjustment and control may become the crucial facts of life. And this can occur only at the expense of a concentration upon the external problems in your life. Not only do your real-life problems become submerged under such circumstances, but you lose the keenest use of your intelligence to solve your problems, the sharpest focus of your anxieties to point the way to the source of your problems, and the most sensitive attention to your hopes, desires, aspirations, and values.

Chester Bennett has objectively described the personal effects of drugs on intellectual behavior.[5] He took a variety of drugs and performed the same high-powered task under the influence of each of them—working a *New York Times* crossword puzzle. None increased his ability to complete the puzzle, and all but one reduced it. No drug can increase the inherent intellectual resources of a human being. Sometimes, without your having to pay a heavy price, they will permit you to use your resources better than when you are psychologically disturbed. But you probably will never do as well with them as without—if you can find effective psychological ways to solve your problems. Furthermore, it appears that behavior-change effects produced under drugs will not persist once the drugs are withdrawn.[6]

THE RATIONAL USE OF DRUGS

Basic to the rational use of drugs to aid psychotherapy is their effect on the solving of life's problems. If they do not do that, their use is, in the long term, not rational.

You should also ask your therapist about the precise physiological effect of the drugs and ways of taking advantage of their effects to advance your problem-solving. If a tranquilizer appeared useful in calming you so that you made a better appearance at a job interview, then that is when and how you should use it. You would similarly be taught to gauge the effectiveness and value of any other major drugs that might be useful to you.

Disturbed persons probably tend to react as irrationally to drugs as they do to other influences in their lives. It is rational people who are most likely to gain the effect the drug physiologically has—and they need it the least.

On a panel a decade ago, this author expounded on the problem of getting mental-health-center patients to reduce their dependency upon drugs. He was followed by a state hospital administrator who described his problems in getting psychotic patients to take them.

---

[5] L. Uhr and J. G. Miller, *Drugs and Behavior* (New York: John Wiley & Sons, Inc., 1960).
[6] D. K. Kamans, "Selective Review of Effects of Discontinuation of Drug Treatment," *Psychological Reports*, XIX (1966), 743–749.

Thus it rests with the particular therapy and therapist to set the patient on a course of drug usage or nonusage which makes sense in terms of his problems and the drug's physiological effects.

EXERCISING PERSONAL CONTROL

To use drugs rationally—and to ensure that you as the consumer are being guided wisely in this regard—you need to know about your therapist's attitude toward them; you need to have informed attitudes yourself; you need to be able to recognize and adjust to dosages, side effects and combinations of drugs; and you need to be able to use drugs to advance you toward your goals.

Physicians seldom have or take enough time to inform you thoroughly about drugs and their effects. So you must often try to gain information on your own initiative.

You may legitimately disagree with your physician in his general attitudes toward drugs—as in anything else he or you believe in which is not factual. After all, there are many fundamental differences within the medical profession itself. He may lean heavily on the use of drugs personally and for his family, or he may tend to reject them. You must decide for yourself finally what your use will be.

The physician's bible which he uses extensively to find out about the composition, effects, and dangers of drugs is the *Physician's Desk Reference to Pharmaceutical Specialties and Biologicals*. It is published annually and might be available to you in your local community or college library. A Harvard Medical School physician, Richard Burack, has also recently published *The Handbook of Prescription Drugs*[7] for public use.

You should be informed about the name of the drug you are taking, the kind of chemical it is, its established physical and psychological effects, possible side effects, the time needed to take effect, its duration of effect and range, and the varieties of dosage. You can thus be alert to your particular problems of usage, keep your therapist fully informed about effects, and make adjustments for maximum safety and usefulness.

Above all, by being well informed and in control of your drug usage, you can squeeze maximum benefits from medication. You can use the drug only as and when it seems likely to advance

[7] New York: Pantheon Books, 1967.

you toward your goals; you can use it in the minimum amount and length of time needed to help you; you can give it up when you feel undesirable effects building up.

Some physicians believe that you must take a drug for some time before you gain its benefits. Others believe that you should take it indefinitely to keep your mood at a certain level. Some act as if a psychotropic drug by itself compensates for a kind of body deficit, as insulin does for the diabetic. Some believe that they alone should determine dosages and judge effects—that they alone should control your use of drugs.

One would hope that your relationship with your therapist would be well enough established in the free, equal way recommended throughout this book so that drug use would be subject to the same relationship. Your therapist would act as a technical expert able to give you psychological information about drugs and his beliefs about usage, encouraging judicious, medically supervised experimentation, with your focus always on solving your problems—not merely on changing your mood. Here too one would hope you would function as an informed consumer, choosing and judging wisely for yourself the service being rendered you.

Part V

SAMPLES OF THERAPY
SESSIONS

CHAPTER 15

Problems of Choice and Editing

IT IS with considerable trepidation that we will attempt in this section to illustrate what goes on in the major forms of psychotherapy. Whenever one tries to illustrate someone else's methods, he is a sitting target for pot shots accusing him of parody, ignorance, or malice. Legitimately any practitioner can say, "But that's not the way I—or my colleagues—do therapy." Yet how can you, as a prospective consumer, be fully informed about what goes on in psychotherapy without finally being able to hear or read something like the actual conversations that occur between therapists and patients behind closed doors?

These interviews are not for professionals who tend to carp at deviations from their special perception of truth. You, as a consumer of therapy, will not be as concerned as the professional with detail and elaboration. You may even see more clearly through trivial professional arguments about the course of some dialogues to the larger factors that appeal to you as offering the best hope for help, or giving you at least a sound basis for shaping an opinion.

Actually, in the training of therapists, an increasing amount of such illustrative material is being used. Only a little over two decades ago, this author was a relatively lonely protagonist and user of wire recordings to teach not only psychology students but also patients about what went on in his practice of therapy. Still, a variety of arguments then, and even now, are used by therapists against making recordings or transcriptions of their interviews.

Often therapists say: "But making a recording—and knowing it is being made, by therapist or patient—will make a difference in therapy itself, in how they will talk to each other." Most therapists and patients, however, quickly become acclimated to the situation.

Usually this concern is merely the excuse of a therapist or patient who, without any such experience, is simply anxious about being recorded.

Another negative argument is that the recording misses important nuances in the interview such as facial expressions of anger or grief, or a smile, body tenseness, the questioning lift of an eyebrow, or foot tapping. Some therapists have filmed or televised interviews to take fuller account of what goes on, and such a procedure surely is more complete. But the written or recorded reports are so much more practical in many situations, and verbal communication so especially important to most therapy, that the occasional incompleteness of recordings seems insufficient reason not to use them educationally.

Some therapists comment that recording interviews is unethical in that it somehow violates the confidentiality of the interviews. We agree that recordings violate confidentiality if they are made without the knowledge of either of the participants. If *both* therapist and patient are fully informed of the purpose, however, and if the recordings are never used for any but the stated purpose, and if both parties have full freedom to accept or reject being recorded at any time, then professional usefulness and ethical considerations should be satisfactorily reconciled.

In a more positive vein, let us review the advantages both of making—and of having available—verbatim transcriptions of psychotherapy interviews to consumers of the service. They have already become widely available and are used within the profession for training and research purposes despite the continuing reluctance of many therapists to go on live display even to colleagues. They have become increasingly popular for this purpose because there is no better way to convey to students what therapy is than to show it to them live or verbatim; above all other reasons, this is our purpose in presenting "verbatim" sessions in this book—and suggesting how you might get others.

The possible artificiality or deceit injected into the interview because the recording is being made would seem to be outweighed by the advantages of having the therapist go "on stage." The main difference going on display seems to make to the therapist is that he tries harder to perform at his best. He may speak more clearly or more fluently than usual, his interpretations may be more careful, he will surely not doze off or daydream. If the recording is not typical, it is likely at least to show him better than usual, feeling pressed to do the best job he can instead of just his average.

By all means try to get and hear or read a recording or verbatim transcript of the therapist you are considering, or of someone else who presumably practices a similar approach to his (or whom he recommends as similar).

Also, from reading the protocols to follow here or others, you can understand better what to expect from alternative forms of therapy you may wish to consider. You may likewise gain an idea of how your therapist might feel that certain behavior on your part may advance your therapy. You may gain the courage to reveal a sexual secret when you hear how acceptable and helpful it can be from the example of others. Or you may find it can be of benefit to express anger, when criticism does not follow.

THE CHOICE OF INTERVIEWS

Of course, the usefulness of interview transcripts hinges on what materials are chosen. Are they representative of the kind of therapy being illustrated? Do they typify what has gone on in this course of therapy? Are they fair samples of the therapy, therapist, and patient?

Actually, therapy is usually extremely boring to listen to or read —most professionals will tell you that. There are many, sometimes lengthy silences when nothing happens, endless minutes of repetition, embroidery, and dull talk on both sides. You would not want to read or hear hours of such stuff.

To avoid such tedious material, we have used a method we call "Time-Lapse Protocols." This method, adapted from the similar method in photography, makes use of excerpts at timed intervals to give the flavor of a continuous process without requiring you to observe the many intervening hours involved. We will attempt to do this by making brief selections of typical periods throughout the therapy and within a session. Thus, the entire process can be sampled and the exact kinds of conversation observed. What is necessarily missing are long periods of seeming inactivity, repetition, irrelevancy, and embroidery which are an integral part of almost all therapy.

THE CHOICE OF EDITORS

Despite the above cautions, it is likely that a single author-editor will bias his presentation in so delicate a matter as presenting practices with which he may disagree. Certainly no single editor can achieve typicality in his selections that most others would agree with. Nor, for that matter, can two editors, nor probably twenty-five. Still, special care should be taken to be fair and representative in selection and editing. This has been attempted by beginning with verbatim accounts by therapists of the approach being illustrated, and choosing additional editors who represent the form of therapy being excerpted. The editors do not necessarily agree with the way therapy is being done, or excerpted, but they agreed to help shape the nonfiction version into a slightly fictionalized one that seems to them to be more representative of the way they do therapy.

ACCURACY OF THE ACCOUNTS

The accounts to follow, then, will be case histories and interviews of real patients, disguised in name and other background details just sufficiently to be unidentifiable. They have also been edited just enough, by representatives of the different approaches, to be more reasonably representative of the cases and interviews, of the approach being portrayed.

Can verbatim reports edited as indicated thus be made more real than nonedited reports? No one has ever, to our knowledge, been publicly congratulated for an accurate portrayal of a "typical" case of any kind of therapy. Probably a "typical" case cannot be portrayed, and that is not the primary purpose here. The purpose is simply to give you a feeling for the more important things that will probably impress you in your therapy if you go to one of the four kinds of therapists, and will distinguish him most distinctively from the others you might choose.

Instructions to the editors were as follows: "These are case histories disguised just enough to be unidentifiable, selected from interviews to represent a form of therapy such as you practice in early, middle, and final stages of treatment. Will you please suggest revisions to make the case presentation accord reasonably well in major respects with the practices of your kind of therapy? Your suggestions will then be incorporated. Your participation does not indicate your full agreement with the presentation or procedures, but simply that you have been willing to modify the protocol in the direction of your practices."

Remember, then, that the dialogues to follow did not occur as smoothly or progressively as portrayed. And some of the distinctiveness of particular patients and therapists has purposely been edited out to make the portrayal somewhat more universal. The sessions mostly were halting, dull, and seemingly useless for long periods of time in ways not portrayed. A single interview given verbatim might take up ten to fifteen printed pages in this book, with many pauses, repetitions, and boring detail. You must, then, take into account as you read the examples that they are intended to give you an overview of method and process; what cannot yet be effectively conveyed in print are the hard work, tedium, and sometimes the anguish of much of the therapy you may experience.

The cases as edited have turned out much better than the author believes they usually do in psychotherapy. Unedited accounts have proceeded much less smoothly with much more disappointment by patients and fumbling by therapists.

Most cases simply are not as successful as in the way portrayed. The therapist's effort may be similar, but following the statistical results of therapy, you are simply not likely to achieve such clear and satisfying solutions.

Remember that most current patients have previously had less than successful therapy. Most patients dribble away from therapy unclear as to when they should terminate, and with no mutually agreed upon solutions to their problems which would indicate to them when to quit. These illustrations show what your therapist wishes would happen and tries to make happen. He may tend to blame you if it does not, but of course you also wish it would end this way. So we can only hope that these illustrations will help you to choose the *kinds* of therapy and therapist that seems most likely to help you move successfully toward your goals.

The relative passivity of the therapist also may impress you. "What *is* he supposed to be doing to help, anyway?" you may ask yourself. The therapist who may roar like a lion at case conferences or in writing about how he accomplished this and forced that, surely must impress the general reader as a tame feline indeed in these accounts. Usually when he is being recorded or otherwise portrayed, he has the soft voice of a gently questioning or becalmed observer who seems to leave the work of therapy and of outside guidance to the patient. This may be as it should be, but it is a rare therapist who will not claim credit for more.

COMMENTARY AFTER REVIEWING THE INTERVIEW EXCERPTS

Clients come to the various therapists prepared to talk about different matters, in different ways, often according to what they think the therapist is interested in, believes, or considers important. Analysts are thought to be interested in dreams and the unconscious generally; nondirectivists in feelings about one's self and others; eclectics in advising vacations, tranquilizers, and hobbies. Or the client learns these things about his therapist in the interviews.

Thus, the therapeutic relationship can easily become a self-contained world, the only sure guarantee against which is some more objective way of discovering and stating the patient's problem. Perhaps what is needed is a problem diagnostic center completely independent of the treatment, where determining the nature of your problem is the sole concern, as at automobile diagnostic centers which are separate from repair garages.

Therapists tend to keep their necks retracted. The editors who reviewed these excerpts almost invariably wanted the therapist to do less, to move more slowly, to speak more cautiously. Is this out of fear that the therapist might be wrong or be too subject to criticism? The passivity of many therapists may be a proper safeguard against stupidity or arrogance, but is it a proper substitute for views, suggestions, advice, or any other active steps by the therapist designed to press the client toward change—if presented in a humble and/or tentative way for the patient simply to try out?

These patients all completed a substantial number of interviews and reached some kind of mutually acceptable termination point. Most patients do not stay this long. From the standpoint of the therapist, most of them quit "prematurely" and without his blessing. He seldom knows why, although he speculates about why and tends to blame the patient for being unable to follow through.

Usually patients express doubts and apprehensions in entering therapy—and when quitting it—even more strongly than when it is in progress. And why not? It is generally so costly and mystifying a procedure at the start, and so pervasive a part of daily living by the end, that apprehensions seem quite reasonable.

To GIVE YOU the flavor of psychoanalytic therapy in short interview excerpts is particularly difficult. The process ordinarily takes up to hundreds of hours more to unfold and progress than do other forms. In addition, beginning with Freud, psychoanalysts have been especially committed and sensitive to nuances of theory and practice and intolerant of deviations, and have made much of slight differences among them. They have tended to follow intently bypaths of theory suggesting that they are unique among their colleagues—even while they defer to Freud's ideas.

The consequent troubles in portraying what it is like to be the patient of a psychoanalyst or psychoanalytic therapist are several. Few analysts practice alike in their interpretations and counsel; their similarities tend to be more of form, such as using a couch. They do not publish verbatim accounts of their interviews. They tend to handle cases much longer than do practitioners of other forms of therapy. In sessions, they tend to be relatively silent or passive for long periods. Finally, they tend to believe that slight differences of interpretation make great differences as to the outcome of therapy.

Altogether, then, it is especially unlikely that psychoanalytic practitioners will agree upon any presentation as representative of the field. You as a patient, however, may see more similarity than do professionals. In this case, a highly experienced and conventionally trained psychoanalytic practitioner has agreed that what is portrayed in this section is, within broad limits, characteristic of what might happen in many cases of psychoanalytic therapy. Actually this account, as did the other cases, started as the true report of actual psychotherapy, but it has been edited to meet what the analyst-therapist regards as a more universal picture.

PSYCHOANALYSIS OR PSYCHOANALYTIC THERAPY

An assumed difference between "psychoanalysis" and "psychoanalytic therapy" has been described in the section on psychoanalytic therapy. The following excerpts from Jonathan Pratt's therapy are closer to psychoanalysis because that form furnishes a kind of model of therapy toward which less formal analytic forms are oriented.

The more diluted or unique forms of psychoanalytic therapy can resemble almost any kind of psychotherapy—including direct advice in a few interviews, as described by a leading analyst, the late Franz Alexander.

Despite the variety within the psychoanalytic school, the illustration will be as conventional as possible. Less orthodox psychoanalytic therapy which works through sessions once or twice a week, ending in a year, or devoted much more to current behavior or immediate interpretations, or much less concerned with transference or the unconscious, represents an effort to preserve some important aspects of psychoanalysis—but to accomplish results in less time.

CASE HISTORY

Jonathan Pratt is a thirty-nine-year-old married man with two sons, eighteen and twelve, and a daughter, sixteen. He teaches social studies in a large high school in a Midwestern city, lives in a $20,000 suburban home, and earns extra income writing a column for his weekly community paper. Since childhood he had suffered no serious physical complaints, although his stomach tended to be sensitive to upset.

After years of considering it, he finally decided to seek psychotherapy because of chronic fatigue and dissatisfaction, constant bickering with his wife, and a sense of missing something important in life by not learning whatever psychoanalysis could teach him about his feelings, the world, and how to get more pleasure out of life. Several of his friends who had recently had therapy liked it and spoke glowingly about having really "had their eyes opened" as a result of it. He considered no therapy except psychoanalytic which he looked upon as a venture with a profound educational experience. No therapists or therapy except the analytic appealed to him as sophisticated, exciting, deep, and complex. He expected in some vague way to become a wiser, more creative, more profound, happier person as a result of therapy, though he had never pinned down how he would want to handle his life differently.

He wrote a letter to Dr. Rappen describing some of his background and problems, and asking for an appointment. He chose Dr. Rappen because two of his friends had gone to him and had spoken of him if not glowingly at least not negatively, and because the doctor had such strong credentials as a clinical appointment at the local university medical school, membership in the American Psychoanalytic Association, and ten years of experience since completing his training. Dr. Rappen had his secretary call Pratt to arrange a "preliminary" interview, at which it was agreed that there would be three interviews weekly at $25.00 a session, although Dr. Rappen said he "preferred at least four sessions a week." His usual rate was $30.00, except that Mr. Pratt could be given a "professional discount" (not *all* professions got such a discount from Dr. Rappen, only the more poorly paid and those in the mental-health field). Pratt, already knowing of the approximate cost, had arranged a loan of $1,500 from his father, and had decided to wait until that was used up to make further plans.

Pratt's interviews with Dr. Rappen occurred on Tuesdays, Thursdays, and Saturdays at 4:15 P.M., and they lasted forty-five minutes. He lay on a couch, while Dr. Rappen rocked gently in a chair at his head where he could glance at Mr. Pratt when he wished to, but not be looked at. Pratt mostly kept his eyes closed and tried to talk freely about whatever came into his head, except for occasions, which took up perhaps a third of the time, when he concentrated on Dr. Rappen's questions or interpretations. Most of the time Pratt talked about his current feelings, with the rest of the time divided between his past history and feelings and his dreams. When Dr. Rappen talked (about a third of the time), it was mostly to interpret, ask questions, and summarize. He was mainly interested in Pratt's feelings about Dr. Rappen, Pratt's apparent inconsistencies or exaggerations in describing past and present events, and his patient's efforts to defend himself against what Pratt inferred to be Dr. Rappen's criticism.

Most of the time when he was on his way to Dr. Rappen's office (or thought about going), Pratt felt anxious and fearful, as if he might fail somehow or turn out to be hopeless or that Dr. Rappen would become disgusted with him. He would at times be as eager and anguished as a lover looking forward to meeting an uncommitted object of his love. Often he left the office somewhat dazed, preoccupied with inner thoughts and ferment which seemed "out of this world," and he sometimes remained somewhat in a reverie through the evening. Except as his job or family or other outside business forced him into action, he tended to spend his time thinking about himself, the turmoil of his thoughts and feelings about himself, and about Dr. Rappen.

He also kept a notebook by his bedside so that he could make notes, immediately upon awakening, of any dreams he had, and he used the notebook during the day to jot down interesting associations and connections in his thoughts. But he quit keeping his notebook after about two or three months since he had too much to discuss properly even without it—too many dreams, associations, and random ideas about his past and present.

J.P.: Excerpts from First Interview (interview went on before and after these excerpts)

* * *[1]

Dr. R.: You lived in Zenith all your life?

J.P.: Yes, I was born there and lived there until I went to college.

Dr. R.: Tell me about your home and parents.

J.P.: Well, Dad was a hard man. At least he seemed tough to me when I was a kid. Mean sometimes. Wanting me to keep pushing, get good grades, work for him in the house all the time. He doesn't seem hard to me anymore. He seems soft now, in fact. Mother was always criticizing him for not being more aggressive on his job. They argued a lot. She was always crying to me about him. I hated it. He was assistant city attorney for thirty years. Never did get the number one job. He said he never wanted it. But I don't know. I think he did.

Dr. R.: How did you feel about your father?

J.P.: I hated him when he made me do things. I hated him to be mean to mother. But I felt sorry for him too.

Dr. R.: And your mother?

[1] *** indicates sections omitted.

J.P.:   She was complaining all the time about him and crying. I felt sorry for her. Sometimes I couldn't see what was so bad about him. Sometimes I thought she was right. But why should she always cry to me about him?

Dr. R.:   How did you feel about her crying to you?

J.P.:   It tore me up. Why me? Why couldn't she keep it between them? Why get me into it? I was just a boy.

Dr. R.:   What did you feel toward your mother for doing this?

J.P.:   I hated it. I hated every minute of it.

Dr. R.:   And her? How did you feel about her?

J.P.:   I hated it. I don't know. It wasn't her fault, I guess. She couldn't help it. She needed someone to talk to.

Dr. R.:   It's hard for you to say how you felt toward her then?

J.P.:   I don't want to say I hated her. But I must have. I guess I did. But it was all mixed up with feeling sorry for her, having her husband mean to her like that.

Dr. R.:   And what about your father, how did you feel about him? If you hated your mother and also felt sorry for her, I suppose you also had some mixed feelings about your father?

* * *

J.P.:   . . . So I decided I would never fight with *my* wife in front of our kids. We could fight tooth and nail in private. But never when the kids were around. That's why I hate my wife so much now. I can't get away from her. I can't stand it fighting in front of the kids all the time. But I can't get away from it.

Dr. R.:   You hate your wife now?

J.P.:   Well, not always. Only when she gets after me—especially in front of the kids. I can't stand that. I hate her then.

Dr. R.:   What about the rest of the time?

J.P.:   The rest of the time she's all right. She tries hard. She's smart enough. She can be good company. But sometimes I just can't stand the sight of her, I want to be gone.

Dr. R.:   Umm.

J.P.:   I shouldn't, I know. It's just that I can't stand her sometimes.

Dr. R.:   When else do you hate her?

J.P.:   When she gets after me. She really gets to me with her complaining sometimes. Finally I tell her to go to hell and then the fat's in the fire. She really blows up then and gives me hell.

Dr. R.:   You can't stand her complaining?

J.P.:   I'll say I can't. Whining and complaining. The kids too. I've got no patience with it. Never have had. Since I was a kid.

*   *   *

J.P.:   Are you interested in my dreams?

Dr. R.:   Why do you ask?

J.P.:   I don't know. I know that analysts are supposed to be interested in dreams. I just wondered.

Dr. R.:   Yes, they can be useful. Did you have a dream you want to tell me about?

J.P.:   I had a great one this morning just before I got up. I was being chased. I was running as fast as I could, but the crowd chasing me kept getting closer and closer. It seemed like I was trying to reach a safe place. But I couldn't seem to get there. *(Considerable questioning and answering about details follows: Where did it seem to be? Whom did the people look like? How did you feel about this? What does that make you think of?)*

Dr. R.:   It seems you were afraid. What occurs to you about being fearful?

J.P.:   Sure I'm afraid. About a lot of things. Like losing my job. Having my wife leave me. Going crazy completely.

Dr. R.:   But now. What are you especially afraid of now?

J.P.:   Now? Well, now, I suppose it's mostly being here. You. Whether you can help me. Whether I can ever get any better. I guess that's it.

Dr. R.:   You're anxious about being here and about whether you can be helped?

J.P.:   Yes, I am. Quite a lot. Can you? Do you think you can do something for me?

Dr. R.:   Well, maybe we should meet another time or two and see how things go. Perhaps when I know a little more about you, we can come back to this. You also mentioned about going crazy. What do you feel about that?

*   *   *

Most of the rest of the interview consisted of the beginning of an extensive recording of a case history, with Dr. Rappen asking detailed questions about Pratt's early life on up to the present time. This continued into the next session.

J.P.: Excerpts from a Middle Interview (after 162 sessions)

*   *   *

J.P.:   I had some peculiar ideas about you and my wife this week. I wondered a lot about what you were thinking about me. I even got the suspicion that my wife might be calling you and reporting on me. And you and she would plan together how to treat me. Sometimes I'd think that maybe I was really crazy and that you were keeping it from me. And protecting me. Like I was helpless.

Dr. R.: Umm.

J.P.: Sometimes it all seems so unreal. I imagine all kinds of things. About you—my wife—me. What's happening anyway? Am I going psychotic?

Dr. R.: No. Not psychotic. You're experiencing strong feelings now that must come out—here—toward me. Maybe toward your wife too. You will see these things later, they'll come together for you at the end.

J.P.: You haven't, you haven't really talked to my wife have you? About me. You wouldn't do a thing like that I'm sure. Still . . .

Dr. R.: You worry, don't you, about what I might do? How I might turn against you. Or let you down.

J.P.: I sure do. It would be terrible if you did. I could never trust anybody again. That would be it. You wouldn't really, I guess.

Dr. R.: Umm.

J.P.: You know, I guess I depend on you quite a bit. It's not like my father. I never did feel close to him. He was always pushing me. He never seemed to really care. I never could get close to him or trust him. He would never get very emotional about anything—except to criticize.

Dr. R.: Now you're feeling different?

J.P.: I certainly am. I can really let myself go in here. I trust you. You're trying to help me. It's hell to go through, though. Sometimes I really don't know what to make of you. You act so damn aloof sometimes. Like you don't care. But I guess I really know you're not going to work against me.

Dr. R.: What about my acting so damn aloof?

J.P.: I don't mean it just that way. But you know, I get such strong feelings about you and you just go sailing along. I'm just another patient to you. You've got your work to do. But it's so damn frustrating sometimes. I feel like telling you to go to hell.

Dr. R.: You get pretty angry with me, don't you?

J.P.: You're damn right! I get so mad I could blow the whole thing right up. You sit there acting like you know it all. Give me nothing. Not what I want. Just sit and nod.

Dr. R.: What do you want?

J.P.:   I want a human being there, a real live one. A good guy who likes me. Not another stone-wall father passing judgment all the time.

Dr. R.:   Do I remind you of your father?

J.P.:   You certainly do!

Dr. R.:   How do you feel about being treated that way?

J.P.:   Like hell! Like I was a baby or something. Who are they to be treating me like this? Who the hell do they think they are? I could kill them. They've got power over me. They can do anything.

Dr. R.:   What could they do to you?

J.P.:   Anything. They can do anything they want. I'm helpless.

Dr. R.:   What associations do you have? Anything that occurs to you.

J.P.:   I don't know. Just that it gives me a terrible feeling.

Dr. R.:   Umm. Go on.

J.P.:   Nothing, I can't think of anything. Just being helpless as a baby. Wanting something. But terribly afraid.

Dr. R.:   Wanting something? What could it be?

J.P.:   I don't know. Just something warm and good. Something to make me feel good.

Dr. R.:   What's the first thing that comes to your mind?

J.P.:   A breast, I suppose. Me—a baby. Having something to suck on. But how could I? I'm too old. It's foolish to want something like that. They'd get after me.

Dr. R.:   What could they do to you?

J.P.:   I'm just a kid and she could murder me, or anything, my mother. It's terrible. Terrible. (*sobs*)

* * *

Dr. R.:   And me. How do you feel about me?

J.P.:   The same way. You could too. You've got me helpless. You've got complete power over me. What can I do?

* * *

Dr. R.:   What connection do you see between your feelings of helplessness and fear and hatred now, and when you were a child?

J.P.:   Yes, yes. I guess I'm beginning to see it. They're the same. It's starting to make sense. It's hell to go through, though.

Dr. R.:   And your fear of helplessness with your wife now? And your hatred of her?

J.P.:   Yes, I know. I could see it at home last night. That's what happened. She was telling me to wipe off my shoes before coming into the house. I could feel myself getting angry with her. Like who did she think she was talking to, one of the kids?

Dr. R.: And what happened?

J.P.: Well, it wasn't so bad this time. I don't know why. I seemed to have a little better control or something. It's a funny thing. It was just different somehow.

* * *

Dr. R.: And you thought I might be in with your wife on this? How did you feel about me?

J.P.: It wasn't so bad about you. You're OK. I know you wouldn't do anything like that.

Dr. R.: But what were your feelings about me when you thought about me conspiring with your wife?

J.P.: You're sure it's all right? You won't take offense? I know it's just a feeling. I know better. It's just that—does it matter? Do you have to know?

Dr. R.: Yes, it's important to say anything that comes to your mind. Anything.

* * *

J.P.: Excerpts from the Final Interview (after 353 interviews)

J.P.: Well, this is it—the last interview. I never thought we would come to this. You know, I still have very mixed feelings about it. How I'll get along. Losing you as a friend. Being on my own. I'm so used to coming here. Life won't seem the same without it.

Dr. R.: Leaving it is almost always hard, but you'll get used to it.

J.P.: I suppose. (*Sighs*) Still, you know coming here three times a week for two and a half years—you get used to it. It's like part of you.

Dr. R.: Umm.

J.P.: I feel way ahead, of course, of where I was when I first came. I don't feel very different in some ways. But I've learned a lot. I can see things much better. I was really pretty blind at first.

Dr. R.: There's always a lot to learn about yourself.

J.P.: I suppose I still haven't got it all. I mean there's always more. You've always got the dreams and other unconscious stuff to work on. But I'm sure I've got to go out on my own now and see whether I can use what I've learned.

Dr. R.: Yes. You can always continue to learn.

* * *

J.P.: So, you see, I've still got some of these symptoms. I still don't like to go home for visits and face my folks. I still get angry with my wife. I still get depressed or anxious at times. In fact just yesterday I felt kind of low.

Dr. R.: Yes, I know. Sometimes these things even flare up a little when you are ending therapy. It's quite common.

J.P.: But shouldn't I have them under control by now? Shouldn't they be all over?

Dr. R.: No. You can't ever be entirely rid of problems and this kind of feelings. You remember, we talked about that.

J.P.: Yes—but I guess I keep hoping. And especially now, finishing up. I want to make sure I'm not overlooking anything.

Dr. R.: Well, these feelings are quite natural. This happens quite often. You're not thrown by them, are you, like before?

J.P.: No, I guess not. Not at all. I'm certainly a lot better off. I get over them much faster. And I really understand them now.

* * *

J.P.: So I was wondering. I know you said I could always come back if I got stuck on something. But then, would you really be willing to see me just for a little while?

Dr. R.: Yes, I'd always be willing to see you. But I wouldn't expect you would need to see me for a while at least. Sometimes you'll get upset. But I think you can work most of these things out on your own.

J.P.: I know, but I was just wondering. Sometimes I think I still need you. It's been so long since I've been on my own.

Dr. R.: You remember, we've talked about this quite a bit lately. Everyone has to go through this at the end of analysis. It is hard to face. Still, it must be faced. And you can handle it even though you might be a little anxious about it now.

J.P.: I know that the day after tomorrow when I would be due here I'll feel lost. It will seem empty and strange.

Dr. R.: This feeling may last for a little while. It's natural after regular interviews for so long. But remember, I've taken vacations before. You'll get used to it and fill in with other things.

J.P.: Sure. I'm sure I will. I'll have to. I've got no choice. Oh, I know it'll work out all right. In fact, I kind of look forward to it at times.

* * *

J.P.: Well, it wasn't the big deal I thought it would be at the beginning. I don't feel any great big bang. It's kind of gradual the way I got better. But I don't feel like I'm walking on air or anything. Or that I'm a completely new man.

Dr. R.: You've changed a lot of the feelings you had, haven't you?

J.P.: Sure. I feel a lot better. I don't get nearly as upset or depressed as I used to. Just about everything's better. But no great big deal, you know.

Dr. R.: Are you disappointed?

J.P.: I guess so. A little. No big thing though. I've learned a lot. I feel better. No, it was worthwhile all right.

* * *

J.P.: You know, when I think back over some of the things I've said—I've talked about here, I just wonder.

Dr. R.: Wonder?

J.P.: Yeah. How I could have done it. Oh, I knew a little about psychoanalysis and how it was supposed to go. And I know that you told me to say anything. But still, you know, the things I've talked about!

Dr. R.: It still surprises you, what goes on inside?

J.P.: I'll say it does. And I still can't figure out just how that made me get better. Why it worked.

Dr. R.: You remember about uncovering your deepest feelings, and seeing how they affect you, and . . .

J.P.: Sure. I know all about that. But what I mean is, well, it's why it all works this way. I know all the reasons. And I believe them. It's just that sometimes I wonder.

Jonathan Pratt remained in psychoanalysis for a little over two years. During this time, in the terms of his analyst, he worked through some of the problems of his early Oedipal situation, matured in his relationship with his wife, and developed more adult interactions (i.e., of equality) with authority figures and friends. In his therapist's view, his basic characterological structure remained (and perhaps this is usually said) unchanged—that of a man marked by early overwhelming parental influence as permanently defensive, one who tends to protect his status by blaming others for his problems.

He never returned to therapy, although he was still plagued by many problems and was often severely depressed. Yet these causes of his misery did not result in serious external troubles such as divorce or dismissal from his job. He had gained confidence in himself and now felt affection for at least one person in his life, his therapist. This feeling, which was reciprocated, seemed for years to give him a source of personal strength he had lacked.

CHAPTER 17 *A Nondirective (Existential)*
Case

ORIGINALLY, in the late thirties, the principal technique of non-directive therapy was to encourage the client to feel, think, talk, and work out his own problems bathed in the warm glow of thera-pist empathy, understanding, and support. Presumably under this approach, the client's better nature and hidden resources would slowly unfold. The therapist conveyed his empathy by judicious nods, repetitions of the patient's words and feelings and, occa-sionally, tentative summaries or extensions of the client's state-ments—but nothing more of personal views or counsel.

Some nondirective therapists have continued to practice in this way, but others, led by Carl Rogers, have reached out for a philosophy about life which has become similar to the views of some existential therapists. Nondirective and existential therapists often sound similar now, philosophically, in their approach to human problems. Emphasis upon human values, place in the world, self-understanding, and love are often the common denominators.

While there are few practitioners who call themselves nondirec-tive or existential, their influence upon the field of psychotherapy has been considerable. Many eclectic therapists at times use their approach. The writings of these nondirective and existential thera-pists have been extraordinarily influential, and you will very likely, at least sometimes, meet up with their views in whatever therapy you receive.

CASE HISTORY

Marion Ganders, a twenty-nine-year-old housewife with three young children, has just been shocked into severe depression and anxiety upon discovering that her husband, a middle-level executive in a medium-sized manufacturing company, had an affair with his secretary for a month during the summer when she and the children were at their lake home. Until this event, her life with him had been conventional, comfortable, and placid.

She had always thought of herself as an enlightened young wife whose main job was to serve her husband and children, but who also, for their benefit and hers, should pursue her education and civic activities. She had usually taken at least one course each semester at the excellent university in their city, and it was through its counseling center that she was referred to a private practitioner when she sought help for her problem. She knew something of the nondirective and existential approach from the instructor in a psychology course on human problems she had taken, and had been impressed with his sympathetic manner with students. The instructor, Dr. Bitler, spent half his time teaching at the university, and was a clinical psychologist with accreditation through the American Board of Examiners in Professional Psychology and state licensing as a psychologist.

Dr. Bitler's sessions with Mrs. Ganders ran fifty minutes. He saw her once a week, except for twice a week at the beginning when she was exceptionally anxious and in the third month when she had a brief recrudescence of the early extreme state. He charged her $20.00 an hour.

Marion Ganders always looked forward to her sessions with Dr. Bitler. He appeared invariably calm, understanding, and sympathetic. He never pressed her, except to trust herself and her feelings. She almost always felt that he was interested in her, that he thought well of her as a person, that he wanted to help her to develop her better nature and learn to fulfill herself in congruence with her environment.

She spent most of her time talking about her present views of herself, her aspirations, and her difficulties in becoming the kind of person she wanted to be. She discussed her past very little, except to develop the ideas that she had always felt somewhat inferior as a child and youth, had therefore been especially proud to marry a bright, handsome man who liked her, and still became depressed when she was with her original family with its faintly disapproving ways.

Dr. Bitler encouraged her to do most of the talking. He talked only about a fifth of the time. Then it would be mainly to reflect what she was saying, or to try to link her ideas in a coherent way. He might gently nudge her to think and talk more in a certain direction, and just occasionally he would inject into the therapy a philosophy of living having mainly to do with the need of a human being, in this case Marion Ganders, to find an active, gratifying relationship to the world and the people in it, and particularly to those nearest her.

M.G.: Excerpts from First Interview

* * *

Dr. B.:   Well, Mrs. Ganders, what's troubling you?

M.G.:   I've got this thing on my mind—all the time. I can't get rid of it. I know it's silly and all, but I can't shake it. It's terrible. I can't even talk about it now that I'm here. I'm sorry to be wasting your time this way. (*Cries*)

Dr. B.:   Can you tell me what it's about?

M.G.:   I don't know. I'll try. We've got a good family life. Everything was going along very well. We're very busy. We've been married twelve years. Then this thing happened. It was this summer and I haven't been able to get it off my mind since.

Dr. B.:   Hmmm.

M.G.:   My husband, he's a wonderful man really. He's kind and generous. He's good to the kids and me. Then this thing came up. (*Cries*) It'll never be the same again.

Dr. B.:   Oh?

M.G.:   I don't think I'll ever get over it. Nothing will ever be the same again.

Dr. B.:   Please tell me about it.

M.G.:   Yes, of course. I've got to settle down. It happened this summer when the kids and I were at our lake cottage. He was staying alone in the city during the week and coming out to stay with us for long week ends. He had an affair with his secretary the month we were gone. That's it. But I can't get over it.

Dr. B.:   It really gnaws at you?

M.G.:   Yes, that's it. I keep thinking about him and her, and keep saying to myself, "How could you do it to me? How could he do it to me?"

Dr. B.:   You put it on a personal basis—as if he were actually doing it to you—thoughtlessly or deliberately directing it against you?

M.G.: Well, it's sort of like that, yes. He must have known how I'd feel, and he did it anyway. How he could come to me week ends and go to bed with me—and all the time be thinking of that other woman. (*Cries*)

Dr. B.: It really hits you on a sore spot.

M.G.: That's right. It makes me feel like nothing. He didn't even think of me. I was just there, but it was as if I didn't really matter.

* * *

M.G.: I never did have a very high opinion of myself. I thought I was pretty lucky to marry my husband. My family thought so too, I think. They never said so, but I sensed it. I was like the ugly duckling in the family. I'm not really as pretty or sharp as my sisters.

Dr. B.: Now this affair has opened up all the old wounds?

M.G.: Yes, that's exactly it. It's like I'm back where I started. All those years wasted. Just when I thought I had finally succeeded at something. It was all just a dream.

Dr. B.: You feel now that nothing you built in your marriage matters, that you've lost everything.

M.G.: Well, not really. We're still there living together with our children. But all my self-confidence is gone. I feel completely battered.

Dr. B.: In other words, even though your specific achievements are still there—your home, your children, your place in the community—your sense of personal worth is lost. Something you felt about what you had accomplished is gone—but not actually what you had accomplished.

M.G.: Yes, of course, we've still really got what we had at the beginning of the summer. It just seems hollow and meaningless to me.

* * *

M.G.: So I don't know whether you can help me. I'm so utterly devastated. Maybe I should give up and get a divorce. Often I think I should, that it's all over between us.

Dr. B.: So you feel like giving up. And what then?

M.G.: That's it. It seems like there's nothing else to do. But I just can't shake it. It's not fair to my husband and children to just go around like a zombie. But what can I do?

Dr. B.: It's hard to decide what to do, I know.

M.G.: You're my last hope. I've tried to struggle along with this myself. But it's not getting any better. It seems just as bad as when I first discovered it. Do you think you can help me?

Dr. B.: You hope I can help you, that somehow I can help you get over this. Yet of course you also know that the real help has to come from within you somehow. You've struggled on yourself, unsuccessfully. Now perhaps I can help you to form a better relationship with your husband. You can perhaps come to feel more like an equal who can then see him more objectively with all of his problems.

M.G.: I hope so. If I could only feel that way. I know he has his problems too. I wish I could help him.

M.G.: Excerpts from Middle Interview (after 18 interviews)

M.G.: You know, I think I'm beginning to see why this seemed so terrible to me. Really see and feel it, I mean. It was as if he couldn't love me—and also want her. I took it personally. But he didn't mean it that way.

Dr. B.: Umm.

M.G.: I'm beginning to feel more compassion for him. A real sympathy. And it makes me feel good when I can think about him this way, and ways I can help him—and us.

Dr. B.: First you were angry with him. But now you're thinking of ways you can improve your marriage?

M.G.: Definitely. What I really need is a place—to be needed. It's altogether different when you can begin to feel things outside of your self, and do things for others, and feel worthwhile.

* * *

M.G.: I can't stand to look at that girl. They can't fire her, so she still works in the office, only she's someone else's secretary now.

Dr. B.: She still bothers you?

M.G.: Yes. I think of her sometimes out of the clear blue. Other times it's after I happen to see her near his office.

Dr. B.: She still gets to you? How do you mean?

M.G.: Well, I think of her seducing him, probably thinking I'm no good, that I'm an old bag, or something. He's sort of innocent. She probably wound him around her finger.

Dr. B.: So now, even though you've got the situation with your husband somewhat in hand, you still are troubled about the other woman.

M.G.: I guess she hits home more. She's a woman like me. It's harder to be objective.

Dr. B.: Do you mean she's more like direct competition, or that you feel inferior relative to her?

M.G.: She's younger and prettier and she's got no responsibilities. I hate her. Still that's not fair either. She probably didn't mean any harm either.

Dr. B.: Umm.

M.G.: I guess if I could completely get over the thing with my husband, I could get over it with her. Except that I don't see her much. How can I learn to control my thinking of her?

Dr. B.: Perhaps you can develop yourself further as you want to be, a sympathetic person. Have you considered what adopting that attitude toward this girl might mean?

M.G.: A little. I haven't tried very hard though. I know what you mean. I do want to understand her better and I'm sure that when I do, I'll feel the same kind of sympathy for her that I do for my husband.

* * *

M.G.: But doesn't the therapy really turn on what I think of myself? I've discovered that when I think well of myself, then I can take most anything. It's when I feel like a miserable failure that almost anything throws me.

Dr. B.: Hmm.

M.G.: I feel good more of the time now. It's like a haze lifting from all around me. I'm beginning to feel like an equal to others more and more of the time. I just wonder how far I can carry it. Can I really feel that way all the time?

Dr. B.: You can't quite believe that this new way of feeling can really be you—all the time?

M.G.: I guess not. It would seem too good to be true. It just wouldn't seem like me.

Dr. B.: But you sound quite hopeful.

M.G.: That's right. But I'll get there—maybe. I hope so.

* * *

M.G.: So then I asked him if he really wanted to do that, that it would hurt his little sister, and how would he feel about that?

Dr. B.: You were trying to help him feel for the other person?

M.G.: Yes. Like I'm trying to do for myself. And it seemed to work. He stopped right there. He didn't say anything. He just turned away without a word.

Dr. B.:   So you feel as if you had accomplished something with him —as you had with yourself?

M.G.:   Exactly. Here I can actually teach him based on my experience. It's wonderful to see how it works. Things in the house are more relaxed, too.

Dr. B.:   Hmm.

M.G.:   I'm getting back on my feet again. But I still get these bad spells sometimes when everything seems right back where it started. Then I think of how things have been going, and remember some good things about myself, and it seems like I can get over it after a while.

Dr. B.:   You still sometimes have bad periods then.

M.G.:   Yes, I get pretty depressed at times yet. Not as bad as before, but still there, and I know I've still got to work to improve myself and my views of myself.

M.G.: Excerpts from Final Interview (after 32 interviews)

M.G.:   We went out last night and it was like old times. It was like wonderful. We could be comfortable with each other. We liked each other.

Dr. B.:   You felt in harmony again?

M.G.:   Yes, only even better than before. We had come through something together. And it was better than before. As if we had shared something very big and important.

Dr. B.:   So you felt as if you had actually gained through this experience?

M.G.:   Oh yes. We had really gained—a sense of growing together. It was like you said before—that it's better to go through bad and good together than to have nothing happen. This is really living.

Dr. B.:   I wonder whether this isn't a kind of lesson that will permit you to continue to grow together?

* * *

M.G.:   Of course, I still don't want to go visit my family. In that sense I guess I'm not done with my problems.

Dr. B.:   What have you done about them recently? You haven't discussed them for a while.

M.G.:   Nothing at all. As little as possible, I mean. We don't go bundling up the kids in the car once a month and drive up to visit them like we used to.

Dr. B.:   And you feel all right about it?

M.G.: Yes and no. When the first of the month comes up—when we used to go—I still get a kind of twinge, like I should, if I were a good girl.

Dr. B.: But you decide not to?

M.G.: I just don't go. Oh, we'll still go for the big holidays, I guess, but otherwise not. It's just not worth it.

Dr. B.: Apparently you don't feel you have to keep visiting them— even when you don't want to. And you're satisfied with this.

M.G.: I guess so.

Dr. B.: You still have reservations though.

M.G.: Yes. I wish it could be different, that we could be closer, with mutual respect and equality. But they're always making these remarks, like I was still a little girl, and it still bothers me. And I decided, why bother. It's not worth it.

Dr. B.: So you've decided simply to accept this part of you, of your resentment, and operate accordingly. Which in this case means not visiting them very much?

M.G.: Hmm. It seems kind of weak maybe. Do you think—oh, you won't tell me, I know—but, I was going to say—do you think I should keep working on it? Everything's going fine otherwise.

Dr. B.: Of course you must make this decision for yourself. You might want to feel your way along with it for a while. You'll continue to change, you know, just as you have in here. Deciding how you want to be, how you want to relate to the world around you, and moving in that direction.

M.G.: I know. I really don't have to decide everything now, do I? Maybe someday I'll want to be closer to them and I'll feel comfortable about doing it.

* * *

M.G.: I know this is the last interview. And I asked it to be. But I still have my doubts. I just wonder whether I can make it on my own. I feel a lot better of course.

Dr. B.: One part of you made the decision to quit, on what seemed quite reasonable grounds. But another part keeps wondering, has doubts—feels perhaps a bit scared?

M.G.: Scared is right. Oh, not bad like I was when I first started coming to see you. But enough to make me wonder. Then I remember what you said a while ago: that this, too, this kind of fear, was a part of me, it was me, and I could learn to live with it or handle it, if it wasn't actually too bad and seriously affecting me or what I did. I know you're right. It's just that this being the last interview, it's a little scary.

Dr. B.: So you know you're better able to handle your problems than before. But you don't yet have full confidence in yourself. And breaking off here is like a complete cutoff from the source of help?

M.G.: I guess so. It's not really, though, is it? It's more like—well, just going off to try it on my own. I know I can always come back if I need to.

Dr. B.: You might be able to think through these things for yourself now. Even the scariness you felt. Even the uncertainty.

M.G.: I can see that I've got to try it. I decided that a month ago. It just takes a little extra talking with you to remind me that I'm handling things pretty much on my own now. And that I can continue to.

Dr. B.: I wonder if it's so much a nudge from me as it is a kind of thinking for yourself. At least it seems to me that this time you've pretty much done it for yourself—even though I was here and made a few remarks.

M.G.: That's about what you've done all along. Of course I do feel more now like I am on my own. And it helped a lot to have you on my side and pointing out things from my own standpoint. Not like someone judging me.

Marion Ganders returned to Dr. Bitler for two more interviews about three months after her last session, reported above. Her anxiety about her husband's affair had returned for a couple of days, and even though her fears were not as strong, she worried that they might continue. By the time she had her appointment, however, they were gone, and Dr. Bitler simply reflected her concern that her complacency at her new confidence had been shattered, even though her anxiety no longer disrupted her life.

As usual, his presence as a kind and understanding friend reassured her, and she decided that her fears were groundless. She therefore stopped seeing him and led a stable, conventional life, grateful for Dr. Bitler's continuing availability if she needed help.

CHAPTER 18 *An Eclectic Case*

ATTEMPTING to portray a "typical" eclectic case is foolhardy. By definition eclectic therapy can cover the entire gamut of possibilities in therapy such as: what sounds like psychoanalysis but is not professionally accepted as such because it is done by an unaccredited therapist; almost completely passive therapy by a therapist who seldom commits himself to anything; aggressive therapy where the therapist "lectures" his patient for most of an hour about exactly what he should do; "sub-convulsive" electric shock which mildly stimulates, followed by a few random remarks by the therapist about the weather and taking up hobbies; hospital rest with or without tranquilizers and ten-minute daily "therapy" interviews consisting of the brief exchange of pleasantries; conversation about whatever happens to come up, indistinguishable from what two strangers might be talking about when they sit next to each other on a bus.

A model of eclectic therapy will be presented, however, which will represent no extreme as listed above. There are many honest, bright, well-intentioned, experienced eclectic therapists around who have fashioned a handy amalgam of physical aids to relaxation such as vacations, drugs, and recreation; practical advice such as changing activities, joining social groups, talking to people nearby; and suggestions for attitude changes such as asking yourself, "What's so bad if that did happen," or saying what is on your mind instead of suppressing it.

It is this first-aid, practical kind of eclectic therapy that will be portrayed. It is no more certain here, however, than with the other methods of therapy that you will not run into strange practices by accredited practitioners that will require your most careful examination. For example, there are therapists who treat

275

several patients at a time during an hour, keeping them semi-comatose on drugs in small separate rooms, while they go from one to the other simply asking each to let his mind wander freely over any thoughts that arise. Others ask only for accounts of dreams and then interpret them, never asking what is happening in daily living.

At its best, however, eclectic therapy is aimed toward results to be gained, as directly as possible, and serves the invaluable social function of giving people in trouble a place to go where they can sometimes get prompt help in a concrete way that is easier for most people to understand than the other forms of therapy. In this sense it requires the least education, sophistication, or commitment from you as a patient. It is probably the most susceptible to change at your behest.

CASE HISTORY

Ralph Figare is a sixty-one-year-old truck driver with a long history of troubled personal relationships—with his family, his co-workers, and fellow members of organizations. Now he is extremely depressed about everything in life, feels that he has been a total failure at everything he has done, and cannot rid his mind of the idea that everyone hates him for the trouble he has caused them in the past. He also worries about having cancer and heart trouble even though he is in good health.

In past years when he was depressed, something had always happened eventually to make him forget it. He was very active at work, with his family, and in his church. For over a year now, however, a pall had hung over him that he had not been able to shake. He had quit all his extra activities, and that did no good. He had gone on two extended vacations, and he came back to the old feelings.

He felt desperate, and at his wife's urging had asked his family physician for help. The physician had suggested trying a new tranquilizer that had just come in the mail. While this drug relaxed Figare somewhat, his depression did not lift, nor did a subsequently prescribed "antidepressant" pill relieve him except perhaps for the first few days he tried it.

Finally, his physician suggested he see a psychiatrist in the same building and, at Figare's request, called and made an appointment for him. When Figare asked his physician about what the therapist would do and charge, he was told that he should discuss such matters at his first interview.

At the first interview, he was afraid to ask about the therapist's methods and charges. And he never did get around to asking, ever. At the end of the month, his bill indicated that the once-weekly sessions of forty-five minutes were costing him $25.00 each.

He spent most of his time discussing his complaints and troubles. Dr. Epstein talked about a quarter of the time, giving him advice about how to change his attitudes and suggesting various positive steps he should take. Occasionally, Dr. Epstein also interpreted some underlying hostility or wish he thought Figare was showing without realizing it.

R.F.: Excerpts from First Interview

* * *

R.F.: Doc, I don't know what's happening to me but I'm just not my old self. Nothing is going right for me. I don't know how much longer I can go on this way.

Dr. E.: Are you thinking of suicide?

R.F.: Yes I am. Oh, I would never do it. I'm too much of a coward I guess. But all kinds of thoughts go through my mind. I just can't get rid of them. I feel terrible all the time.

Dr. E.: How bad do you feel? Do you think you can go on?

R.F.: Oh yes, I can go on all right. I guess I can. It's pretty tough though, Doc.

Dr. E.: You don't feel that you need to get away for a while then? Go to the hospital for two or three weeks?

R.F.: No, nothing like that, doctor. I've got my wife to support, and I don't know what I would do in the hospital. I don't want to leave home unless I have to. Do you think I should?

Dr. E.: Well, no. At least I think we can try it this way for a while and see how it goes.

R.F.: That's good. I'd like to stay out of the hospital if I can.

* * *

Dr. E.: What's the main thing you're depressed about, do you think?

R.F.: I don't honestly know, doc. Everything, it seems like. Sometimes it's one thing and sometimes it's another. Right now I've got a big hassle going with a fellow I drive with sometimes. He bugs me with his stories about his different girl friends. He's a married man but he plays around a lot, you know. And he's always bragging about this girl and that, what a good lay she was. I told him last week to shut up, I was tired of it. Now I wonder what he's going to do to get back at me.

Dr. E.: What do you think he might do to you?

R.F.: I know he won't really do anything. He's just a big blowhard you know. But I get to worrying what he might say to the other drivers about me behind my back. Or bring charges against me with the union.

Dr. E.: Can he really hurt you?

R.F.: No, not really. I've been with the union for twenty-five years now and I'm pretty well thought of, you know. And I've been through this kind of thing before—a lot. Nothing can really happen.

Dr. E.: Then why should you worry? Could you remind yourself of how these things always turn out in the past?

R.F.: I try, doctor, all the time. I know that he can't hurt me. But right now that's what I worry about. I can't get it out of my mind.

Dr. E.: We have a fairly new kind of drug, you know, that often controls depression. I think we should try it and see.

R.F.: I've tried those already. Dr. Shaffer gave me some. They did a little good, but not for very long.

Dr. E.: I know. He told me about that. But I have something different I've used with pretty good success. I think it would be worth a try. Meanwhile of course we'll keep talking like now about what's bothering you and try to get at the cause.

R.F.: All right, doc, whatever you say. I'll do anything to try to shake this.

* * *

Dr. E.: We're getting near the end of the hour. Is there anything else you would like to bring up?

R.F.: Well, I don't know, doctor. Do you think you can help me? Have you ever seen anyone like me before?

Dr. E.: Many times. There are thousands of people with your problems all over the United States right now. Of course, no two are exactly the same. But this kind of depression is very common.

R.F.: Have you ever cured anyone with it? I mean, does anyone ever get over it?

Dr. E.: Oh yes, many people get over it by understanding it better. And by making some adjustments in their life. And of course

R.F.:   we get some help from these new drugs that raise your mood some. There are many things we can do to help you feel better.

R.F.:   I'm glad to hear you say that. You know I think I'm worse off than anybody else. I've never known anyone that felt as bad as I do. But I suppose you see lots of them.

Dr. E.:   Yes I do. And I can help most of them. Everyone seems to think he's worse off than anyone else.

R.F.:   I feel better already, doc. I'm sure you'll be able to help me. I hope you don't mind my questioning you. I just don't know very much about it.

Dr. E.:   No, of course not. You should ask me about anything that comes to your mind. Anything. This is one place where you can talk about anything at all. It will help you a lot to relieve yourself of it. And it will also help me to understand you better and be able to help you.

R.F.: Excerpts from Middle Interview (after 28 interviews)

R.F.:   I'm really down today, doc. Worse than ever. I knocked off from work and just lay around the house.

Dr. E.:   What happened?

R.F.:   Oh, no big thing happened. It's just my son. He as much as said to my face yesterday that he didn't believe me, and I thought, "What's the use." I've about had it.

Dr. E.:   What was it all about?

R.F.:   It was just a little argument about the school his kid goes to. I had heard that it was too easy for the kids and I mentioned that to him. He took offense at that. He said it was a good school, it was just that this kid was a kind of show-off and got into trouble because of it.

Dr. E.:   Why did it bother you so much?

R.F.:   I just thought I would try to help. But he didn't pay any attention to me. In fact, he as much as said I didn't know what I was talking about.

Dr. E.:   Why should it bother you so much? You should know that arguments are perfectly natural. You have to learn to take them, even with your own children. You can still be friends. Can't you do nice things for them?

R.F.:   I don't know, doc, it's pretty bad. He probably thinks I'm just a troublemaker. I never did get along with him so well since he got married.

Dr. E.: But you have gotten along all right, haven't you? Even after disagreements. If you can remember that.

R.F.: Oh yes, we never completely broke off with each other, if that's what you mean. No, I guess we get along all right. He seems to like me all right usually. You're right. We'll get over this I know. But then something else will come up.

* * *

R.F.: Then I've got this sex problem, doc. I've never told anyone about it before. I'm really ashamed of it. Those notes you're making. Nobody gets to see them, do they?

Dr. E.: No, absolutely not. They're strictly confidential. You don't have anything to worry about, about them.

R.F.: I've never talked about it at all. It's on my mind a lot. Do you think that's what could be causing all my trouble?

Dr. E.: Tell me about it. Then we can see how it fits in.

R.F.: It's pretty hard for me to talk about. But my wife has always been worried about having babies, see. After we had our third one and she had such a hard time. So, see, we started to do something. I think it's perverted or something. And it always bothers me.

Dr. E.: Umm. What was it?

R.F.: Well, doc, I wouldn't go through with it. I'd pull out before anything happened. That's wrong isn't it? How bad is it?

Dr. E.: There's nothing so bad about it. It's a common way of birth control. It's not a very good way since it's not sure and it often leads to tensions. But it's nothing like a perversion.

R.F.: Anyway, that's it. I've been worried about it for a long time. It's on my mind quite a bit. You don't think it's so bad, huh?

Dr. E.: No, it's not bad at all. Does anything else about it bother you?

R.F.: Only that people might find out about it. Then they'd talk about me, and knock me down about it. They'd think I wasn't much of a man, you know.

Dr. E.: Well, is it straight in your mind now? There's nothing the matter with it from the standpoint of manhood. It's common.

R.F.: Yeah, that's all good to know. I guess it's all right.

* * *

R.F.: I don't know, doc. I still feel pretty depressed. Is there something else you can do about it? Something that could make me feel better?

Dr. E.: What do you have in mind?

R.F.: Like some medicine, or something you can tell me that would straighten things out. Get me going again.

Dr. E.: I can give you a different kind of drug we can try out. But you know we haven't had much luck with the ones we've tried. At least not for very long. We can keep trying, though.

R.F.: How about some other form of treatment, like psychoanalysis? I've heard about hypnosis too. Or shock treatment.

Dr. E.: You have the free choice to try them of course. I'll be glad even to make referrals for you if you want me to. But I wouldn't particularly recommend them. I think with drugs, outside activities, understanding, etcetera, we can solve this thing.

R.F.: I don't know anything about them, you know. I was just wondering if I'm getting anywhere.

Dr. E.: It's always hard to decide about that. But you don't seem to be as depressed and hopeless as when you first came in. And you don't seem to get quite as upset about everything that comes along as you used to.

R.F.: That's right, doc. I know you're doing a good job. I just get to feeling pretty hopeless, that's all.

Dr. E.: As far as hypnosis and psychoanalysis are concerned, here's what you could do. *(He explains them, his willingness to make referral, and his own views, somewhat negative, of their appropriateness)*

R.F.: You don't think I should change I guess. What about shock treatment then?

Dr. E.: This would probably be more appropriate, and I can make arrangements for that any time you want to try it. It's often used in cases like yours and produces good results. It would probably be worth trying.

* * *

R.F.: Excerpts from Final Interview (after 55 interviews)

R.F.: Well, doctor, I've decided that this will be my final session with you.

Dr. E.: Oh?

R.F.: You've done a lot for me, but I've decided to try it on my own now.

Dr. E.: I see. How did you decide that?

R.F.: You know, I've been thinking about it for a while, spending so much money, not doing everything you tell me, and all. But mainly wanting to try it on my own for a while. I think I can make it all right now.

Dr. E.: You feel in pretty good shape to handle things on your own now?

R.F.: Yes I do. I feel quite a bit relieved of the old depression. I've still got quite a lot of it, you know. But I don't feel like I might commit suicide anymore or go crazy or anything like that.

Dr. E.: Is there anything special you've decided to do?

R.F.: My wife and I are going on a vacation. We're leaving next week for a month. We've always wanted to go out West, so we're going to travel around to the parks and that. You said that would be a good idea.

Dr. E.: Yes, I think it is. Anything else you're planning to do?

R.F.: I joined that health club last month, you remember, and I'm still going there. I like that. And my wife and I are still going to that bridge class we started with in the winter. We're pretty busy.

Dr. E.: And you feel better because of it?

R.F.: Yeah, I guess so. At least it keeps my mind off those things that used to bother me.

*   *   *

R.F.: So I've quit going to the union meetings, doc. They were aggravating me too much. I'd come home all stirred up. That's OK isn't it? I talked to you about it before. Remember?

Dr. E.: Yes, I remember. I think that's all right. As long as you're doing other things. Does it help not to go?

R.F.: I don't get mad, at least. I came pretty close to taking a swing at some of the guys there. Then I'd get worried about it afterwards. Don't you think that's all right, to quit?

Dr. E.: Oh, I think it's all right. You're just keeping away from a trouble spot for you, and that makes sense. What about at work otherwise?

R.F.: That's all right. I don't get into any fights or anything. I'm a good driver, I've got a good record, and I don't cause any trouble anymore. I just don't open my mouth.

Dr. E.: You don't talk out as much as you used to?

R.F.: I don't hardly say anything around there any more. Sometimes one of the guys'll ask me what's the matter with me. I don't say anything. Just, like "I'm OK" or "nothing." They leave me alone.

Dr. E.: That's OK with you?

R.F.: Sure. It's a lot better than it used to be. At least I've got nothing to worry about. Sometimes I think about what they might be saying behind my back about me. But not much. I just mind my own business and they leave me alone.

Dr. E.: That's quite a gain. Do you think you can keep it up?

R.F.: Yes, I think so. It's working out pretty well. I don't see why I can't keep it up.

* * *

Dr. E.: And how are things going at home with your wife?

R.F.: Pretty good. I haven't gotten mad at her for quite a while. She's trying hard to please me and all. I really don't have much cause to get mad at her.

Dr. E.: That's good to hear. You always did say that she didn't give you much cause, but you got mad anyway.

R.F.: I know I did. I just couldn't control myself. Now we do some things together. I just don't get mad much anymore at anything, doc.

Dr. E.: Has the depression gotten worse?

R.F.: I don't know. No, I guess not. At least I don't get into much trouble anymore.

Dr. E.: And you are vacationing and going out and keeping busier.

R.F.: Yes I am. I guess I really am feeling better. Sometimes it's hard to tell. But I want to quit coming in anyway and see how things go.

Dr. E.: That's perfectly all right. I think you may as well try. You can always come back.

R.F.: I'm glad to hear you say that, doc. If I get into trouble again, I'll sure be back. By the way, have you got any reading I could do that might help?

* * *

For about six months after sessions ended, Ralph Figare managed to keep moving on his own in the directions discussed. Then he returned to Dr. Epstein for three more sessions, and over the course of the next five years, consulted four other therapists. Even though their orientations were somewhat different, including the prescription of drugs by two of them—all of these therapists finally suggested that the patient keep busy, take up hobbies, schedule frequent vacations, and join congenial groups. One also gave him electric-shock treatment, but stopped when Figare demurred.

Essentially, Figare controlled his therapy more than did the other patients described earlier. Due partly to the patient's age and partly to his insistence on practical help, none of the therapists tried to impose a systematic approach. It is an open question whether any one approach could have accomplished more than any or all of the others, unless a therapist had tried successfully to convince Figare to work patiently with a systematic method, thus putting it—and others—to the test.

CHAPTER 19

A Behavior-Change Caes

THE BEHAVIOR-CHANGE case is perhaps the easiest to portray. Because it is the most recent, most concretely problem-centered, and most research-oriented of the methods, it has so far developed the fewest idiosyncrasies and individualistic leaders. A moving excitement, as if with a kind of new toy, seems to insulate it, at least temporarily, against within-group jealousies and competition.

Various behavior-change therapists may show an interest in or elicit different problems from the same patient, and they will have different solutions to suggest for trial. They are, however, more likely to accept a problem as originally put to them by the patient as the problem to be worked on. They are less likely than other therapists to impose or interpolate a problem dictated by their theoretical bias.

A major difference that is emerging, however, among behavior-change therapists involves the awareness and nature of the client's participation. Behavior-change efforts can be made with or without the subject's knowledge. Many experiments have been done and change accomplished without the subject being aware of what was being done to him.

Whether you should always know what your therapist is doing and why is a philosophical and ethical question, not a scientific one. This question is not special to the behavior-change approach. Psychoanalysts usually do not mention the especially potent effect of the transference relationship they encourage until toward the end of therapy. Nor do nondirectivists usually describe to their clients explicitly the special power they attribute to their warmth and understanding with their clients. Nor do eclectic therapists commonly make explicit the implied magic of their pills or apparent assurance in giving advice.

But behavior-change therapists speak and write more openly than do the others of "manipulating" or "shaping" behavior. They analogize between mice or pigeons who learn to solve problems by being given food pellets on an efficient schedule when they move in the direction the experimenter wants them to move, and the human being who is given compliments for the same purpose. This therapy is rooted in the findings of scientific laboratories and research projects. Its theory has been derived directly from laboratory observations. It imposes the least philosophy, speculation, and "intuitions" upon its practitioners and patients. It carries with it high hope for a scientific psychotherapy.

In our effort to take the consumer's view, we place ourselves on the side of the patient's right to know whatever is being done to or for him and why, and therefore will portray only that kind of behavior-change therapy that does keep him informed. In this view, there is no place for manipulations of which the patient is not informed, although many experimenters and therapists of all persuasions consider the patient's ignorance no handicap to therapeutic success, and often an advantage.

Behavior-change therapy also has several faces. One is that of the rigorously direct conditioner who, like Wolpe, may try to cure a phobia of dogs or airplanes by presenting stimuli in little doses, moving the patient in small steps toward a final confrontation with the fullblown, originally feared object; and there is the hospital psychologist who gives psychotic patients candy or money when they do something useful to their rehabilitation. Also there is the therapist, most notably Albert Ellis, who tried to change the words the patient tells himself that trigger his self-defeating behavior.

We will portray here a more complex behavior-change effort with a patient and problems comparable to the patients and problems portrayed in the other approaches. It attempts to change self-defeating behavior both by blocking its occurrence and by substituting for it more positive, rewarding behavior. The major limitation of behavior-change therapy today, aside from the paucity of good research (a fault even more characteristic of the other therapy forms), is the narrowness of its applications. It usually is applied to small segments of behavior. It is conducted in the laboratory, where it seems too simple-minded to be significant for the real problems of human beings in the world. After all, teaching a schizophrenic patient in a hospital to eat with a fork instead of his hands, by giving him a token or piece of candy, seems an infinitely easier task than teaching a lawyer to treat his wife nicely so that she will go to bed with him—even though the principle is the same.

However, we exercise the same privilege here as in presenting the other interviews, namely, that of portraying a model of what successful behavior-change therapy *can* be.

CASE HISTORY

Sara Forman, social worker, is a 41-year-old single woman who recognizes, faintly, that she is turning sour toward people, and is increasingly handicapped in her usually vigorous life by extreme fatigue and frequent headaches. She has been professionally successful to the point of becoming an upper-level supervisor in a fairly large agency and was president for a year of the local chapter of the social-work association. But she still lives alone and feels increasingly shut off from or bored by her old social activities—church gatherings, professional meetings, and visits to relatives.

She had long considered seeking psychotherapy, first at 24, when she had just graduated from the school of social work, partly to learn more about her "unconscious," and partly to discover why she was afraid of men and seemed to scare them away from showing her the affection that she really desired. But she was afraid to commit herself to the time, cost, and involvement of psychoanalysis, which was the only therapy that appealed to her as profound.

At thirty she had again almost entered psychotherapy, after an affair with a man who left her after six months to marry someone to whom he had been secretly engaged for a year. Again she pulled back and decided instead to blow her savings on a trip to Europe.

Finally, at forty-one, she had decided to go through with therapy. She was gripped chronically by vague fears of something that was about to happen to her. She wanted both relief from this misery and help in learning how to enjoy life again. For two years she had debated with herself about whom to choose. She had heard too many rumors about the weaknesses of various therapists to decide easily. A lecture given at her agency by a behavior-change therapist finally decided her.

Aside from being good looking, articulate, and assured in his manner, the behavior-change therapist. Dr. Ewing, made good sense to her when he spoke about trying to solve problems directly and concretely as possible. She was excited by the prospect of having him cast his bright eye on her and her problems and tell her what she must do to gain vitality in living.

She called Dr. Ewing one afternoon, had to leave a number with his answering service, and got a return call from him that evening. When he gave her an appointment for the following Saturday afternoon, she felt that her problems were already half solved.

He saw her twice a week for the first two months of therapy, and then weekly for fifty-minute interviews that cost her $25.00 each. She oriented her other activities to the appointments. So much planning went on that each interview determined how she spent her time until the next one.

Dr. Ewing was full of ideas about ways she could try to change her habits the better to reach her goals. Frequently he talked up to half the time, sometimes interrupting her. He frequently changed the subject on her, or asked her to try to concentrate on this problem or that. He asked her to make up a time budget, and money budget, and to report at the beginning of each interview on how she had applied the suggestions made at the previous meeting.

She often left his office a little depressed at her failures—but always hopeful of doing better by next time. She wanted desperately at times to get away from him and therapy, to relax and be left alone, and sometimes looked forward to holidays and meetings as she had an excuse to leave town and therapy. But her attitude was infused with an anguished optimism; she felt that if only she worked hard enough on her problems, they would yield and she could command her life and resources almost as she wished.

S.F.: Excerpts from First Interview

* * *

S.F.:   So I find myself pretty critical of my workers. They're sloppy in their work. They're always late with their reports and I just get plain fed up with them. They're pretty low level or something. They're just not smart in the way they do things.

Dr. E.: So you've a problem of how you're going to get along with them. What you want the relationship to be?

S.F.: I suppose you could put it that way. I think sometimes I'm in the wrong field—or wrong place. I can't stand dumbness. And here I am trying to nursemaid a bunch of pretty slow people.

Dr. E.: All right then. You don't like the workers you supervise. You get impatient with them. Is there anything else at work that is a problem to you?

S.F.: I don't think so. Oh, well, I suppose you might say that the administration of the agency is, sort of. I've been kind of leader among the supervisors in trying to get some changes made in the way the agency is run. Some new ideas. Like lectures. Time off to take classes. That kind of thing. But it's pretty hard to get them to move.

Dr. E.: Does this bother you much? Does it upset you to the point you can't move well toward your own goals?

S.F.: Well, that is one of my goals, to keep the agency alive. But it is true, sometimes, that I could scream at the sheer inertia of it all. Nobody seems to want to do anything that might rock the boat. I get pretty disgusted and give up.

Dr. E.: So perhaps your impatience with the administration also does more than upset you, it actually may reduce your effectiveness even in bringing about change.

S.F.: Yes, I guess so. I hadn't thought of it that way. But I guess that's right. Of course, I've got friends there too. I don't want to give you the wrong picture. I have strong loyal friends among the other supervisors and we talk these things over quite a bit. I'm not the only one that feels the way I'm talking to you.

* * *

Dr. E.: These other supervisors, are they the friends you referred to before? Are they your main social friends?

S.F.: Yes, they are. I have very few friends outside of work. We've sort of grown up together. I've been in the same place for ten years now. There's some consolation in that.

Dr. E.: Is your social life a problem to you?

S.F.: Yes and no. I have these few good friends from work and we visit around with each other quite a bit. But it's really not enough, I guess. I'm quite lonely, really, quite a bit of the time. I think of going back home to live.

Dr. E.: Do you come close to doing it?

S.F.: I think so. I'm quite close to it now. At my age, you know, it begins to look good to live among your kin again. I've been thinking seriously about it.

Dr. E.: What would you want to have socially? How would you like things to be?

S.F.: I haven't thought about that. I suppose I'd like a home of my own. I guess I'll never have that now, though. Otherwise I just don't know. Hmm. I'll have to think about that.

Dr. E.: So you have a social problem, perhaps of loneliness or lack of intimacy, though you're not sure what it is or what you want?

S.F.: Yes, I'm sure I do. Something very important is lacking.

* * *

Dr. E.: Well, if you have these ideas, and want to do something about them, why don't you? What stops you?

S.F.: Just the sheer problems of living. I barely manage to keep up with my work day by day. I don't really keep up. I'm always behind. And feeling harassed. And I'm tired all the time, Dr. Ewing. Often I can barely drag myself around.

Dr. E.: How do you spend your time, exactly, during an average week?

S.F.: I work a forty-hour week, you know, eight-thirty to five-thirty, five days a week. I often stay over half an hour or an hour trying to catch up. I go home, cook supper, straighten things up a bit, read the paper, and go to bed. That's about it, and it isn't very good.

Dr. E.: And week ends?

S.F.: I'm always trying to catch up on housekeeping and shopping and letterwriting. I never do catch up. I try to go out at least once on a week end, visiting, a movie, walking or something.

Dr. E.: It sounds as if you're unhappy with this kind of schedule.

S.F.: Yes, I am. I'm not going anywhere. I'm like on a treadmill. But what can I do? I hope you can help me.

Dr. E.: I will have a number of suggestions for you to try out. But first I hope we can come to a working statement of your most important problems, at least as you see them now. This treadmill thing we'll try to break up by your deciding on a priority of activities you want to give your limited time to, then making a weekly schedule, hour by hour, that works in the higher-priority items—even if you have to drop some lower-priority activities to do them.

* * *

S.F.: So my money seems to slip through my fingers too. I probably send too much home, for one thing. I send my parents money each month even though they probably don't need it. I really don't know how they stand financially. Anyway—I don't have enough to furnish my apartment properly, or travel during my vacations as I would like to do.

Dr. E.: Have you ever made out a budget?

S.F.: No. I've always wanted to be more spontaneous than that. I don't like people who count each penny and lay out their lives neatly. I want to be freer.

Dr. E.: Do you enjoy freedom when you feel that your money slips away from you and you don't have it for what you really want?

S.F.: No, I guess not. I really don't know where it goes. I should, I guess. Do you recommend that I keep a budget?

Dr. E.: Yes. At least until you know how you spend your money, and gain control of it so that you're using it the way you want to, through planning.

* * *

S.F.: Excerpts from Middle Interview (after 30 sessions)

Dr. E.: How have things been this week?

S.F.: Pretty good. Better. The schedule is beginning to work. I still don't really like to do it, but I'm getting to like the way I get things done with it. I'm getting a lot more done.

Dr. E.: What kind of things?

S.F.: Well, I peg away at my household chores a certain amount of time each day, and then I quit and go on to letter writing. And every day I also set time aside for reading and studying. My batting average has gone up too, you see. *(Gives him her schedule to look at.)* I'm getting things done on schedule about three-quarters of the time.

Dr. E.: Hmm. You certainly have improved, it looks like, both on what you schedule and what you accomplish.

S.F.: Once I force myself to get going, I feel all right. I've got more energy. The hardest thing is to get started.

Dr. E.: Are the goals you are accomplishing with your schedule satisfying to you? They can always be adjusted, you know, to move you where you want to go.

S.F.: They're all right. I guess I haven't broken through yet to anything that would inspire me. It all seems kind of routine. But it's a lot better than before, at least. And I'm starting to think of other things. A lot more seems possible.

Dr. E.: Like what?

S.F.: Like a different job, for example. I don't *have* to stay in the same old rut. I never before saw it that way; it was always like I was behind the eight ball. But maybe I can do better —or at least enjoy a change.

Dr. E.: Have you thought specifically of what you might change to?

S.F.: That's the next step. I've got a friend who is wanting me to come to work there with her agency. And there's the university School of Social Work. Maybe I could teach. Oh, there are lots of possibilities I never considered before.

* * *

Dr. E.: And the week ends? What about them?

S.F.: I still can't get them organized very well. I really don't want to stay home and do the same old routine. But I don't know just what to do to get out.

Dr. E.: We've talked some about how to find congenial company and recreation. How have you been going about this?

S.F.: You remember—I've always been somewhat shy in groups. And most of my friends seem to be married, and week ends are for families. I did try that church group you suggested but only four people showed up, and they were all younger than I am.

Dr. E.: Have you checked yet on the Foreign Center group and the others we listed?

S.F.: No, not yet. I'm going to work them into my schedule, though. Beginning after the holidays, I'm going to try one per week.

Dr. E.: You seem to have had quite a bit of trouble getting yourself started socially.

S.F.: I'm kind of afraid to go. I'm afraid I'll be too old. Or dull. They won't like me. Most of the groups I've gone to aren't very friendly to newcomers. I get easily discouraged and usually don't go back.

Dr. E.: You're afraid they won't like you so you quit before that can happen?

S.F.: It seems like it.

Dr. E.: All right then. Do you see that you are anticipating failing so you act on behalf of the others—instead of in your own interest? Your interest lies in making yourself an effective member of the group, so your energies should be directed toward making that come about. You can help the process, regardless of whether the group shows interest in you or is indifferent. If you imagine or call its neutrality "unfriendliness" directed at you, you defeat yourself. If, on the other hand, you extend yourself to be friendly, interested, and participating, you can control the situation in your favor to a great extent. It's another example, isn't it, of your taking the self-defeating approach instead of the problem-solving one?

* * *

S.F.: So there I was, trying to supervise this very hostile man, and starting to shake inside. I was afraid I'd lose control so I excused myself and went to the rest room and stayed there about ten minutes. When I came back to my desk he was gone and I let it go. I really should call him in again to finish the interview but I'm afraid.

Dr. E.: He was hostile in what way?

S.F.: Oh, in just the way he talked and looked at me. As if to say, "Just who do you think you are?" You know how hostility always has devastated me, and here I was supposed to tell him what to do, to criticize him, on top of everything.

Dr. E.: What do you mean "on top of everything?"

S.F.: I mean, I never did like him anyway, even before he was transferred to me for supervision. He always looked kind of sarcastic—you know? I tried to get out of it but it was my turn.

Dr. E.: Have others reacted to him this way too?

S.F.: Nobody likes him. In fact, everybody tries to avoid him. And nobody wants to supervise him. So it's not just me.

Dr. E.: But you act like it's just you, don't you? That is, if this is just an unpleasant task that must be done—maybe like catching up on back reports—you probably would not have such a strong reaction. You seem to be reacting as if he were passing some important kind of judgment on you, that he is not just an employee who is troublesome to everyone.

S.F.: That's true, but how can I get over it? Just noticing him yesterday upset me. I could feel it.

Dr. E.: Well, then, what's so bad about having this kind of man acting sarcastic toward you? You can try to remind yourself that this is the way he is, that it has little to do with you specifically, and get on with your job. Your job in this situation is to be as good a supervisor as you can—regardless of him. And to find reward in that.

S.F.:   I'll try it. At least it won't hurt to try. I'll call him in first thing tomorrow morning. So far your suggestions have worked pretty well.

Dr. E.:   All right. And I think you will begin to sense—here, as in other situations you have handled—that this feeling of being able to control the situation, to try out new ways of handling it, to be a kind of master instead of victim of the conditions, will make you feel better and function better.

S.F.: Excerpts from Final Interview (after 62 sessions)

S.F.:   It's hard to believe that I'm finally going.

Dr. E.:   When do you leave?

S.F.:   Tomorrow! If the movers come. I'll leave right after they do and I'll be on my way to the new life. It's kind of scary, after all these years here. But I know it's the right thing, to try it, whatever happens. You do think it's a good idea, don't you? I guess I'd just like to hear you say it again.

Dr. E.:   You seem to have some anxiety about the change. But I think you can handle it all right yourself.

S.F.:   I know I can. Just looking for a little extra support. Anyway —I got a very nice letter from my friend in Chicago welcoming me, and painting a rosy picture. I'm sure it won't be all that good. Incidentally, she also gave me the name of a psychiatrist there.

Dr. E.:   How come?

S.F.:   You know she knew about my seeing you. I've written her about it from time to time. Anyway, I must have made some remarks about wondering about leaving here and seeing you, you know, and she must have picked it up and thought she could help by suggesting someone there.

Dr. E.:   Was she right? Do you want to have someone to go to there?

S.F.:   Yes and no. I'm not too clear about it. Mainly, though, no. I have no intention of continuing therapy right away. I don't think I need to. My problems are pretty well in hand. Still, it's nice to be able to talk to someone when you need to, and I've gotten kind of used to coming in here.

Dr. E.:   You're making a distinction, aren't you, between needing help to solve your problems, and simply having someone to talk to?

S.F.: Yes, I am. I'll have to remember that. Because I don't need to pay just to have someone to talk to. I remember—we talked about that before.

Dr. E.: That's right. You've made a beginning with friends here, and your friend in Chicago. And you can continue to work on that and to improve these friendships which have begun to serve that kind of purpose. The technical help was something else again.

S.F.: Yes, of course. I really don't think I need more technical help now. Maybe I will, though.

Dr. E.: Certainly you might. And I'm sure you will be able to recognize your need for such help and how to get and use it better now than before.

* * *

S.F.: Then I had a final interview with my boss yesterday. He was very nice, said I had done a good job and wished me well and all. I think he mostly meant it. And all the others, too.

Dr. E.: You seem to be less cynical than you used to be.

S.F.: Some of it, I'm sure, is just the fact that I'm leaving and everyone always says nice things then. But partly I think they really mean it. I don't feel so tied up as I used to. I just can like people more. I feel more on top of things. Sure, they've got weaknesses—we all have—but they're not against me particularly. You taught me that, that they're just showing their own problems to me. I can get as much good out of them as they've got in them, if I try. If I just don't act helpless about it.

Dr. E.: I'm glad you could see and apply this. Whatever happened with that man you were supervising, by the way? You haven't said anything for a month or so.

S.F.: Well, I quit supervising him the beginning of this month. I was glad to be rid of him. He's a kind of nuisance, you know. I got better with him. At times he even seemed to act like a human being. Then I felt sorry for him. But I could never really like him for very long. He'd always do something to spoil things.

Dr. E.: Apparently you maintained your own stability with him, though. I remember you gradually got over being completely thrown when you saw him. I wonder how, in retrospect, you think you learned to handle it. And how you could handle future situations.

S.F.:   Pretty much like I already said. I suppose I'll run into men or women like this again. I just have to keep reminding myself that it's their problem, not mine. Not to let it get to me, as if it's personal. I feel like I can handle it now even if I don't like it. I can control the situation.

* * *

S.F.:   One last question. What if my feeling better is just based upon the excitement of the change? What if I start to slip back into my old ways again after a while?

Dr. E.:   Well, there's a lot that we could talk about, about that, if we had the time. But you might remember—I'm sure you would if we had the time to go over it—the course of your help. How you began to move in on your problems with your own efforts. How you tried different ways of attacking them. How you continued with the methods that helped you. You know, this change you're making is really the end product of all that, not just something that happens to stir you up temporarily. It only happened after you had done everything else. If you ever start to slip again, you should be able to remember and use the attitudes and methods you've learned. Of course, you should also be able to recognize if you are losing control of situations, are not applying what you know you should, and don't seem to be able to rouse yourself to the effort. Then you could get professional help again—until you were able to get yourself underway again with good problem-solving efforts.

S.F.:   Yes, yes. I know all that. I guess I just wanted to hear you say it again. I really do feel that way. I hope you don't get the idea that I'm pessimistic or worried.

Dr. E.:   No, I'm sure you're showing some natural reactions to leaving here, going into a new situation.

S.F.:   I'm really looking forward to it and feel quite confident of myself. But I guess I'll always wonder a little. It's just a question of where the balance lies.

Sara Forman changed her living conditions in concrete ways as a direct result of her therapy. Specific and planned changes to reach her goals were the major and immediate business of her therapy. Her therapist has not heard from her again, and can only guess either that she has never needed further help, or that, if she did, it was probably for different problems from those discussed with him. If the latter, he could feel confident that she would request specific help for fairly well-defined difficulties from whomever she saw, and that she would approach her future problems in a relatively objective manner aimed at solving them directly.

Epilogue—How to Use This Guide

THE EFFECT of most self-help guides is fleeting. Books appear, thousands of copies are sold, and then the titles are forgotten with the arrival of new products.

Mostly, the trouble is that such books are read once, and their ideas applied for only days or weeks, when a more sustained interest is necessary for substantial results. We urge you to try to review this book whenever an issue it discusses becomes a problem to you. It is not intended as a spectacular bouquet. Look upon it rather as a bunch of straw flowers whose merit hopefully lies in durability.

We would prefer the sustained effect over the spectacular. Whatever merit this book may have should lie in its continuing usefulness to you as you struggle to match your problems with the resources which our society provides to help you with them. Try applying it—and keep trying its suggestions as long as they seem to hold hope of advancing you toward solutions. Try talking about it with friends—and keep talking with them as long as your conversations yield useful results in changing attitudes and actions that may follow.

Time will change psychotherapy, but we expect the change to be in the directions to which this book points. That is, two to ten years hence, you may expect to see the psychoanalytic and non-directive approaches fade further into a background in which their distinctive identity as therapies is lost, although their substantial contributions to theory and method remain.

The direction of the science seems almost certain to be toward more precision in determining what kind, amount, and timing of rewards ("reinforcement schedules," in Skinner's language) will most efficiently produce desired changes in behavior. Mental-hospital patients and severely disturbed children are already being trained in this way. For you the rewards to be associated with new behavior will most likely have to be clearly described, and ways of obtaining them specifically outlined by psychotherapists; thus in concrete small steps you can earn and enjoy results from your changed behavior.

Hypothetically, the places and professions for help should meld, so that a new profession of behavior changers would develop, cutting across the wasteful and often meaningless professional distinctions that exist today among the practitioners of psychotherapy in pastoral counseling, psychiatry, social work, school counseling, and clinical psychology. But desirable though they may be, social institutions do not work so rationally. Only great crises, such as military necessity, have forced such major professions as medicine and education to strip to their essentials and become more efficient in training and practice.

Perhaps a major social war on poverty, on unemployment, or on family disruption would force professional counselors to learn better how to produce practical results. This is perhaps the best hope for a more effective therapeutic profession whose results will be demanded by and judged in a broad consumer market.

Meanwhile, you will have to content yourself with the more modest goal of finding within the existing professions the help you need. If, as we believe, the current state of psychotherapy requires you to work your own way through a jungle of professional services colored by a "let-the-buyer-beware" attitude, let that fact be faced. You can gain if you master the skill you need to find your way. An optimist might even decide that learning how to perform well the task of choosing and directing one's help is a proper part of therapy. After all, if you have learned how to handle yourself capably in this regard, you are also more likely to be able to tackle your other problems successfully.

The ultimate best use for this book should be as a pad under hot dishes. It should serve this purpose well when you have developed your own good ways to get help when you need it, and when you have used up whatever loan value the book may have with friends. After all, it is the purpose of most help—parents to children, teachers to students, physicians to patients, lawyers to clients—to obviate the need and thus to terminate the relationship.

Annotated Bibliography

To list here a few references among the thousands of books available for further reading may be viewed as idiosyncratic or even presumptuous. This is, simply, a selective survey of books which I often loan to my patients who request supplementary reading in the areas listed. These books have proved to be specific, accurate, and useful. You can try them out for yourself and accept or reject what they offer according to their particular value for you.

They also are fairly new books, which means that they tend to be current and easy to buy. They are neither highly technical nor overly simple. They are widely read by professional people as well as by students and laymen of college-level intelligence. All should be available in or can be ordered by any fair-sized library. Some may be reserved for adults only, or be kept in medical libraries.

1. CHILD TRAINING

Discipline, Achievement, and Mental Health, by E. L. Phillips, D. N. Wiener, and N. G. Haring, Englewood Cliffs, N.J.: Prentice-Hall, 1960. This book, written for teachers and parents, considers that children's behavior problems derive from poorly planned and conducted training programs. Discipline (or effective planning and practices to reach goals) is viewed as leading to achievement, and achievement of one's goals to good "mental health." Common problems of children are analyzed and concrete solutions, involving specific systems of planning, rewards and penalties, and follow-up, are described.

2. CLINICAL PSYCHOLOGY

Clinical Psychology, by N. D. Sundberg, and L. E. Tyler, New York: Appleton-Century-Croft, 1962. An unusually well-written, comprehensive, and fair-minded textbook, this description of the field of clinical psychology will answer most questions about psychologists, psychological tests, and methods of counseling and psychotherapy. It includes a list and brief description of the most commonly used tests, and can (but need not) be studied in depth, since it is a graduate-school textbook.

3. DIAGNOSTIC DEFINITIONS

Diagnostic and Statistical Manual, Mental Disorders, by Committee on Nomenclature and Statistics, American Psychiatric Association, Washington, D.C.: The Association, 1952. Although an increasing number of psychotherapists consider the current diagnostic system to be unreliable, outmoded, or irrelevant for the solution of personal problems, diagnoses continue to be required for legal, insurance, pension, employment, and other purposes. If you want to know what these diagnoses are supposed to mean, you can consult this manual for the most standard definitions in current use.

4. DRUGS

Physician's Desk Reference to Pharmaceutical Specialties and Biologicals, Oradell, N.J.: Medical Economics, Inc. (published annually with quarterly supplements). New drugs still come out so frequently, and new cautions and other information about old drugs pour forth so voluminously that your physician will frequently consult this guidebook to find out about drugs you may already be taking or that he wants to prescribe. Its language is simple. You can find color pictures of many pills to help identify yours, and a description of content, dosages, effects, and cautions.

5. HISTORY OF PSYCHIATRY

The History of Psychiatry, by F. G. Alexander and S. T. Selesnick, New York: Harper & Row, 1966. This is a comprehensive new history of psychiatry, the result of a collaboration between a dean of American psychiatry and psychoanalysis and one of his students. Reading this history for the first time provides a fascinating opportunity to compare ancient and modern witchcraft, and ancient and modern wisdom. It leaves many readers feeling that the intervening years between old and new practices shrink drastically, that man has progressed very slightly, and that he remains incredibly ignorant about how to handle himself as compared with how to handle his physical environment.

6. MARITAL RELATIONS

Creative Marriage, by A. Ellis and R. A. Harper, New York: Lyle Stuart, 1961 (also in paperback as "The Marriage Bed"). While some readers disagree with Harper and Ellis's seemingly casual attitudes toward some common moral beliefs, most say they have found useful attitudes and guidelines in this book to apply to their marital problems. In particular, the authors cut through the cant surrounding a "love-will-conquer-all" attitude, specify self-defeating attitudes and behavior, and propose specific ways to make marriage work better.

7. PUBLIC ATTITUDES RE MENTAL HEALTH

Americans View Their Mental Health, by G. Gurin, J. Veroff, and S. Feld, New York: Basic Books, Inc., 1960. Earlier in our guide we cited results of polling a representative sampling of the American population on their problems and uses of help. This book is a detailed compendium of views which will summarize for you the attitudes and experiences of your fellow citizens relative to their problems and professional help. The sampling is sketchy but the data are the best available in this field.

8. SELF-HELP ON PERSONAL PROBLEMS

A Guide to Rational Living, by A. Ellis and R. A. Harper, Englewood Cliffs, N.J.: Prentice-Hall, 1961 (also in paperback). Although this book is an early treatise on the particular system called "rational psychotherapy," it is so full of descriptions and practical solutions of common problems that you are likely to find it useful even when you do not agree with its theory as a complete solution to your problems. In stripping psychotherapy of mystique and calling attention to how what you say to yourself can make your behavior either self-defeating or successful, Ellis and Harper have provided usable self-help aid.

9. SEX INFORMATION

The Art and Science of Love, by A. Ellis, New York: Lyle Stuart, 1960 (also in paperback). This is currently the best selling sex-information manual. It is an excellent compendium of specific, accurate information, physical and psychological, about sexual functions and techniques. While you may demur at the offhand way Ellis treats conventional attitudes and practices he considers irrational, he presents his facts straightforwardly and has brought rationality and pleasure to what should be one of the most satisfying and valued human activities.

10. THEORIES OF PSYCHOTHERAPY

Psychoanalysis and Psychotherapy: 36 Systems, by R. A. Harper, Englewood Cliffs, N.J.: Prentice-Hall, 1959 (also in paperback). Harper's book describes briefly but clearly a wide range of theories about psychotherapy. It may give the impression that there are many more useful theories than there clearly are. Many differences are, in practice, picayune, and represent more each author's effort to appear original than truly useful innovations, but this is the way the field often appears. It is, in any case, a very useful guide in which to look up the names of theorists and the tenets of the various theories.

PROFESSIONAL MEMBERSHIP DIRECTORIES

1. *Biographical Directory of Fellows and Members of American Psychiatric Association*, New York: R. R. Bowker, 1963.
2. *Directory of the American Psychological Association* (published every other year, with Annual Address List), Washington, D.C.: American Psychological Association, 1966.
3. *Directory of Professional Social Workers* (published occasionally), New York: National Association of Social Workers, 1966.

Index

Education (*cont.*)
See also Training and education
Educational counselors, 102–05
Elavil, 237
Electric-shock treatment, *see* Shock treatment
Ellis, Albert, 85
Emergency care, 115
Emotional problems, 5, 215, 217, 235
  concrete, converting vague or indirect complaints into, 49–50
  determined by available help, 11–13
  living problems, mental illness vs., 32–34
  serious, sensing, 29–30
  vague, specific vs., 34–35
  worry about unimportant or serious problems, 37–38
Employment agencies, counseling service by, 104–05
Employment information, sources of, 61
Ending treatment, setting conditions for, 159–60
Environment, unfavorable, obstacle to progress, 197
Equanil, 236
Existential psychotherapy, 69, 75–77
  case study of, 266–74
Expectations from psychotherapy, 193–95
  realistic, 15–27
  unrealistic, 16
Eysenck, Hans J., xii, 20

False hopes from psychotherapy, folklore and, 17–18
Family counselors, 87, 105, 107–08
Family-management information and planning services, 62
Fear of change, obstacle to progress, 195–96
Federal government, informational pamphlets of, 62
Fellowship Club, 57
Financial-planning advice, sources of, 61
Final interview
  behavior-change case, 294–96

Final interview (*cont.*)
  eclectic case, 281–83
  nondirective (existential) case, 272–74
  psychoanalytic case, 262–64
  setting conditions for, 159–60
  structuring, 210
First interview, 137–60
  appointments, missing or changing, 159–60
  behavior-change case, 288–91
  confidentiality, limits of, setting, 150–52
  consulting arrangement, setting conditions for, 159–60
  cost of treatment, deciding on, 155–57
  diagnosis, asking for, 142–43
  eclectic case, 277–79
  ending treatments, setting conditions for, 159–60
  first lesson, preparation, 138–39
  frequency of sessions, deciding on, 157–58
  information from the therapist, seeking, 149–50
  intake process, handling, 139–41
  length of treatment, estimate of, getting, 152–55
  nondirective (existential) case, 268–70
  payment for treatments, deciding on, 155–57
  personal questions, asking, of the psychotherapist, 146–49
  preparing for, 138–39
  psychoanalytic case, 257–59
  results of treatment, estimate of, getting, 152–55
  time of treatment, deciding on, 158–59
  treatment method, asking for, 142–43
  trial period, utilizing, 143–46
Folklore, false hopes from psychotherapy and, 17–18
Frequency of interviews, adjusting, 177–78
  deciding on, 157–58
Freud, Anna, 75
Freud, Sigmund, 11, 42, 69, 71, 89, 217, 254

ABOUT THE AUTHOR

Daniel N. Wiener is an associate professor of psychology at the University of Minnesota, teaching in the School of Social Work and the Psychology Department, as well as a research psychologist with the Veterans' Administration. He has conducted private practice since 1948 and has lectured at several colleges. A graduate of the University of Minnesota, where he also earned his doctorate, Dr. Wiener served as a psychologist with the Air Force during World War II and as a clinical psychologist for the state of Connecticut.

Currently chairman of the Insurance Committee of the Minnesota Psychological Association, Dr. Wiener was chairman of the committee that wrote Minnesota's psychologist accreditation law, vice-chairman of the state's first Board of Examiners, and chairman of the State Ethics Committee.

His other books are *Dimensions of Psychotherapy, Short-term Psychotherapy and Structured Behavior Change*, and *Discipline, Achievement and Mental Health*. He has also published numerous articles.

Born in Duluth in 1921, Dr. Wiener lives now in St. Paul.

Format by Katharine Sitterly
Set in Linotype Times Roman
Composed, printed and bound by The Haddon Craftsmen, Inc.
HARPER & ROW, PUBLISHERS, INCORPORATED